Praise, Motivation and the Child

Anyone who spends time with children knows that praise works. It is a powerful motivator – praising children for good behaviour or good work builds self-esteem and self-confidence. Children love to collect stickers, certificates and rewards – so what better way is there to shape behaviour, encourage good work habits and produce confident learners? Teachers and parents alike know that praise is effective – we use it every day and we see the positive effect that it has on our children.

However, constructivist practitioners would argue that praise in any form creates hierarchies and competition in the classroom, has little effect on genuine learning and is invasively judgemental rather than supportive. Constructivists would further argue that self-esteem cannot be built by external agency – teachers and parents can only create an appropriate environment in which a robust sense of 'self' can grow and develop.

This book challenges traditional, embedded thinking about the role of praise. It questions the assumptions we make about developing self-esteem, about the ability of children to form their own independent judgements and the choices that children make regardless, rather than because of, contingent praise.

What happens when children are praised? Read this book, listen to what children really think and challenge your own assumptions.

Features include:

- Case studies and children's work samples
- Points for reflection which could be used for CPD sessions
- Appendices containing behaviour policy samples
- Pupil, teacher and parental perspectives.

This book is aimed at practising and training Primary school teachers. It would also be suitable for NQTs who are starting to shape their own practice, experienced teachers who want to develop and question their own practice and students on BA Hons and PGCE courses.

Gill Robins is the former Deputy Head of a Hampshire school. She received the John Downing Award in 2010. Until 2011 she chaired the English Association Editorial Board for the *English 4–11* journal.

Praise, Motivation and the Child

Gill Robins

Routledge
Taylor & Francis Group

LONDON AND NEW YORK

First published 2012
by Routledge
2 Park Square, Milton Park, Abingdon, Oxon OX14 4RN

Simultaneously published in the USA and Canada
by Routledge
711 Third Avenue, New York, NY 10017

Routledge is an imprint of the Taylor & Francis Group, an informa business

British Library Cataloguing in Publication Data
A catalogue record for this book is available from the British Library

Library of Congress Cataloging in Publication Data
Robins, Gill.
  Praise, motivation, and the child / Gill Robins.
    p. cm.
  ISBN 978-0-415-68173-5 (hardback)—ISBN 978-0-415-68174-2
  (paperback)—ISBN 978-0-203-11768-2 (ebook) 1. Motivation in
  education.   2. Classroom environment.   3. Praise.   4. Self-esteem in
  children. I Title.
  LB1065.R55 2012
  370.15'4—dc23
                                        2011052706

ISBN: 978-0-415-68173-5 (hbk)
ISBN: 978-0-415-68174-2 (pbk)
ISBN: 978-0-203-11768-2 (ebk)

Typeset in Galliard
by RefineCatch Limited, Bungay, Suffolk

FSC
www.fsc.org
MIX
Paper from
responsible sources
FSC® C004839

Printed and bound in Great Britain by
CPI Group (UK) Ltd, Croydon, CR0 4YY

Contents

List of figures and tables   ix
Acknowledgements   x

Introduction   1

1   **What's wrong with these pictures?**   3

Three contrasting classrooms 3
   Jane's classroom 3
   Marcus's classroom 5
   Sue's classroom 7
Behaviourist and constructivist paradigms 10
Points for reflection 11

2   **The emergence of educational theory**   12

Early educational philosophers 12
   John Amos Comenius (1592–1670) 13
   John Locke (1632–1704) 13
   Jean-Jacques Rousseau (1712–1778) 15
   Johann Heinrich Pestalozzi (1746–1827) 16
   Friedrich Froebel (1782–1852) 17
Points for reflection 18

3   **Behaviourism – the perspective**   19

A review of behaviourist theory 19
   Ivan Pavlov (1849–1936) 19
   John B. Watson (1878–1958) 20
   Edward Lee Thorndike (1874–1949) 21
   B.F. Skinner (1904–1990) 22
An evaluation of behaviourist theory 24
Points for reflection 25

4   Behaviourism contextualised – translating theory into practice   26

The behaviourist paradigm evidenced in national policy 26
   The Steer Report 26
   Charlie Taylor's behaviour checklists 27
The behaviourist paradigm evidenced in school policy 27
The behaviourist paradigm evidenced in classroom practice 28
The behaviourist paradigm evidenced in research literature 31
The behaviourist paradigm evaluated 33
Points for reflection 33

5   Constructivism – the perspective   35

A review of constructivist theory 35
   John Dewey (1859–1952) 35
   Jean Piaget (1896–1980) 36
   Lev Vygotsky (1896–1934) 37
   Carl Rogers (1902–1987) 37
   Jerome Bruner (b. 1915) 38
An evaluation of constructivist theory 39
Points for reflection 39

6   Constructivism contextualised – translating theory into practice   41

The constructivist paradigm evidenced in national policy 41
The constructivist paradigm evidenced in school policy 42
The constructivist paradigm evidenced in classroom practice 44
The constructivist paradigm evidenced in research literature 45
The constructivist paradigm evaluated 46
Points for reflection 47

7   Praise, motivation and positive psychology   49

The development of self and the role of praise in motivation 49
   Harry Harlow (1905–1981) 49
   Edward Deci and Richard Ryan 50
   Abraham Maslow (1908–1970) 51
   A.S. Neill (1883–1973) 53
   Carol Dweck (b. 1946) 54
   Mihaly Csikszentmihalyi (b. 1934) 56
   Daniel Pink (b. 1964) 56
Points for reflection 57

8   Praise – help or harm?   58

Seligman and learned helplessness 59

Schunk and attribution theory 59
Dweck and self-theory 61
Deci and Ryan and a continuum of motivation 62
Fryer and financial rewards 63
KIPP schools, Duckworth and the Grit Scale 64
Kohn and the purpose of praise 65
Dopamine and the brain's reward centre 68
Cheating 69
Does praise help or harm? 69
Points for reflection 70

9   **Praise – what do young children think?**   71

Praise and age-related self-perception 71
Praise Posters and public praise 74
Points for reflection 80

10 **Praise – discerning intention and defining value**   82

Reward hierarchies 82
Contingent praise 86
Students' perceptions of the reasons for praise 87
  Effort 87
  Concentration 87
  Encouragement 88
  Building confidence 88
  Feedback 88
  Challenge 89
  Learning behaviour 91
  Motivation 91
  Self-evaluation 92
  Self-esteem 93
Using social networking sites to praise children 96
The views of teachers 96
Points for reflection 98

11 **Praise – privacy and preference**   99

Students' views and preferences 99
  Gold Book 99
  Good News notes 100
  Feedback marking 101
  Certificates 102
  Proud Book 103
  Merits 103

How praise is valued 104
Private versus public praise 106
Points for reflection 106

12 **Praise and motivation in a cultural context**   107

Amy Chua 107
Cross-cultural studies 108
International differences in socio-cultural expectations 110
Implications for the future 110
Points for reflection 112

13 **Creating a culture of compliance**   113

Jack – a case study 113
Controlling teachers 118
Public policy and high-stakes testing 119
Points for reflection 122

14 **Creating resolute and resilient learners**   123

Mastery 123
Interest 124
Self-efficacy 125
Paideia 126
Mercer and 'exploratory talk' 126
Quest to Learn 127
Social media and learning 128
Points for reflection 131

15 **Protocol and pedagogy**   132

Pink: The 3.0 motivation upgrade 132
Reflection on personal pedagogy 134
Points for reflection 136

Appendices   137
Bibliography   144
Index   151

Figures and tables

Figures

1   A motivation continuum as defined by Deci and Ryan   66
2   Mind Maps®   83
3   Reward hierarchies   84

Tables

1   Certificate analysis table   90
2   What happens when children are praised?   135

Acknowledgements

I would like to thank the staff and pupils of those schools who have participated in this research study anonymously, and the staff and pupils of Dunannie, Bedales pre-prep school, for their enthusiastic involvement in this project, their willingness to share their views and their consent for them to be published.

Pseudonyms have been used in all interview transcripts and case studies.

Thanks to Paul Dix, of Pivotal Education (*http://www.PivotalEducation.com*), the copyright holder of the Praise Posters which appear in Appendix C, for his kind permission to use them.

Thank you to my son Benjamin and my daughter Laura-Jane, for consent to publish their childhood views and stories which are contained in the Introduction.

Thank you to my husband John, who has not only designed and managed my websites and sorted out all my technology issues but has patiently listened to, and commented on, the many theories that I have explored during the writing of this book.

Introduction

Praise may seem an unusual subject for a book. After all, anyone who spends time with children, either professionally or as a parent, will be familiar with star charts and the power of reward as an incentive to learning. Praising children is a time-honoured and proven way to shape behaviour. Or is it?

I was first asked this as a parenthetic question at a seminar when discussing the effectiveness of praise as a behaviour management strategy. The seminar leader asked me if I really believed what I was saying. A debate of gladiatorial proportions ensued because I was sure that I was right – I was an experienced teacher, parent and voluntary youth worker and I knew that praise always worked. My reaction was Schopenhaueresque in its proportions: he reputedly said that, 'All truth passes through three stages. First, it is ridiculed. Second, it is violently opposed. Third, it is accepted as being self-evident.' But the question had been asked and my curiosity was aroused. And one memorable occasion came into my mind several times in the ensuing few days which started to convince me that maybe the truth of what the seminar leader had said was, in fact, self-evident.

I saw a picture of my son, then three years old, walking along twirling a blue umbrella. He had seen the umbrella several weeks earlier, pressing his nose flat against the shop window and begging me to buy it for him. I saw this as an opportunity because my son sucked the two middle fingers of his left hand and I really wanted him to stop. So I made him a star chart and told him that if he stopped sucking his fingers for a set time, I would buy him the umbrella. As far as I could see, if the chart lasted long enough, the habit would be broken and he would be rewarded for the achievement, so it was a win–win situation. Twice every day he took great pleasure in sticking a star on his chart, watching them increase as days, then weeks, passed. He did not relapse once, not even at night. I used to watch his fingers creep towards his mouth whilst he was falling asleep, but they never went into his mouth even when he was deeply asleep, such was the strength of his determination. We duly bought the umbrella and celebrated. At least, my son celebrated. I was horrified to see his fingers go straight back into his mouth the moment I had made the purchase, and there they remained for a further two years. He even made up for the lost weeks by sucking his fingers more often for a while.

I should have learnt important lessons about the power of desire in motivation, the immense strength of a three-year-old's self-control and the uselessness of bribery as a parenting strategy. I thought I was changing a habit. He thought he was behaving in a certain way to get a desired object, and after all, nobody had told him he was expected to stop the habit for ever – in his mind, it was a simple equation of performing task A to get desired possession B. Our two purposes were poles apart, but it still did not occur to me that it was my strategy that was at fault. I merely concluded that I had not applied it for long enough to break the habit.

After the seminar discussion, I was wondering if I had been wrong. So I talked to my two, now adult, children about the role of praise when they were at school. My son usually remembered to bring certificates home by way of proving that he did some occasional work, but he did not value them, taking greater pleasure in fulfilling his self-defined role as a 'gifted non-producer'. Primary school was largely an inconvenient irrelevance which robbed him of valuable time with construction kits and the chance to absorb vast quantities of facts from the encyclopaedias which were not considered 'proper' reading in school. My daughter, whose favourite childhood mug said, 'Overachiever and proud of it', took pride in earning stars and certificates, but said that they made no difference to her view of herself as a learner of the things which interested her. Both of them, even as adults, were animated about the injustice of praise and reward being used as behaviour bribes whilst their good behaviour was taken for granted, and this comment reminded me of an exchange I had recently witnessed. I was working in a school with a great deal of challenging behaviour and the Head used to walk around the Hall giving out merits whilst I was singing with the children. One day she gave a merit to a child whose behaviour had been particularly unacceptable for all but the last two minutes of the session. One of the quiet children said, 'Can I have a merit, please? I sat really quietly', only to be given the answer, 'No, dear, you always sit beautifully. You don't need a merit.'

I finally decided that there was good reason to pursue a study of the role of praise and reward when I overheard a conversation between two boys, both very able and sensitive writers, on the issue of a poem they were writing:

Joe: Just write it down.
Robert: But we could do better. I don't like this word.
Joe: Just hurry up and write it down. If we write it we'll get a merit.
Robert: But this word isn't very good. Let's think of a better one.
Joe: (starting to get impatient) Just write anything. We'll still get a merit.

The class was being taught by a teacher who routinely offered reward contingent on task completion. But here was evidence of reward impacting negatively on learning, even in a collaborative situation where one child tried hard to consider the quality of the work.

Contingent reward takes a wide range of forms in schools, from stickers, house points, cups, certificates and extra privileges in the Primary sector to financial or material rewards in the Secondary sector. But is the widely held assumption correct that rewards are motivational? Is motivation a simple matter of cause and effect? What actually happens when children are praised?

Chapter 1

What's wrong with these pictures?

Three contrasting classrooms

Jane's classroom

Jane is a very experienced teacher. She teaches a mixed ability class of 32 children, 17 boys and 15 girls, all in Year Two. Her classroom is attractive and well organised – trays are labelled in order to foster the children's independence in locating and using resources. Some trays are labelled with her name and children know that they should not touch these. Tables are tidy, with a pot for table points centrally placed. Book shelves are attractively arranged, stock is regularly rotated and there is a range of fiction reading material to satisfy the choice of boys and girls across the ability range. All books are colour coded so that children know which band they can select their book from. Any request from a child to read a book above their current banding is met with a quiet, but firm, conversation about assessing progress in reading. An 'Author of the Week' stand highlights a writer whose books Jane has chosen. An extra box of non-fiction books labelled 'TOPIC' awaits use during the relevant lesson. Display is colourful and relevant. Boards supporting literacy and numeracy learning are obviously updated regularly and children's work on the current topic of 'The Victorians' is neatly mounted and demonstrates a high standard of attainment. Children know where to put completed work for marking and where to locate their books when needed for the next lesson. In the cupboard are rows of files, each labelled with a subject and a term. Long, medium and short term planning is sequentially filed with differentiated activities and worksheets ready to photocopy.

One board displays the class contract – a child explains that everyone in the class agreed these rules from a list which their teacher gave them and everyone has signed their name to indicate engagement. The rules are positively structured; one, for example, says, 'We will walk into the classroom quietly'. When they break a rule, there is a sanction. On the same board is the merit chart, with each name neatly written at the start of a line of stars. Another child explains that their teacher gives them merits for working hard, meeting the success criteria for a lesson, behaving well or doing a good piece of work. Merits add up to certificates, with Platinum being the highest. One child is wearing a different coloured sweatshirt from everyone else – he explains that he is the Golden Student for the week, so he gets to wear the sweatshirt, which is awarded in a whole school celebration assembly, for the day and then he can wear it home. His certificate says he was chosen by the Head Teacher for setting a good example when helping his friends at playtime. The Head takes pride in the school's reward structure and often comments to visitors that if they have a problem in school, they create a reward to address it. She knows that public awards are a really effective tool in managing a cohesive school community. Another look at the rewards board shows that children can work for Golden Student, Best Table, Tidy Classroom, Tidy Cloakroom, Top Table, Considerate Play and Lunchtime Award. Generally, all the children appear to be polite to each other and considerate of each other's feelings. All classes conform to the same protocol, so there is a feeling of uniformity around the school.

The task board for the day shows subject lessons and the day's activities, so the children know exactly when they can change their books, go to the Library or collect the merits from their teacher that she has written in their books. Jane feels that this gives the children security about their day and gives her control over where the children are and what they are doing. This is particularly important for special needs children or those children who are inclined to misbehave when given too much freedom.

As the children move quietly to their ability groups and settle down for their first lesson, the classroom becomes very peaceful. The teacher waits until the last child is settled and ready to listen, then she starts to teach. The lesson is clearly well planned, she knows what outcomes she expects and knows what learning she is going to assess. Children put their hands up if they want to speak – this ranges from asking to sharpen a pencil to answering the teacher's questions. Jane targets her questions carefully, ensuring that they are structured to initiate a response. Offered answers are nearly always correct, so the children are demonstrating their prior learning effectively. Inaccurate answers are met with a supportive comment such as, 'Good try'.

Occasionally, the children are asked to discuss something for two minutes before sharing their ideas with the teacher. On one rare occasion, a child speaks directly to a peer without raising her hand, which elicits a gentle reminder. When she calls out an answer a couple of minutes later, her name is written on the board. She glances anxiously at the class contract board, reminding herself that if her name goes on the board again during this lesson, she will lose five minutes of her playtime. Even when the child calls out again, the teacher remains calm as she writes up the name next to a sad face. Everyone in the class knows that redemption of the sanction is no longer an option. Before resuming the lesson, Jane writes a couple of names on the opposite side of the board next to a big smiley. These children smile themselves as they know that they will get a merit if their name is still there at the end of the lesson. They continue, with the class focusing on their differentiated, independent tasks in silence.

Jane teaches her 'hidden' group during the guided session, those children who passively come to school every day, work and play compliantly and then go home. They do not make expected progress, so Jane focuses on them regularly. Any talking is initiated and mediated by Jane, who understands the importance of speaking and listening in a child's development. The silence is broken only by a request to borrow a ruler, to which Jane responds, 'Of course; you may collect a ruler from the tray'. She is proud of the child's independence in locating the correct tray, collecting the ruler and returning to her place without disturbing anyone.

At the end of the day, Jane meets with her Teaching Assistant to review pupil progress for intervention programmes, then works until all of the books are marked. She makes an encouraging comment in each one, knowing that praise from their teacher will encourage the children to work hard and strive to achieve. Sometimes she awards a merit, where she feels that a child has achieved the task well or has worked hard. She methodically ticks the boxes against each child's name in her assessment folder, making a list of the children who did not meet the success criteria. For these children, she follows the encouraging comment with a note about what they need to do next.

As she is tidying up and setting out worksheets for the next morning, a parent drops in to ask about her child's spelling test scores. Jane is a very popular teacher with parents. She always has helpful data in her mark book, showing weekly spelling and tables test scores, current phonics steps, book bands, ability grouping justified by testing and data to show progress. Her classroom is ordered, rules are kept and children feel secure. Learning follows clear, measurable steps, parents know exactly what to expect and they are confident that their children are making steady progress in Jane's care. They appreciate her overt control of their children's social and academic learning. This is reinforced each year during her performance management when the children's progress is reviewed and new targets are set. Jane is very confident about her professional practice and willingly embraces the school ethos. Her Head categorises her as very good and is glad to have such a well-respected teacher on her staff. She really misses Jane when she is unwell or on a course, because supply teachers can never control the class quite like she does.

Marcus's classroom

Marcus is a young teacher who likes to reflect on practice, both his own and that of his colleagues. In the reference for his current post, his previous Head commented on his innovative approach to much of his teaching, in particular in expressive arts. Without really knowing why, he had felt uncomfortable in his previous school and was ready for a change. He teaches a mixed ability class of Year Four children, 16 girls and 14 boys. There is quite a high concentration of special needs, both in his class and across the school. Marcus's classroom is similarly well organised and he takes care to label resources to encourage independence. Fiction books are also banded in this school, but only as a guide to the children. They can choose any book they wish and because Marcus believes that a wide choice of reading material, both fiction and non-fiction, will promote a greater enjoyment of reading, the shelves contain a mix of different books. Those relating to the current topic are on a separate shelf, but are freely available – the children are just asked not to take topic books home because everyone in the class needs access to them. Sometimes Marcus overlooks this if a child is desperate to read a particular book and promises to bring it back the following morning. Most of the time they remember, because they understand their responsibility to their peers.

Children whose reading is supported are on a staged reading scheme which is managed by the Teaching Assistant, but these children, too, are allowed to read anything they wish during private reading times. Picture books are popular across the school so there are plenty in evidence. Comments from parents that, 'They're only looking at the pictures', are met by Marcus with a wry smile and, 'Reading pictures is an important part of reading, too'. Display boards are creative and colourful, although one board looks quite untidy as it has large pieces of sugar paper on it, covered with children's writing. Marcus explains that this is the working wall for their current science theme and the children have been forming and discussing hypotheses before they start their investigations.

The class contract is displayed, complete with class signatures. Marcus is pleased with this – he believes that power should be shared with the class whenever possible, so he did not provide them with any rules; the children came up with them. The fact that they resemble all the other class's rules demonstrates how well the children understand what good behaviour is. At least, he feels, they have ownership of their contract. The merit chart is displayed on the same board, together with the reward and sanction list. Merits add up to certificates and the house cup. A child explains that the teacher chooses two children every week for Gold Certificates in the celebration assembly. This could range from a particularly good piece of work, to effort or good behaviour. Otherwise, there are few rewards – the Head believes that children should not be praised for what the whole community does anyway, that is, keeping their cloakrooms and classrooms tidy, being polite to each other and showing consideration. He expects the staff both to model this and acknowledge examples of it from children by simply saying, 'Thank you'. The children agree with this, saying that reward, '. . . would be a bit odd because you should do it anyway', another child adding, 'Thank you is a kind of reward'.

The task board lists the learning for the day – this is a mixture of subjects (notably maths and English) and topic areas. Today, the afternoon is titled 'The RainForest: Tree Layers' (research, art, DT – design and technology). Nothing is listed about clerical tasks – Marcus explains that children collect their own merits when they have a spare moment. He is not aware of cheating and feels that he would see this fairly quickly if it happened, even if other children did not notice it first. Within reason, books can also be changed at any time and children can go to the Library whenever they wish as long as they check with him first. Marcus believes that if he gives children responsibility for their own decisions, they will act responsibly. If they do not, he will address it privately with the individual child.

Planning files in this classroom look like a work in progress. English and maths files are clearly labelled with lessons sequentially filed, but there are very few worksheets in evidence. All teachers in this school are committed to making learning as relevant an experience as possible, so real-life problems are gradually replacing maths worksheets, and writing for a real purpose drives the teaching of sentence and text structure, rather than the other way round. Staff have observed an increase in engagement as a result of this development; standards are rising and there seem to be less 'stuck' children. They are waiting for a complete cycle of data to prove this empirically. Coincidentally, staff have also noticed that some children are keener to read feedback comments and less keen to hunt for merits. The rest of the curriculum is topic based and Marcus wants to tie English into this wherever possible. This will not only make writing even more relevant, but will also lead to less duplication of tasks, freeing up more time for quality drafting and writing. Some maths links are obvious, too, although he wants to ensure that skills are progressing – keeping maths as a discrete subject serves this purpose.

As Marcus prepares for the first lesson of the day, he asks the children to finish off whatever they are doing; some are reading, some are completing work and some are discussing the Early Morning Challenge. Nobody moves from their place, as the classroom is rarely ability grouped. The lesson is well paced; Marcus demonstrates excellent subject knowledge and the children are soon engaged in their learning. There are regular peer discussion opportunities with feedback discussed by the whole class. Sometimes, if he is unsure of their understanding, Marcus will probe a group until he is satisfied. Many of his questions start with, 'Why do you think . . . ?' and he seems more concerned with the quality of the thinking than the correctness of the answers. Where answers are wrong, he will often throw it open for class discussion with a question such as, 'Do we agree . . . ?' Frequently, it is the child who gave the wrong answer who is the quickest to explore alternatives. Marcus does not agree that this is demeaning to any child who gives wrong answers as the children trust each other not to be critical and so they learn from each other's mistakes.

Because there is a lot of talking in this lesson, sometimes a child will call out or talk inappropriately. Although there are sanctions in place for this, Marcus prefers to raise an eyebrow in the direction of the child, which is usually enough of a reminder about taking turns. As they prepare for independent tasks, the children start to move around. They explain that grouping is based on what they need to learn next. They can indicate this by colour coding the previous day's work or their teacher can make the decision. The guided session is with a seemingly disparate group, but it quickly becomes clear that they are all at the same point in their understanding. This session, too, is characterised more by probing questions than didactic teaching. Marcus is slightly frustrated at the number of interruptions from children in other groups; he hopes that their ability to work independently will develop over the year. He has taught them strategies (use your brain, use a book, ask a buddy) but they do not seem to be embedding yet.

The classroom becomes noisier during the afternoon, when art and DT get underway. Children leave the classroom to collect resources and they show independence in their organisation. Some children sketch independently, whilst others work in groups to investigate the strength of different paper structures which simulate tree trunk thicknesses for different layers of the rainforest. Marcus circulates, prompting and probing to help children find solutions.

At the end of the day, Marcus also sits down to mark books. Each book has been colour coded by the child and Marcus spends minimal time on those coded green. With orange or red coding, he spends time reading any notes the child has written and deciding how to group them the following day to move their learning forward. It seems more like a partnership, as each book gets a responsive comment, phrased either as support or challenge. Some merits are given and these appear to be for effort. Marcus feels frustrated again as he looks back through the books, as children are still not building on his feedback comments effectively. Assessment will take place at the end of the unit.

Parents are generally happy with Marcus teaching their children, because their children are enthusiastic about going to school and they like their teacher. They are slightly concerned about the testing regime that Marcus has introduced, which involves peer testing of spellings and tables. Also, he does not ability group the class and some parents of able and special needs children are beginning to feel that this is disadvantaging their child. Some of his ideas, particularly about testing, seem progressive and this has been mentioned by parents, casually and in passing, to the Head. At his performance management meeting, this is discussed openly. Marcus and the Head agree that they need to communicate Marcus's philosophy more clearly. The Head is glad to have him on the staff, feeling that he will make a significant contribution to the next stage of the school's development. He has no hesitation in categorising Marcus as a good teacher, with many outstanding qualities.

Sue's classroom

Sue is a very experienced teacher, having taught across the whole range of Primary education. She has a wide array of teaching strategies and knows when to teach didactically and when to facilitate collaborative learning. This year, she is teaching a mixed ability Year Six class of 29 – 14 boys and 15 girls. Two boys have behaviour plans, a further four children are on the Special Educational Needs register and three children are on the Gifted and Talented register. Sue feels impatient about labelling children, as she believes that it creates hierarchies both in the classroom and amongst parents. She also wonders if there is a better way of supporting learning than an Inclusion Register. All Individual Education Plans are written with the children, who define their own learning needs. The Behaviour Plans are particularly carefully written in partnership with each child, as Sue believes that permanent change, whether it's social or academic, only happens when a child chooses to learn. Conversations with parents are open and frank; the child, the parents and Sue are clear about the support that she will give and the child and parents are clear about their responsibilities. Sue knows that she will achieve far less if parents do not engage in this partnership.

The classroom is well organised with labelled resources and attractively arranged bookshelves. Children can choose what they read, even if they are also on a reading scheme, and fiction, non-fiction, picture books, graphic novels and manga texts are all neatly arranged. Books are organised and rotated regularly by the children in consultation with the Learning Resource Assistant, selected from a well-stocked central resource area. Only topic books are restricted to the classes currently needing them. Children across the school can request the purchase of books and there is a community ethos of enjoyment of reading. Children volunteer to choose a focus author, often compiling simple presentations which are then saved on the network for everyone to use.

At the beginning of each year, most display boards in Sue's room are empty. In the first few days of term, display boards become colourful as they are quickly covered. The children maintain these themselves, choosing what they need to support their learning and what work they want displayed. In this way, they feel that fairer choices are made. One wall is given over to a working wall, which is full of questions such as, 'Does anyone know about democracy? Did it start in Greece?'. Someone has responded with a web address. There is a star chart on one board, but there are no names. This is because of concern that a named chart created hierarchies, promoted competition to win stars that did not necessarily support genuine learning and prompted unkind comments. As Emily says, '. . . people go off and talk about it and then say you didn't really deserve that'. So each child keeps their own, private chart and the public chart just shows the accumulation of merits for each House. The children appear happy with this and also talk enthusiastically about Good News Notes, which go home to parents. There are corresponding Bad News Notes, but they cannot remember the last time one was used. There is also a weekly celebration assembly in which two children from each class are awarded a Head Teacher's Certificate – Sue is uneasy with this because she knows that every week several children in her class are disappointed not to be chosen, but she makes sure that if a child is proud of something, a Good News Note goes home.

There does not appear to be a class contract, but you are pointed to some large colourful words which say that the children are all working together to make their classroom: Fun, Co-operative, Happy, Peaceful, Creative, Caring and Polite. Sue explains that these words were chosen by the children. First they brainstormed a list of words and then they removed duplicated words. This had led to a great deal of discussion about word meaning, including whether 'collaborative' was the same as 'co-operative', whether a peaceful classroom was a room with no noise and whether everything in the curriculum could be creative. Sue had taken part in this discussion as a peer, with occasional prompting questions, as the session had been led by the Class Councillors who had been elected the previous day. A child explains that they chose this instead of a list of rules because it described good things and anything that you might do wrong could be discussed in the context of one of these words. For instance, if you called someone names, your teacher would ask you which words you had forgotten about, which were not only 'Caring' and 'Polite' but also 'Happy' and 'Peaceful' because you have stopped the other person feeling these things.

The task board for the day lists activities, but there are no subject lessons in evidence. A Big Picture on the board states that the current theme for this class is 'Eureka!' and shows a central outcome, an inner circle containing 'Skills we will learn' and an outer circle stating, 'How we will learn them'. Closer examination shows that the theme is Ancient Greece. As the day begins, Sue explains that they are going to start with an investigation. She asks the children what they know about Pythagoras and then what they know about triangles. Most children contribute and the atmosphere is relaxed, with some spontaneous humour. Sue asks a lot of questions, then the children start working collaboratively on the investigation while Sue moves between groups, probing knowledge and challenging statements. At one point she stops the class so that one group can share what they have found. Questions are asked by various children, which all sound like thinking aloud – they begin with, 'How do you know . . . ?' or, 'What do you think . . . ?'. Sue is pleased with this interaction as she has worked hard on this aspect of speaking and listening. Frustrated with group talk in which some children took over whilst others complied, she trained the class to 'talk their thinking' including challenging each other's ideas. This was difficult at first, as the class felt that it was rude to question a peer in the same way that their teacher did, but once they overcame this, independent working followed quickly. All except for a few children, who still followed her round the classroom asking if they had got the right answer or whether they had written enough.

Throughout this exchange, Sue sits at the back of the classroom, apparently handing control to the children. Just before break, Sue asks the children to make a note of what they have learnt so far, what they would like to explore next and anything that they want to highlight in their self-assessment files. The classroom is quite noisy, although Sue explains that there are times in the day when they are completely silent, usually when working or reading independently. Children come and go for intervention sessions almost unnoticed. At various points, the Teaching Assistant comes into the classroom with a child, sitting with them to ensure that their one-to-one learning is being accessed and utilised. Sue works closely with her Teaching Assistant to ensure that all support work ties in to wider learning so that children gain maximum benefit.

At the end of the day, Sue looks through the children's comments, sometimes writing a comment and sometimes a question. Using Assessing Pupil Progress documents for six children, she highlights a statement and makes a note to confer with these children the following day to see if they agree with her. Assessment is a continuous partnership process in this school, with teachers updating tracking documents regularly. There is very little formal testing, but standards are rising rapidly.

Parents are sharply divided in their views of Sue. All parents are delighted that their children are such enthusiastic learners who love going to school, but a significant minority is very unhappy that there are no formal spelling or tables tests (peer testing is every child's responsibility), creative writing seems more important than neat handwriting and Home Learning (why not call it Homework?) is often an open-ended task that has no right answer for parents to check before it is given in. Further, they worry about the amount of time that Sue spends apparently sitting in the classroom, rather than standing at the front, teaching properly. She does not have a list of weekly test scores, declines to discuss their child's achievement in comparison with the rest of the class and seems to think that asking questions rather than teaching is developing their child's ability. They are particularly concerned that their children often work with peers of much lower ability and they interpret this grouping as a bottom set, assuming that Sue is unaware of how bright their children are.

They claim that their children should be moved to the top set. Parents have discussed this with the Head, who explains how children learn at the school, including the difference between setting and flexible grouping according to learning need. In addition, she adds, parents have been consulted about all these changes through the Parent Council and the ethos is consistent from Early Years through to Year Six. But it all seems very liberal and progressive; '. . . playing is fine when they're little, but not now,' remarked one parent. And the teacher their children had last year did not agree with these 'new-fangled' ideas even though it was school protocol and she continued to teach didactically and test weekly.

One day, during an OFSTED (the Office for Standards in Education, Children's Services and Skills) inspection, the parents, concerned about their children's readiness for 'proper learning' at Secondary school, complain about Sue to the Inspector who comes to the school gate to talk to them. Parents are keen to say that their children like coming to school, but are worried that they are going backwards. This triggers a thorough investigation into progress in Sue's class, which finds that not only do the children in her care make better than expected progress, they make significantly quicker progress than in previous years as they are prepared for end of Key Stage SATs (Standard Assessment Tests). Sue remains unperturbed as she believes that her teaching strategies are nurturing confident, inquisitive learners. At her annual performance management review, Sue discusses ideas for making pupil voice more meaningful. She is not interested in categorisation, viewing lesson observations as a vehicle for sharing ideas rather than an opportunity for judgement.

Behaviourist and constructivist paradigms

So, what's wrong with these three pictures? That depends on the perspective from which you view them. If you are a teacher, you will almost certainly see yourself in one of the three pictures, you can probably identify other teachers that you know and some of the profiles probably provoked strong reactions in you. For instance, you may think that Jane is much too controlling, not allowing pupils any opportunity to think for themselves or show any initiative, but Jane would not agree. Her school, which serves a large, sprawling estate with all the attendant problems of urban decay, has a very high proportion of challenging children. Staff believe that they are providing the children with the structure, stability and organisation that is lacking in many of their lives. They also believe that praise, consistently applied, is the only way to teach children the difference between acceptable and unacceptable social behaviour. They believe that children learn self-control when they are controlled and that working for praise motivates learning. Parents support this view and appreciate the order and control, which they feel makes for a good education.

You may agree with Jane's approach and feel that Sue is liberal, progressive and sloppy. Sue's school is in a mixed social area where you might expect that children would cope with a more relaxed ethos because they display quite mature social behaviour. But she also teaches some very challenging children and these are the children who flourish most in her care. Contrary to being sloppy, Sue believes that her teaching is rigorous and focused. She believes that distributing power in a classroom increases trust, facilitates learning, fosters ownership and empowers the community. She thinks that 'self' cannot be taught – she can only create the conditions in which self-control, self-confidence and self-esteem grow. Praise is a form of acknowledgement which the children value, but she is clear that she is not making a judgement and praise is never contingent on behaviour. When parents express concern, Sue encourages them to think back to a particular teacher or project that inspired them in their own education. They talk about an inspirational teacher or a project that captured their interest and even as adults they still remember how it felt to engage with effective learning. They never describe spelling and tables tests scores, handwriting practice or rote learning, yet they use these as benchmarks by which to judge their children's learning.

The three teachers actually share much in common; they are all caring, committed practitioners who want the very best for each child that they teach. They work hard, planning and assessing carefully and they know that effort is vital in the pursuit of excellence. They all demonstrate secure subject knowledge and the majority of their pupils make good or very good progress. They are all well respected within their schools, playing their part in creating cohesive communities. But what divides them may be more significant that what unites them.

The belief that a person can be trained to behave in chosen ways by the use of praise stems from behaviourist theory. It is so embedded in our thinking that most of us accept it without question. It pervades policy, both at national and local levels, and dictates much of what happens in a school community. Contrastingly, constructivist theory postulates that people construct their own knowledge through the filters of previous experience. Effective learning takes place when a teacher not only understands this, but welcomes cultural experience into the classroom, encouraging children to use these filters to make new meaning.

So why the concern with praise and reward? Because a school's position on this together with sanction (the opposite side of the same coin), is an effective indicator of its place on the behaviourist–constructivist spectrum. The same is true of teachers and parents and the debate is controversial; it creates a traditional versus progressive, or conservative versus liberal, dichotomy. It challenges beliefs and directs those who engage in it to examine the difference between their beliefs and their assumptions. The following chapters examine behaviourist and constructivist theory and the implications of these theories in classroom practice.

Points for reflection

- With which of these teachers do you most readily identify? Why?
- How did you react to the teachers who are different from you?
- In Jane's class, a child sought permission to collect a ruler. What does this say about power distribution in this teacher–pupil relationship?
- What praise and reward systems do you use in your school?
- What effect do you think praise has?
- How much do you know about your students' views of praise and reward?
- Think about your answers to the previous two questions. Separate your assumptions about praise and reward from your knowledge.

Chapter 2

The emergence of educational theory

The debate about effective strategies for motivating children to learn is not a modern one. This chapter outlines the thinking of the most influential educational theorists from the eleventh to early twentieth centuries. The dialogue has remained remarkably consistent for the last one thousand years – curriculum content, teaching styles, outdoor learning, the shaping of academic and social behaviours, motivational learning, healthy lifestyles and the role of parents.

Early educational philosophers

In the eleventh century, the views of Anselm of Canterbury (c.1033–1109) were widely respected; he opposed the use of coercion in raising and educating children, reflecting instead on the need for a child to be nurtured 'like a young plant' (Cunningham 2006: 29). The following conversation with an Abbot who had complained that the boys in his care were 'incorrigible ruffians' despite regular beatings, demonstrates his view:

St Anselm: Now tell me, my lord abbot, if you plant a tree shoot in your garden, and straightway shut it in on every side so that it has no space to put out its branches, what kind of tree will you have in after years when you let it out of its confinement?

the Abbot: A useless one, certainly, with its branches all twisted and knotted.

St Anselm: And whose fault would this be, except for your own for shutting it in so unnaturally? Without doubt this is what you do with your boys . . . you so terrify them and hem them in on all sides with threats and blows that they are utterly deprived of their liberty. And being thus so injudicially oppressed, they harbour and welcome and nurse within themselves evil and crooked thoughts like thorns, and cherish those thoughts so passionately that they doggedly reject everything which could minister to their correction. Hence, feeling no love or pity, goodwill or tenderness in your attitude towards them, they have in future no faith in your goodness.

(Cunningham 2006: 28–9)

Anselm understood that a child's character is formed by social environment and the quality of care within it, and that the future of the adult is also shaped by this early experience.

The theory of education forming the child was commented on by the Dutch humanist Erasmus (1466–1536), who described a child as, 'nothing but a shapeless lump . . . you must so mould it that it takes on the best possible character,' (Cunningham 2006: 111), a view which echoes that of Aristotle, writing in *De Anima* (*On the Soul*, Part 3) some two thousand years earlier, 'mind is in a sense potentially whatever is thinkable, though actually it is nothing until it has thought. What it thinks must be in it just as characters may be said to be on a writing tablet on which as yet nothing actually stands written: this is exactly what happens with mind.' The French philosopher René Descartes (1596–1650) took a different view, postulating that the human mind contained innate ideas from birth and that the function of education was to question everything that an individual assumed to know since sensory information might not be accurate. Reason was the route to knowledge.

John Amos Comenius (1592–1670)

Comenius, who is considered to be the father of modern education, was a practitioner, not just a theorist. He believed that education should be for everyone, regardless of gender or wealth. He organised schools and he was the first educator to apply the Cartesian theory of investigation and reason to learning. In 1658 he published *Orbis Pictus*, thought to be the first known picture book written specifically for children and containing pictures of the world. It was certainly a departure from previous textbooks.

Comenius also explained his beliefs in his book *Didactica Magna* (*The Great Didactic*), completed in 1631. He stated that children would engage in learning if their parents valued learning, supported their child's teacher and encouraged hard work. He also thought that classrooms should be attractive, clean and bright, with pictures, charts and maps displayed on the walls, an outside area in which to play and a garden in which students could study and appreciate plants. He exhorted teachers to be gentle and persuasive, to praise industry occasionally and to teach with some humour in order to make learning more pleasant. He even advocated dialogic teaching and group discussion in order to support the formation of knowledge. Civic leaders should attend school presentations and public performances, 'praising the industrious ones and giving them small presents (without respect of person)' (Comenius, 1967: 132).

He believed that children should start learning from familiar objects, moving to explore less familiar things to develop knowledge. He also believed that the acquisition of knowledge should be a pleasure, not just a task. He advocated emulating nature in that 'Nature compels nothing to advance that is not driven forward by its own mature strength' (ibid.: 137) and that teachers should teach only as much as a child can absorb, not the amount that the teacher wishes to impart. In summary, he wrote,

> The proper education of the young does not consist in stuffing their heads with a mass of words, sentences, and ideas dragged together out of various authors, but in opening up their understanding to the outer world, so that a living stream may flow from their own minds, just as leaves, flowers, and fruit spring from the bud on a tree.
>
> (ibid.: 147)

John Locke (1632–1704)

The Enlightenment thinker, John Locke, refuted Cartesian theory, revisiting the ideas of Aristotle and Erasmus in his 1690 *Essay Concerning Human Understanding* in which he wrote about a child's developing mind, 'The senses at first let in particular ideas, and furnish the yet empty cabinet, and the mind by degrees growing familiar with some of them, they are lodged in the memory . . .' Locke viewed a child's mind as a tabula rasa, or an empty (literally erased) slate, onto which information is impressed. He also describes the mind as, 'white paper, void of all characters, without any ideas,' which people paint on, 'with almost endless variety' through experience and reflection.

This book was followed in 1693 by a series of essays entitled *Some Thoughts Concerning Education*, which remained an authoritative text for the next century. In its dedication, Locke wrote that he felt the book was necessary because, '. . . the early corruption of youth is now become so general a complaint' and there was an obvious need for, 'virtuous, useful and able men' (Locke 2008: Dedication, location 49).

Locke's understanding of the word 'education' was holistic and he clearly saw parents and teachers as partners in whole-child education, making little distinction between them in his advice. He shared his views on play, clothing, exercise, sleep, healthy eating, parental authority and discipline, and the building of character. He argued that,

> he that has found a way how to keep up a child's spirit easy, active, and free, and yet at the same time to restrain him from many things he has a mind to, and to draw him to things that are uneasy to him . . . has, in my opinion, got the true secret of education . . . what he is to receive from education, what is to sway and influence his life, must be . . . habits woven into the very principles of his nature, and not a counterfeit carriage put on by fear, only to avoid the present anger.
>
> (ibid.: section 42, location 532)

Locke argued firmly against the use of corporal punishment, which he felt not only bred resentment, but was also ineffective in shaping internalised behaviour. He believed that a child would moderate behaviour only to avoid punishment or whilst being watched. In other words, he did not see any cause and effect between punishment, particularly corporal punishment, and good character in a child. He also reminded readers not to overload the children in their care with too many rules and to deal with misbehaviour, unless it was wilful disobedience, with, 'advice, direction and reproof' rather than punishment, additionally stating that, 'a look will be sufficient in most cases.' He suggested that educators should appeal to children's reason which they understand, 'as early as they do language', arguing that children, 'love to be treated as rational creatures' (ibid.: section 81, location 1062).

He also considered the role of reward in education, arguing against its efficacy with the same clarity with which he argued against corporal punishment, stating,

> when you draw him to do anything that is fit by the offer of money, or reward the pains of learning his book by the pleasure of a luscious morsel; when you promise him a lace-cravat or a fine new suit, upon performance of some of his little tasks; what do you do by proposing these as rewards, but allow them to be the good things he should aim at.
>
> (ibid.: section 52, location 593)

In other words, Locke is saying that offering reward focuses a child's attention and desire on the reward, rather than the task in hand. He argued that it is far better for parents or teachers to give their children gifts because they care about them, rather than reward them for doing something that they 'shew an aversion to, or to which they would not have apply'd themselves without that temptation' (ibid.: section 52, location 604). Bribery, he argued, was not good for a child's character development.

Locke also offered advice about management strategies that he believed would work without the need for reward or sanction, namely 'esteem and disgrace'. He suggested that children enjoy being praised, writing, 'First, children (earlier perhaps than we think) are very sensible of praise and commendation. They find pleasure in being esteem'd and valu'd and especially by their parents and those whom they depend on.' Conversely, he saw parental disappointment as a powerful motivator which precluded the need for corporal punishment saying that if parents '. . . shew a cold and neglectful countenance to them upon doing ill . . . it will, in a little time, make them sensible of the difference' (ibid.: section 57, location 630).

Turning to the use of reward in learning, Locke urged teachers not to force children to undertake tasks unwillingly, arguing that even play would become unattractive if a child was forced to play for several hours a day. Instead, he advised teachers to take advantage of willingness and curiosity so that learning is both an enjoyable and a positive experience. 'Curiosity in children,' he said, 'is but an appetite after knowledge; and therefore ought to be encouraged in them' (ibid.: section 118, location 1769). Further, he suggested that curiosity should be aroused by the use of strange or unknown things, in order to provoke questions. He suggested that children's questions should always be taken seriously and answered clearly and honestly.

Finally, he addressed the issue of suitable curriculum content for the education of an English gentleman, with a call not to 'have their heads stuff'd with a deal of trash.' Although specific to the needs of the seventeenth century, the argument about appropriate curriculum content sounds remarkably modern in its consideration of subject value. A complete chapter is devoted to the relevance of teaching grammar.

His suggestion for play-based early learning is also remarkably relevant, stating, 'I have always had a fancy that learning might be made a play and recreation to children . . . it must never be imposed as a task, nor made a trouble to them' (ibid.: section 148, location 2208). He suggested teaching the alphabet by using a ball with 32 sides, each side carrying a letter of the alphabet. He suggested sticking vowels to a die and consonants to three further dice in order to teach blends and he challenged readers to find other ways to teach reading through play. He believed that the human mind builds complex concepts by combining an understanding of simple concepts and also that one of the purposes of education is to teach a child a necessary social balance between liberty and self-control. In the nature/nurture debate, Locke's theories advocated nurture.

Jean-Jacques Rousseau (1712–1778)

Rousseau wrote his treatise on education by creating a fictitious character, whom he named Émile. He disagreed with Locke, believing that freedom and self-control were two separate entities and that childhood should allow a complete freedom through which self-control would develop over time – the nature side of the debate. He described Émile's education from babyhood to adulthood through defined stages of development; an education which was both child-centred and active, based on the exploration of nature in the early years of learning. He wrote, 'He wants to touch and handle everything; do not check these movements which teach him valuable lessons' (Rousseau 2004: 581). Rousseau did not value the acquisition of facts for their own sake, writing that children are taught in this way when a teacher needs to show that,

> there has been no time wasted; he provides his pupil with goods which can be readily displayed in the shop window, accomplishments which he can show off at will . . . If the child is to be examined he is set to display his wares; he spreads them out, satisfies those who behold them, packs up his bundle and goes his way.
>
> (ibid.: 116)

Because of the nature of his active learning, Émile had no bundle to display, but Rousseau believed that his learning was more useful because he had mastered the skill of thinking things out for himself – he had created his own knowledge rather than accepted transmitted facts from an adult or from books. Rousseau advised,

> The art of teaching consists in making the pupil wish to learn. But if the pupil is to wish to learn, his mind must not remain in such a passive state with regard to what you tell him that there is really nothing for him to do but listen to you.
>
> (ibid.: 193)

The transmission model of teaching was not part of Rousseau's thinking.

On the use of coercion or bribery to gain obedience, Rousseau wrote, 'When you try to persuade your scholars of the duty of obedience, you add to this so-called persuasion compulsion and threats, or still worse, flattery and bribes. Attracted by selfishness or constrained by force, they pretend to be convinced by reason' (ibid.: 47). In other words, they comply because it is advantageous to do so, not because they believe it to be the best course of action for its own sake. He understood the externally motivating force of punishment and reward.

Although Rousseau himself described *Émile* as a utopian novel, it gained a strong following amongst some and his theories were widely practised. His ideas are credited with influencing the concept of child-centred learning.

Johann Heinrich Pestalozzi (1746–1827)

Pestalozzi was born and raised in Zurich. He took an interest in the theory of education through acquaintance with Rousseau's *Émile*, although he later expressed dissatisfaction with Rousseau's theory, deciding that self-control needed to be taught. Through watching his own young son, he concluded that children learnt through experience, action, imitation and observation. He understood that learning required effort, determination and concentration. He also concluded that the relationship of the teacher with the pupil was critical. He wrote,

> life for the young child should be happy and free, and education in self-control should be gradual and careful. Punishment and restraint should rarely be necessary. Pressure to learn beyond the child's natural pace is harmful, and the denying of opportunities to learn by trial and error retards the development of character as well as of learning.
>
> (Pestalozzi quoted at *http://www.pestalozziworld.com/pestalozzi/lifeandwork.html*)

He put his theories into practice by creating a community of some twenty children who lived with the Pestalozzi family, learning to read, write and also to farm. He explained his view of education as a social and community enterprise in his first book, *Leonard and Gertrude*, published in 1781. He continued to develop his ideas whilst teaching in Burgdorf, where both the academic and social progress of his pupils was noticed following an inspection which commented that Pestalozzi had discovered the universal laws of teaching. Discipline, which was based on affection, was particularly noted.

In 1801 he published *How Gertrude Teaches her Children*, an 'Attempt to give Directions to Mothers how to Instruct their own Children', which explained his theories, proved through practice. He believed that children should learn in a safe environment which excluded corporal punishment, that learning should be sensory, that children moved from concrete to abstract thinking which meant that early learning should be practical and activity based, that children should think for themselves and that a love of learning was the best motivation to future learning.

Friedrich Froebel (1782–1852)

Froebel, the teacher credited with the creation of the kindergarten, originally started to train as an architect, having shown excellent visual skills as a child. He also had a keen love of nature. After teaching in a school in Frankfurt which was deeply influenced by the ideas of Pestalozzi, he decided to change careers. Opening his first kindergarten in 1840, he developed two ranges of play materials, called Gifts and Occupations, which were formed as cubes, blocks and shapes designed to encourage exploratory play. This pedagogy, although familiar to the modern world, was revolutionary in a system which valued rote learning and transmission of knowledge as the preferred teaching style.

Froebel also shared Pestalozzi's views of education as a community activity, the need for indoor and outdoor activity and the need for a holistic approach which encompassed parents and carers. He believed that education should encourage independence and interdependence, imagination, creativity, social, moral, cultural and spiritual awareness as well as the development of language, mathematical, physical, artistic and aesthetic skills. The ethos of Froebel's schools was one of engagement and encouragement, not punishment.

A range of modern paradigms are rooted in the views of these early philosophers and teachers. These include the need for early learning to be based on guided play, an understanding that learning is most effective when it is enjoyed and that active learning through exploration and observation motivates the most effective learning. There is also a shared belief that learning is a uniquely personalised process, dependent on prior knowledge and understanding. Interestingly, none of these early educators advocated a praise and punishment, or 'carrot and stick' approach to teaching – Locke argued cogently against it and encouragement, rather than punishment, was seen as preferable by most of the other writers.

The belief that knowledge grows through perception and experience is the basis of the constructivist paradigm, the development of which passed to Piaget, Vygotsky and others. But whilst all educators would agree on the need to nurture children, ensuring that they grow, learn and become prosocial individuals, the twentieth century saw less unity of view about how this should be achieved. New theories for filling the 'empty cabinet' (including who fills it and how) were developed, views which were diametrically opposed to the constructivist argument. The filling of the tabula rasa took on a very different face with the emergence of the behaviourist paradigm.

Points for reflection

- Compare Locke's view that a child's mind is an empty slate which needs filling, with Descartes' view that a human mind contains innate ideas at birth. How does your belief about this shape your professional practice?
- Pestalozzi and Froebel both believed in community-centred schools with strong parent/carer relationships. How is their belief reflected in your context?
- Locke warned that giving rewards focuses attention on material gain and so detracts from actual learning. Rousseau called them 'bribes'. What is your reaction to these opinions?
- None of these early educators advocated a 'carrot and stick' approach to learning. How would using this approach have affected their relationships with the children that they taught?
- What do the approaches of these writers say about a) power distribution and b) the trust relationship, in their learning environments? How might you respond to this in your own experience?

Chapter 3

Behaviourism – the perspective

This chapter reviews the emergence and development of behaviourist theory during the twentieth century, from Pavlov's early observations of animal behaviour to B.F. Skinner's formulation of the theory of operant conditioning. Behaviourists believe that behaviours can be studied and quantified through the 'black box' of the mind. The chapter concludes with an evaluation of behaviourist theory.

A review of behaviourist theory

Ivan Pavlov (1849–1936)

Pavlov was a Russian physiologist and psychologist who, whilst researching the neural and physical processes of dogs' digestive systems, observed a previously unremarked phenomenon. He noticed that the dogs started to salivate as an uncontrolled, or innate, reflex action when food was produced. He then observed that the dogs started to salivate when the lab technician was near them as if in expectation of food, leading him to question whether this reflex could be trained. His experiments involved using metronomes and whistles, in addition to the better-known bell. He established that if he used a particular sound just before the food was produced, the dogs would salivate by associating sound and food, after just a few attempts. Eventually, the dogs salivated at the sound alone, leading Pavlov to conclude that an unconditioned reflex could be trained by association to evoke a particular response, a phenomenon which he called classical conditioning.

Later in his life, Pavlov pursued the question of whether conditioning reflexes could have any effect on neurosis. Having, through detailed observation against defined criteria, categorised his dogs as either 'strong and balanced', 'strong and unbalanced' or 'weak' (Pavlov 1941), he varied the volume of sound used prior to feeding. He discovered that if a very loud sound was associated with food, the animal would show fear and not eat. From this, he concluded that a fear response could be engendered and trained through conditioning, although the degree of response appeared to be affected by the excitability of the subject, in this case, the dog.

Although he was awarded the Nobel Prize in Physiology or Medicine in 1904, Pavlov's work was not widely known in England until its translation in 1927. His work attracted great interest, preparing the way for other studies of behaviour. In addition to shaping the thinking of early twentieth century psychologists and scientists, his work had a more popular appeal, notably in Aldous Huxley's 1932 novel *Brave New World*. This is a dystopian narrative in which babies are conditioned from birth for a pre-determined role in a society in which all behaviours conform to the narrow requirements of their work. In a letter to his father on completion of the novel in 1931 (quoted in Huxley 1991), Huxley described, '. . . the appallingness of . . . the effects of such sociological reforms as Pavlovian conditioning of all children from birth and before birth'. In the words of the novel's Director of the Conditioning Centre, conditioning is seen as 'one of the major instruments of social stability' (ibid.). In writing a dystopian novel about the assumed utopia of a conditioned world, Aldous Huxley was quick to discern the future dialectic.

John B. Watson (1878–1958)

John Watson was born and educated in America where he worked as a school principal for a year before moving to the University of Chicago, studying philosophy with John Dewey and Jacques Loeb. Influenced by their thinking and his research studies into the link between sensory stimuli and learning in birds and animals, Watson formulated the theory which he named 'behaviourism'. He believed that differences in individual behaviour were due not to fundamental differences in people themselves, but in their differing experiences. In 1913, he published *Psychology as the Behaviorist Views It*, which is popularly known as the Behaviourist Manifesto. In it, Watson states that, 'Psychology as the behaviorist views it is a purely objective experimental branch of natural science. Its theoretical goal is the prediction and control of behavior' (Watson 1913: 158).

In 1920, Watson, working with graduate student Rosalie Raynor, conducted the Little Albert Experiment. He had observed that children often expressed fear in response to loud noises, but that this was an innate, or unconditioned, response. The experiment tested his hypothesis that, in accordance with Pavlov's theory of classical conditioning, a child could be conditioned to be afraid of a stimulus which they had not previously reacted to, through association with their own, innate, fear response. Accordingly, he exposed a nine-month-old baby, Albert, to a range of stimuli, including a white rat. Albert showed no fear, so two months later the white rat was re-introduced. In subsequent sessions, a loud noise was made behind Albert as he reached out to the rat, and he showed the expected fear response to the noise. After several sessions of associating a frightening noise with the appearance of the rat, Albert cried and demonstrated fear just when the rat was introduced. Not only did Albert subsequently fear the rat, but also other linked stimuli, including white rabbits and dog fur. This led Watson to conclude that stimulus generalisation had occurred; Albert had associated his conditioned fear of the white rat with a group of objects which shared some similar characteristics.

The experiment ended when Albert moved away and he was not deconditioned, so there was no empirical evidence of the extent of his fear or whether it persisted through childhood or into his adult life. In fact, after several years of searching, it was discovered that Albert had died at the age of six from hydrocephalus. Although Watson concluded from this single experiment that the fear response could be conditioned, it had just one subject, it was never repeated and it would not conform to any modern ethical research guidelines. Even so, his work gained popularity with its promise of a science which could control behaviour. Ten years later, he was confident enough of his behaviourist theory to write,

> Give me a dozen healthy infants, well-formed, and my own specified world to bring them up in and I'll guarantee to take any one at random and train him to become any type of specialist I might select – doctor, lawyer, artist, merchant-chief and, yes, even

beggar-man and thief, regardless of his talents, penchants, tendencies, abilities, voca-
tions, and race of his ancestors.

(Watson 1970: 82)

This statement encapsulates his view that behaviours can be shaped to the chosen end of a
behaviourist practitioner regardless of the culture, heredity, consciousness and self of the
individual. Environment is everything – one only has to control the environment to control
the individual.

Edward Lee Thorndike (1874–1949)

Edward Thorndike was the first behaviourist to consistently apply theory to educational
practice, developing an early form of behaviourist educational pedagogy. He may also have
been the first to discuss the concept of behaviour modification. Whilst studying with William
James (a renowned physiologist and brother of novelist Henry James) at Harvard, Thorndike
developed two significant techniques for studying animal behaviour – the puzzle box and
the maze.

The puzzle box was created to test Thorndike's hypothesis that learning was a result of
trial and error. A box was designed with a foot pedal which opened a closed door, allowing
the occupant to access food. A cat was then shut in the box. Initially, the cat would explore
the box, stepping on the pedal and opening the door by accident. As the experiment was
repeated, the cat operated the switch more quickly. Thorndike plotted the speed of escape
on a graph to demonstrate the learning curve, repeating similar experiments with other
species. He found that the curve of the graph resembled an 'S' shape, with initially slow
progress followed by much faster learning until a plateau of learning was reached. From this,
he concluded that learning was a result of connections being made between stimuli (being
shut in the cage) and responses (stepping on the pedal to achieve freedom). He derived
similar conclusions from his work with mazes.

From his research, Thorndike formulated his Law of Effect, which stated that if the
outcome of a behaviour is pleasing, that behaviour will be repeated because the action is
associated with satisfaction. Conversely, if an outcome is unsatisfactory, the behaviour is less
likely to be repeated. His results were published as *Animal Intelligence* in 1898.

By the time Thorndike moved to Teachers College, Columbia, in 1899, he had developed an interest in the application of his learning theories to the field of education; he
remained at Columbia University for the next forty years, developing a scientific approach
to educational psychology. It is worth considering his definition of primary education, as
this is his stated agenda for all teachers. The following was written in 1906:

> . . . physical training and protection against disease; knowledge of the simple facts of
> nature and human life; the ability to gain knowledge and pleasure through reading and
> to express ideas and feelings through spoken and written language, music and other
> arts; interests in the concrete life of the world; habits of intelligent curiosity, purposive
> thinking, modesty, obedience, honesty, helpfulness, affection, courage and justice . . .
>
> (Thorndike 2009b: 4)

It would be difficult to disagree with any of this. The issue is the *how* rather than *what*. His
philosophy, imbued with behaviourist theory, can be summarised in his own words:

It is a fundamental law of mental life that if a mental state or bodily act is made to follow or accompany a certain situation with resulting satisfaction, it will tend to go with that situation in the future. The applications of the law to teaching are comprised in the simple and obvious but too commonly neglected rules. Put together what you wish to have to go together. Reward good impulses. Conversely; keep apart what you wish to have separate. Let undesirable impulses bring discomfort.

(ibid.: 110)

In the course of his working life, Thorndike defined a set of quantifiable measurements of mental traits which he used to assess the learning of all children from 'moral defectives' to 'exceptional children'. Rather than theorising, his aim was to apply the science of psychology to teaching, learning and assessment, and he did this comprehensively; his philosophy of drilling and testing in phonics and arithmetic as an accurate measure of learning still pervades current curricula and thinking. He believed that learning was incremental, therefore the curriculum should be carefully planned and that the pleasure associated with reward would condition children to learn.

B.F. Skinner (1904–1990)

The extent to which behaviourist theory is embedded in the minds of educators is attributed to the work of the psychologist, B.F. Skinner. In 1913, Thorndike formulated the Law of Effect which stated that, 'if an organism emits a response, and that response is followed by reinforcement, the probability of the response's recurring will be increased' (Thorndike, cited Skinner 1968; Deci 1975). According to this theory, behaviour is shaped by consequences. Skinner illustrates this with the example (Skinner 1972) that if a person moves into the shade because he is hot and so cools down, he is more likely to repeat this behaviour the next time the sun is hot. Cooling down reinforces the behaviour choice. If a person then moves into the shade before becoming too hot, Skinner described this phenomenon as 'operant conditioning'.

Skinner perceived that the educational climate of his time encouraged 'aversive conditioning' (ibid.), whereby pupils worked to avoid punishment. He believed that this aversive response was actually reinforcing the behaviour of the teacher. Whilst some positive reinforcement was evident, it was either applied too infrequently or too inconsistently to have a significant effect. He argued that if pupils were consistently praised (positive reinforcement) for learning or behaving in a certain way, they would behave in the same way again, thus creating 'conditions which are optimal for producing the changes called learning' (Skinner 1968: 10) and allowing the teacher to influence the behaviour of pupils at will without resorting to punishment. He further argued that a positive reinforcement schedule would need to be carefully structured in order to maintain the required behaviour, concluding, 'The application of operant conditioning to education is simple and direct. Teaching is the arrangement of contingencies of reinforcement under which students learn' (ibid.: 64).

However, perceiving that human behaviour is too complex to be entirely dependent on the reinforcement of teacher/pupil interaction, Skinner invented a Teaching Machine which rewarded the pupil when obtaining the correct answer. The inspiration for this came from a visit which he made to the school of one of his children. Observing a maths lesson, he noted that whilst some children were moving rapidly through the work with ease and learning nothing new, others were struggling to understand the necessary concepts to even attempt the work. In addition, all children had to complete the work before any kind of feedback was given, although Skinner believed that to be most effective, reinforcement needed immediacy. He also realised that in a classroom full of children at different stages of learning, immediate teacher reinforcement was not possible. Advocating the mechanisation of the classroom to maximise learning efficiency (Skinner 1968), he stated that a 'technology of teaching' could 'maximise the genetic endowment of each student' (ibid.: 103) – personalised learning which predated the availability of online learning programmes.

The first models of his Teaching Machine merely repeated known learning, but within three years he had developed the Machine to the point where material was broken into small, repeated steps, a new concept was introduced and then help and support were gradually withdrawn until the pupil had learnt something new. He understood that the sequencing of steps, with immediate feedback, led to effective learning.

Skinner expounds his philosophy of behaviourism in his Utopian novel, *Walden Two* (Skinner 1976), an extant inner dialogue in which an education and childcare system is scientifically designed so that each child lives in an ideal environment in which they can thrive and learn. At some points Frazier, the fictitious community leader, appears to cogently argue for a constructivist ideal, when outlining an education which is 'practical, relevant and driven by child interest . . . since our children remain happy, energetic and curious, we don't need to teach "subjects" at all' (ibid.: 110–11). The counter-argument is effectively rehearsed through the narrative of the novel, as Burris, a visiting Professor, views the necessary control as 'sadistic tyranny' (ibid.: 99) and engages frequently in a debate about free will and personal choice in the context of social engineering.

The philosophical tension of this novel highlights the assumptions inherent within the behaviourist perspective – that control and structured socio-cultural design are positive strategies. Frazier argues that the application of positive reinforcement in order to design a learning community is an ideal, stating that, 'By a careful cultural design, we control not the final behaviour but the inclination to behave – the motives, the desires, the wishes' (ibid.: 246). In this way, he asserts, those who are controlled still feel free – an argument also posed by Rousseau (*Émile*, cited Skinner 1968) and quoted regularly by Skinner.

Skinner, through the alter ego of Frazier, also highlights a weakness of the behaviourist paradigm – it is too detailed a science to be used without years of training (Skinner 1976) if it is to effectively control behaviour, creativity, thinking skills, problem solving and attention span in the way that Skinner intended. In asking why a young child's curiosity to learn is not replicated in the classroom, he concluded that positive reinforcement is not applied early enough or consistently enough in a child's early life (Skinner 1968), as a result of which teachers must spend their time using praise and reward to re-shape their pupils' socio-cultural habits or reinforce those which are acceptable, both of which he viewed as a waste of teaching time.

Skinner addressed the issue of control, and therefore power, very little in his writing, beyond saying that the pupil also has control over the teacher through their response to aversive or positive reinforcement (Skinner 1972). In a debate with the neuroscientist Donald Mackay in 1971 (analysed in a BBC Radio 4 *Head to Head* broadcast in 2011), Skinner rejected the theory of free will, stating that it was merely a human construct, 'to free oneself from certain kinds of aversive, coercive or punitive conditions'. He further argued that what we perceive to be independent choices are actually choices determined by our environment. He did not therefore think that control was necessarily a bad thing, since he believed that humans are influenced by hidden forms of control anyway – the modern phenomenon of advertising would be an example of such control. Although Skinner wanted to 'design a more effective culture', he abandoned the pursuit of absolute power in education, not through any ethical consideration but because it seemed to be out of reach.

It is clearly necessary to his theory that power rests only with certain individuals, but there is no debate about the inherent weakness in this form of social structure. For conditioning to be effective in the classroom, absolute power must rest with the teacher, who designs and delivers the reinforcement schedules. Apart from any moral argument about autocratic control, there is no discussion about the suitability of the people with whom this power resides to exercise it fairly – presumably Skinner had faith in the teaching profession never to act in self-interest, or inadvertently train its own weaknesses into the community. And although Skinner's theory was in part a reaction to the aversive conditioning of punishment, what alternative does a behaviourist teacher have but to punish when positive reinforcement fails and their autonomy is questioned or threatened?

The issue of motivation is also discussed very little – this may be because it was not important to Skinner, or possibly because motivation had not yet become a subject of detailed study. In *Walden Two* (Skinner 1976), Frazier does suggest that an individual could develop a form of self-control if operant conditioning were successful enough, although control of this should still remain with society (in this context society remains undefined, but presumably means the group of design-controllers who structured the conditioning schedule). In *The Technology of Teaching* (Skinner 1968), Skinner personally appears to argue that motivation is no more than 'the arrangement of contingencies of reinforcement' (ibid.: 11) – that is, extrinsically controlled but with the appearance of intrinsic decision.

An evaluation of behaviourist theory

Critics of behaviourism argue that it excludes other developmental factors, including heredity, external influences such as culture (the 'nature versus nurture' dispute) and the internal influences of thought, feelings and emotions. Conditioning is a passive process on the part of the recipient and thought processes are not considered. The humanist perspective conflicts with behaviourism's deterministic conclusion that all behaviour is conditioned by environment. This denies the existence of an individual's free will in interpreting, reacting to and shaping that environment, or the ability of an individual to adapt their behaviour if they discover new information. Behaviourism also cannot explain how spontaneous learning takes place – a phenomenon that every teacher and parent regularly witnesses – and intuitive or exploratory thinking and the construction of meaning from previous knowledge.

Much behaviourist theorising assumes that humans learn in the same way as animals, so that observed animal behaviours can be assumed to be the same in humans: it is also a reductionist theory in its assumption that all behaviour can be explained as stimulus and response. Perhaps most significantly, there is no consideration of the role of motivation in behaviour – in many experiments where food was the reward, it is possible that the animals were motivated by the desire for food, i.e. the reward was of enough need or interest to the animal to engage in the experiment. Supporters of behaviourism argue the benefits of its application to behaviour modification and also the advantage of its quantitative research methodology, which yields measurable results.

By the 1920s, behaviourist theory was being questioned, in particular by Edward Tolman, who has been described as a cognitive behaviourist. His evidence showed that when rats were allowed the freedom, they explored a maze without external reward. But they not only explored it, they appeared to develop a mental map of the maze, using alternative routes when one was blocked. He concluded that reward was not necessary to reinforce behaviour as some form of cognitive activity was involved in motivating a spontaneous act of learning. In 1942, L.P. Crespi further discovered that the speed that rats moved was directly related to the size of the available reward – the smaller the reward, the more slowly the rats ran. It can therefore be concluded that when reward was offered, it was the size of the reward, not the reward itself, which was motivating the behaviour.

Although the Canadian psychologist, Albert Bandura (b. 1925) is sometimes categorised as a behaviourist, he rejected pure behaviourism as too simplistic. Whilst he considered the concepts of reinforcement and conditioning in his work, he interpreted these through cognitive functioning. In 1961, he conducted his famous Bobo (inflatable) Doll experiment. An adult was filmed hitting and acting aggressively towards the doll. When children were shown the film and then played in a room containing a similar doll, the children replicated the adult behaviour which they had observed and also acted aggressively towards the doll. Since the children were not rewarded or incentivised in any way to copy the adult behaviour, Bandura concluded that the children's behaviour was imitative based on their observation of the adult. His social learning theory moved beyond behaviourism by concluding that much human behaviour is learnt through imitation of other humans. He also believed that environment and behaviour acted reciprocally.

Points for reflection

- Define the strengths and weaknesses of behaviourist theory.
- What are the advantages and disadvantages of applying behaviourist principles to social and academic learning?
- Identify and discuss the inherent assumptions of behaviourist theory.
- In what ways has behaviourism affected your beliefs as an educator and therefore shaped your professional practice?
- To what extent, and in what ways, do you exercise control in your classroom?
- What are the ethical implications of control?
- Rousseau believed that guided freedom led to the development of self-control. Locke believed that both freedom and self-control should be guided and modelled simultaneously. Skinner believed that freedom was a human construct which hindered conditioning and that self-control should be conditioned and reinforced. What do you think?

Chapter 4

Behaviourism contextualised – translating theory into practice

Even though the simplistic approach of behaviourist theory was being questioned by the beginning of the twentieth century, the principles of behaviourism steadily gained a foothold in the thinking of both educationalists and parents. It continued to embed, even as other teaching methods were evaluated and evolved to meet the changing needs of the twentieth century. Several decades of research into learning motivation have still failed to fully impact on the implementation of behaviourist practices, which are evidenced at every level of the education service.

The behaviourist paradigm evidenced in national policy

During the 1970s, the practice of giving prizes, medals and other rewards fell from favour as it was seen to provoke competition and create hierarchies. But in 1989, the Elton Report *Discipline in Schools* gave direction on the use of reward, recommending that all schools should, 'provide a range of rewards accessible to pupils of all abilities'. Praise and reward, as a direct translation of behaviourist theory, quickly became part of everyday school life. In 1993, OFSTED (the Office for Standards in Education, Children's Services and Skills) noted in the report *Achieving Good Behaviour in Schools* that praise and reward must be applied with consistency in order to be effective and that it should be made for genuine achievement, not for conformity.

Currently, behaviourism is so embedded in our educational practice that it pervades much of our training and advisory literature, with the value of its strategies accepted without question. It is promoted as effective practice from the DfE (the Department for Education), in training materials such as the *Further Literacy Strategy* (2002), which contain comments such as; 'Praise and reward good behaviour . . . praise what the group achieve when they work together . . . praise the children for "having a go" even if they make a mistake . . . praise the bits they got right', and in behaviour management, 'Choose one aspect of behaviour to work on – for example if one child always interrupts, tell them that they will be rewarded if they do not interrupt that session' (DfES 2002).

The Steer Report

The Steer Report *Learning Behaviour* (2005) examined issues of behaviour and discipline in schools, stating that, 'As experienced practitioners we know many schools have excellent systems in place to reward good work and behaviour'. One key recommendation is the auditing of reward and sanction as part of school policy (Steer 2005: Section 2, point 24), stating that all good teaching is underpinned by a praise and reward structure (ibid.: section 2, point 22). The use of Praise Postcards was offered as evidence of best practice. One school policy required every teacher to send at least one postcard home every day, with the reward focus being changed weekly 'to ensure that the widest possible number of students became eligible'. Steer also echoed the 1989 Elton Report in asserting that 'All schools should have a wide range of appropriate rewards' (Steer 2005). Further, the final report (Steer 2009: 25) states that 'Clear rules and the consistent application of rewards are essential,' and when describing successful schools, 'Praise is used to motivate and encourage pupils' (ibid.: 79).

There is no consideration in this report of those schools which do not motivate pupils in this way and it is implicit throughout that praise and reward are the only way to motivate good learning and social behaviours. The statement, 'all good teaching is underpinned by a praise and reward structure' actually explicates this cause-and-effect formula – so what of those good schools and teachers for whom this is not the case? How can they be good teachers without using the carrot and stick approach? Consider Marcus's school described in Chapter 1. The Head of his school was clear that children would not be rewarded for meeting community expectations and the pupils themselves regarded it as 'a bit odd' to be rewarded for doing something that everyone should do anyway. Their behaviour (and in consequence their learning) met high expectations without the need for reward. A reductionist view which assumes that praise is motivational, and that it is the only motivational strategy that good teachers should use, pervades national policy.

Charlie Taylor's behaviour checklists

In October 2011, Charlie Taylor, the government's Expert Adviser on Behaviour in Schools, published *Getting the Simple Things Right: Charlie Taylor's behaviour checklists*. It contains 22 key principles for Head Teachers to improve behaviour and a further 21 principles for class teachers. It suggests that every class should display reward and sanction tariffs, with a system for 'ensuring that children never miss out on sanctions and rewards'. Heads are exhorted to praise good staff performance whilst monitoring the amount of praise, rewards and punishments that each teacher gives to ensure individual alignment with behaviour policy. Teaching staff are encouraged to use parallel praise, which praises children 'for doing the right thing more than criticising those who are doing the wrong thing' (DfE 2011).

The agenda of this document is quite clear – children are controlled by praise and sanction and their teachers are controlled through monitoring their compliance with a praise and sanction policy.

The behaviourist paradigm evidenced in school policy

This view then trickles down to the level of school policy which is effected at every level of school life. Consider the statements contained in the sample behaviour policy in Appendix A, an example of an 11–16 Secondary school policy which stems from behaviourist belief. The centrality of reward is clear, together with a belief that this will engender mutual respect. Expectations are made very clear to students through display and regular discussion. The requirements of both staff and students are also defined, so everyone in the community is aware of their role. The Teaching and Learning Policy in Appendix A (from a Primary school) demonstrates how behaviourism affects learning, to the extent that in this policy, children have no part to play in their own learning – a phenomenon described by the writer Alfie Kohn as 'doing to' rather than 'working with' (Kohn 2000a). Detailed lesson plans for the week have to be delivered to the Head each Monday morning, so there is no opportunity for teachers to follow the learning – the Head regularly drops into classes unannounced to ensure that teaching is going according to plan.

But behaviourism also affects curriculum content. Sometimes described as mastery learning, goals are set by the teacher and broken down into incremental steps. Feedback to reinforce right answers is given regularly and fluency is built through repetition. Cues to elicit the right response are given during questioning and the correct answer is then reinforced through praise or reward. This approach is also known as 'skill and drill' or 'teach and test'. Planning is regulated, with the skill for the teacher being in defining the size of the incremental step in each lesson and the place of each child on the learning steps. Regular testing ensures that assessment is a straightforward matter of ticking the target boxes – achievement and performance are quantifiable. Single subject teaching will also be more evident in a Primary context than creative curriculum design and any cross-curricular links would be planned and explicated through teaching.

The use of synthetic phonics as a 'one size fits all' approach to teaching reading in English schools is an example of this, one which has provoked considerable controversy. Whilst nobody is denying that understanding a phonemic code is essential in learning to read, it is also true that reading is not solely about code breaking. This debate has also been held in the US, where phonics versus Whole Language (an approach to reading devised by Kenneth and Yeta Goodman of the University of Arizona) has raged for several years.

The learning environment, which is set by the teacher at the beginning of each school year, is also influenced by the beliefs of the community and the appearance of each classroom is often directed through policy. Every classroom is value-laden and its appearance communicates the sort of teaching and learning which goes on within it. In a behaviourist context, display content is decided by the teacher; the classroom will contain criteria for, and evidence of, rewards and sanctions; the organisation of resources will steer students in particular directions, seating, rules and regulations all communicate the role of the teacher as sole manager and signify expectation of the pupils at each stage of their day. When students enter the room, they will respond to the environment. The nature of questioning from the teacher and the type of talk contained within the classroom (mostly answering questions or engaging in transactional talk) will be controlled by the approach of the teacher.

The behaviourist paradigm evidenced in classroom practice

Although Skinner was interested in the technology of teaching and learning itself, his work today has been almost completely diverted into strategies for managing social behaviour. This is evident in a popular theory devised by Lee Canter and elucidated in his text *Assertive Discipline: Positive Behaviour Management in Today's Classroom* (Canter and Canter 1992). Defined by City University, New York (Weber 2005) as the most widely used behaviour management package in the United States (it was widely used in England during the 1990s, although it has now largely fallen from favour), it provides a comprehensive schedule of every aspect of behaviour management which should be explicitly taught to the class and must then be regularly reinforced with praise.

Teachers are advised to choose the rules that work for them, considering student input but making a final choice of rules which meet the needs of the teacher. Praise is then used to reinforce observance of the rules. Canter urges teachers to display information about available rewards such as being first in the line at break or eating lunch with the teacher, and even advises that positive reinforcement of a direction should be provided every time it is given in the first two weeks, every third time it is given in the following two weeks and every fourth time thereafter. Teachers are advised to write this schedule into their planning documents along with praise opportunities, stating, 'Make praise the most consistent positive reinforcement technique you use. Start thinking now about all the opportunities you have each day to recognise your student's successes' (Canter 1992: 151). He further states that praise is, 'the most powerful support you can give. What's the easiest way to motivate students? Praise. The most effective? Praise. Under all circumstances? Praise' (ibid.: 62).

As there is little doubt that many children will comply with a teacher who demonstrates this level of organised control over every aspect of the classroom and who also has a range of sanctions to apply to each misdemeanour, it would appear that this behaviourist approach is successful. However, no questions are asked about what the teacher is successful at doing – controlling children, clearly, but some bold statements are made by the author for which he provides no evidence, either empirical or anecdotal. These include, 'students learn to respect and trust an assertive teacher', 'positive recognition will . . . increase students' self-esteem', create a 'positive atmosphere in the classroom' and 'establish positive relationships with students'. There is, therefore, an assumption that planned control will necessarily create a positive learning environment. There is no consideration of the possibility that the most effective lesson that children are learning is compliance to an externally imposed code of conduct.

The school visit described below typifies the outworking of behaviourist theory in the classroom. The visiting teacher, who was spending a day in the school, was asked when she arrived not to go into any classrooms without permission. Her request to visit the Early Years setting was met with some reserve, but after about twenty minutes she was escorted to the relevant classroom where 15 four-year-olds were sitting neatly at tables in complete silence, clearly primed to be on their best behaviour. For the following fifteen minutes, the teacher introduced the session's play to the class. She informed the attentive children that the playhouse was no longer a shop; today it had become an ice cream hut. The children were all going to the beach, they were going to purchase their favourite ice cream from the square end window of the hut and then sit nicely whilst they ate their ice creams, before paddling in the sea and returning home. The session would conclude with the children drawing a picture of their experience and annotating it with words chosen from the list provided by the class teacher, who explained that these were words which the children already knew and which were being reinforced. The activity proceeded quietly, the children were all polite and compliant, the resulting pictures were carefully drawn and annotated after the teacher had questioned the class about what they had done and support was given to any child who struggled.

Later in the day, the visiting teacher met with the School Council, who had a thoughtfully prepared list of questions about what her pupils enjoyed doing and learning in her own context. At various points, she asked the children some questions of her own, in the same way that she would have done with her own School Councillors. But the result was slightly different – she was met with a tsunami of ideas, thoughts, comments and conversation, the children tripping over each other in their excitement to join in.

During a conversation at the end of the day, the Head happened to mention how good the Early Years practitioner was and what an excellent example of early education had been witnessed. She talked with enthusiasm about the targets achieved, measurable progress made and the excellent behaviour displayed which was an outcome of the teacher's outstanding management. The words 'spontaneity' or 'creativity' appeared to be anathema when introduced into the conversation, although the Head did express some concern that a young teacher that had just joined the staff took this progressive approach and was raising some concerns because collaborative learning was leading to a noisy classroom. She was creating work for herself because her approach meant that she had to set a lot more individualised targets. It had also been noticed that she was much less able to award merit stars consistently as behaviour was so much harder to quantify – it felt as though the teacher was allowing the children too much freedom. In conclusion, the Head apologised for the outburst by the School Council, although she did, in their defence, mention that they were not accustomed to having their views solicited which was why their response had been so exuberant.

So how had behaviourism influenced the learning environment in this school? Praise for the children was given often in the Early Years classroom and it was given consistently when children conformed to the teacher's requirements. The learning environment was determined and controlled by the teacher, as she had quantifiable targets to be achieved in a given time frame, so a high level of control was necessary. Teacher–pupil interaction was clear; questions were asked and answers elicited to demonstrate learning. The children were confident in their relationship with the teacher and could assume her support and attention when asking for clarification. Pupil–pupil interaction was polite, clearly articulated and mostly transactional. Exploratory conversations were quickly redirected by staff. The school had also bought into the concept of pupil voice enough to establish a School Council. But if its views were not sought, where was the voice of the pupils?

But although praise and reward are used in the majority of schools, the systems in use and the way they are applied vary widely according to context. Most Primary schools use stickers, stars and certificates; in some schools, these accumulate to individual awards and in other schools to house or team rewards. Most schools have some form of celebratory assembly which serves as a corporate reinforcement of the school's values and many schools, particularly in the earlier years of education, involve parents in this celebration. Companies who produce anything from subject stickers to bespoke rewards abound and an internet search quickly reveals a dazzling array of choices. Most children appear to love collecting stars, stickers and stamps and are keen to share them with parents and carers. There is some suggestion that children engage with this less in the later stages of Primary school when peer approval starts to outweigh parental approval. At Secondary school, credit or house points are still used, although many students themselves say that interest wanes after the first two or three years of Secondary school.

An increasing number of schools are raising the stakes in their reward systems by allowing students to accumulate credits to purchase material items. Vivo Miles is one of the fastest growing companies offering this service. Students are issued with a plastic card similar to a credit card on which their miles are logged. The system is electronic, the participating school can decide the criteria for awarding credits and teachers who use it find that it is easier to manage than internal paper-based systems. Set up costs and reward costs are met by the school – one estimate suggests that the rewards can cost about £28,000 a year. The Vivo Miles website states that attendance improves; exclusions fall; academic performance is nurtured; students are motivated; they learn about personal finance; and community cohesion and healthy choices improve in schools which use the system. In spite of its widespread popularity, not everyone is convinced; some parents object to their children being bribed with material possessions for meeting their most basic expectations (such as going to school every day) and others feel that it encourages selfishness in their children, teaching them that everything they do deserves material return. In the words of Lord Darlington 'What is a cynic? A man who knows the price of everything and the value of nothing' (Oscar Wilde, *Lady Windermere's Fan*). Will paying children to do what they should do anyway merely nurture a generation of cynics?

One company (Primary Technology) has developed a software program called 'Eyes to the front' which gives reward points for looking at the teacher. Webcams detect eye movements and use facial recognition to give points to the quickest child to respond and keep looking. Although this may create a short-term attention focus, there is no guarantee that children are actually paying attention, listening and learning – they will focus on what they are being asked to do, which is to look. It could provoke competition without enhancing learning (it may well detract from the learning process as children compete to be rewarded) and it would be quite possible to obstruct peers in order to win reward points, leading to claims of unfairness.

Other schools link with companies to reward pupils. In the United States, Pizza Hut runs a BOOK IT! programme each year which quite simply, 'motivates children to read by rewarding their reading accomplishments with praise, recognition and pizza' (*http://www.bookit.com*). Monthly goals are set by participating teachers and children earn a pizza each time the goal is achieved. The Alumni section of the website includes comments from adults who were involved in the scheme as children. Their pride in their achievement is clear, but the focus of the comments is not reading achievement but the acquisition of the free pizza – it is important to be clear what is being achieved in a reward situation. It would be interesting to know if this early encouragement develops into a lifelong love of reading, if reading progress in participating schools is more rapid than non-participating schools and whether progress is sustained during the months of the year that the programme is not running.

The behaviourist paradigm evidenced in research literature

Several researchers have investigated the use of praise in the classroom. In 2002, Robyn Beaman and Kevin Wheldall of Macquarie University, Australia, reviewed existing empirical evidence on the use of teacher approval and discovered that teachers generally approve of good work and disapprove of poor behaviour, but not with any consistency in either case. They state that, given the considerable amount of literature proving the effectiveness of praise, it is surprising that teachers do not make more use of contingent praise in order to reinforce both academic and social behaviour more systematically and consistently. It suggests that learning could be improved through the consistent application of a behaviourist agenda. There is, however, no consideration of the intrinsic values or limitations of behaviourism *per se*.

In 2004, Karen Chalk and Lewis Bizo of the University of Southampton, England, examined specific contextual praise and found that consistent use of such praise improved on-task behaviour, although enjoyment of learning appeared to remain unchanged. They concluded that specific praise produces self-regulated workers (Reinke *et al.* 2007, concluded similarly) although there was no consideration of the role that enjoyment plays in learning or whether genuine learning had actually taken place. In addition, the method of data collection was observational so any changes within the time frame of the research could only prove contextual, short-term change. Impact on cognitive change would take much longer to prove than the scope of the research permitted and would widen the discussion beyond the limitations of the enquiry. The research also did not allow for the effect of observation on teacher performance – use of contextual praise is likely to be more consistent when a teacher is aware that this is the focus of the observer. So although specific praise produces self-regulated workers under certain conditions, there is no evidence that learning is taking place, or that self-regulated working continues when staff and students are no longer being observed.

In 2005, Australian researchers Josephine Infantino and Emma Little considered the effectiveness of behaviour management strategies on a sample of secondary school pupils. Although there was broad agreement on the effectiveness of various forms of home notification of good behaviour and good work and the value of private, rather than public, praise, they concluded that management strategies were often rendered ineffective because the students themselves failed to value, and therefore comply with, them. They found that students often did not even agree with teachers' definitions of unacceptable classroom behaviour.

There is also an implicit suggestion in the research (similarly noted by Ruth Woods, 2008) that within a behaviourist environment, students will structure their own peer reward system, with misbehaviour usually attracting peer praise and affording status to the student. There is an assumption in this research that behaviourist strategies are the most effective means of creating a learning environment so student opinion was sought within that context. Perhaps a key consideration should be the researchers' observation that strategies were ineffective when students failed to value them – as David Brooks observes in his popular text *The Social Animal*,

> The people in the executive suites believed that the school existed to fulfil some socially productive process of information transmission . . . But in reality, of course, high school is a machine for social sorting. The purpose of high school is to give young people a sense of where they fit in the social structure.
>
> (Brooks 201: 73)

Marcie Steele, of the University of North Carolina, considered the value of the behaviourist approach in teaching children with learning disabilities (Steele 2005), concluding that breaking down goal-oriented learning into small steps aided learning for these children. Intervention programmes, whether computer based or delivered by a learning assistant, all use this approach, often with great success. Modelling, which Steele defines as an idea based on behavioural theory, is a key strategy used by all teachers for all pupils when explaining a new task, but it may be of particular value to children with learning needs. The availability of timetables, rules and expectations are also structures which are needed by some children.

Dr Ruth Woods (2008) provides a useful critique of behaviourism in her analysis of pupil behaviour over an extended period. Prompted by concern about the real long-term benefit of this approach and the fact that much previous research, being quantitative, did not permit a pupil perspective, this research used extensive pupil interviews with a single child for whom the reward and sanction cycle had failed. Transcriptions of the interviews show that many of the rules and rewards failed because the system was too simplistic to accommodate the child's socio-cultural understanding of what was being asked of him. Woods concludes, 'initiatives designed to improve school discipline are unlikely to succeed if they fail to investigate and take into account contradictions between values and morals inside and outside the classroom' (Woods 2008).

Contrasting three learning models (transmission, acquisition and exploration), Barbara Rogoff of the University of California highlighted an inherent problem with the transmission approach resulting from behaviourist theory, stating,

> Adults see themselves as responsible for filling children up with knowledge, as if children are receptacles and knowledge is a product. It has been variously called a receptacle model of learning, or an assembly factory or banking model of learning because children are seen as receivers of a body of knowledge, but not active participants in learning. The children have little role except to be receptive, as if they could just open a little bottle cap to let adults pour the knowledge in. In this adult run model, adults have to be concerned with how to package the knowledge and how to motivate the children to make themselves receptive.
>
> (Rogoff 1994: 211)

The researcher both highlights the question of motivation and implicitly observes the challenge inherent in motivating learners in an adult-controlled environment.

The behaviourist paradigm evaluated

So behaviourist theory, when translated into a consistent system of contingent praise, can be effective in controlling compliant children (although current media and political concern about the level of classroom disruption in English schools would suggest that for a growing number of children, even this is no longer true). The age of the pupils is also a factor – young children value the good opinion of their carers whilst teenagers are more concerned with peer approval. Can one approach suit all stages of school life?

However, evaluations of behaviourist practice also fail to question what children are actually learning, beyond compliance, their position in a power relationship or the effect of control on their development. It is generally accepted that praising a child will increase self-esteem and create positive social and academic learning behaviours, yet for a growing minority of pupils, this does not seem to be the case.

Is this because positive reinforcement has not been started early enough in their lives, because of inconsistent application, or because praise and reward, twin pillars of behaviourist theory, are irrelevant to their cultural and social values? Are positive social attitude, academic learning and the development of self merely a matter of cause and effect? Research suggests that a behaviourist approach is only successful when everyone in the community both understands the choices and shares the same values, and even then, what the community is successful at achieving is only examined in a narrow context. So what happens when students do not fit the methodology? Is there an alternative?

Points for reflection

- Read the policy documentation in your school relating to behaviour and teaching and learning. How strong is the emphasis on praise and reward? How does this shape the ethos of the learning community?

- Look at your own classroom or teaching context. What does it say about your values and beliefs? What does it say about the relationships within the room?
- How do planning and assessment reflect the process of teaching and learning? Is there a 'one size fits all' approach in just some, or all, areas of your teaching?
- What are the benefits of incremental learning? Is it suitable for all aspects of learning? Is it suitable for all learners?
- Considering your own practice, to what extent do you think that Beaman and Wheldall are correct in their observation that teachers approve of good work and disapprove of bad behaviour? How is this reflected in your use of praise and sanction?

Chapter 5

Constructivism – the perspective

It has been suggested that constructivism as a learning philosophy can be traced back to the work of the Italian philosopher, Giambattista Vico (1668–1744). He was a Professor of Rhetoric at the University of Naples who believed that people formed new knowledge from what they already knew, which in itself was based on individual beliefs. The formalisation of the constructivist epistemology is usually attributed to Jean Piaget, who is defined as a cognitive constructivist. It postulates that learning is the construction and reconstruction of knowledge by each individual from their own ideas and previous experiences.

The point of this theory of learning is humorously made in Leo Lionni's 2005 picture book, *Fish is Fish,* which tells the story of a minnow and a tadpole. When the tadpole grows into a frog, he hops out of the pond, occasionally returning to tell his friend the fish about the wonders of the world. He describes a bird as having wings, two legs and many, many colours. But while he visualises a bird which he has actually seen, the fish, interpreting this information through the filters of his limited experience and knowledge, visualises coloured flying fish with fins as wings and two frog-like legs. Descriptions of cows and humans are similarly interpreted. This story demonstrates the core belief of constructivist theory: that people create new knowledge from existing knowledge. Meaning is made within the context of prior experiences and the possibilities for misconception are manifold.

In this chapter, a perspective on the constructivist paradigm will be given by outlining the work of its principal exponents: John Dewey, Jean Piaget, Lev Vygotsky, Jerome Bruner and Carl Rogers. The chapter concludes with an evaluation of constructivist theory.

A review of constructivist theory

John Dewey (1859–1952)

The American psychologist John Dewey is defined as a pragmatist rather than a construc-tivist, but he considerably influenced constructivist theory. He believed that students should be able to learn through practical real-life experience, stating that education was a social as well as a learning process. He argued against passive knowledge transmission in the class-room, believing that curriculum content should relate to students' prior knowledge and experience in order to promote the formation of new knowledge. He believed that the teacher should be a partner in the learning journey. Critics of Dewey regard his views as liberal or progressive and therefore responsible for a decline in standards due to the depar-ture from traditional methods of teaching.

Jean Piaget (1896–1980)

Speaking three years before his death, on a video which he wished to make to explain his thinking, Piaget stated that, 'Knowledge is not ready made. Each of us is continually creating our own knowledge. We are continually organizing what we know, structuring and restructuring our knowledge' (Piaget and Coretta 1977). He concluded that learning was a three-fold process, the stages of which he named assimilation (taking new experiences or information on board and assimilating them into existing cognitive structures), accommodation (changing cognitive structures to add the new experience or information) and equilibration, a process in which the learner restores a balance with the environment which has provided the new information. After a new event has been both assimilated and accommodated, Piaget believed that the learner established a schema, or knowledge structure, which would exist until further information was introduced when it would be used to process the new information and modified in the light of it. It therefore follows that knowledge cannot simply be transmitted by one person and passively accepted by a recipient, as activity must occur in the brain of the recipient in order to assimilate and accommodate the knowledge. Learning must, by Piaget's definition, be active to be genuine.

Through his extensive observation of young children, and analysis of their spontaneous language, Piaget was able to define key stages of cognitive development and the nature of thought at each stage. He believed that the order of these stages was fixed. During the sensorimotor stage, lasting for the first two years of life, a child learns by using reflex and sensory skills such as sucking, listening, looking and holding. The preoperational stage, which encompasses the Early Years of learning and lasts until the age of six, was defined by Piaget as cognitive egocentricity, as the child cannot intellectually manipulate information or empathise with others. Imaginative play and imitating known adult roles through play is characteristic of this stage. The concrete operational stage encompasses the Junior school years. The egocentric speech of early childhood becomes socialised speech at around the age of seven or eight. Children begin to reason about concrete events and as they increasingly gain control over socialised speech they engage in and internalise undirected thought. Piaget defined this internalised thought as residing in the imagination. He argued that it is through the relationship of directed thought and word that concepts are increasingly used to learn. In the final stage of development, the formal operational stage, which commences around the age of eleven, children begin to develop the ability for abstract thought, reasoning, logical planning and the use of logic in discussion. Hypotheses can be formed and evidence logically presented to support or disprove them.

Piaget's work, although widely applied to educational theory, was criticised for the narrow research samples which he used (including his own three children), which, critics argue, limited his work to a narrow socio-economic band. Some suggest that the ages at which children pass to the next stage are not applicable to all children and that the impact of environmental factors on development was not considered by Piaget.

The application of Piaget's beliefs to education inspired the concept of active learning. He believed that children needed to explore, discover, discuss with their peers and consider their mistakes in order to learn. The role of the teacher was therefore one of facilitator and also to create disequilibrium to promote further enquiry. As Piaget said, 'to understand is to discover, or reconstruct by rediscovery, and such conditions must be complied with if in the future individuals are to be formed who are capable of production and creativity and not simply repetition' (Piaget 1972: 20). Speaking at a conference in

Kyoto in 1971 (cited Davidson 1968) he questioned the goal of education, asking, 'Are we forming children who are only capable of learning what is already known, or should we try to develop creative and innovative minds capable of discovery from the preschool age on, throughout life?'

If Piaget's observations are correct and a child learns in incremental steps, nothing will move a child forward until the child itself is ready to let go of a view and assimilate a new one. Adult intervention cannot directly influence; the input is merely absorbed into, and interpreted through, the child's current experience and understanding. Piaget, who was working at the same time as the leading behaviourist thinkers, believed that children are intrinsically motivated as learners and therefore do not need rewarding. This being the case, praise or reward is at best an irrelevance and at worst an interference in the child's self-determined learning journey.

Lev Vygotsky (1896–1934)

Vygotsky, a Russian psychologist sometimes described as a socio-constructivist, was born and worked in Russia in the early years of the twentieth century. He died from tuberculosis as the age of just 38, and his work remained largely unknown in the West until the 1960s, when translations were made.

Similarly to Piaget, he researched the function of language in child development, although he differed at some key points from Piaget. Where Piaget was interested in language as a window onto the incremental building blocks of learning, Vygotsky understood language to be culturally determined and integral to a child's learning. He believed that egocentric and communicative speech were simply two strands of social speech rather than indicative of consecutive stages of development as stated by Piaget. (Piaget, writing in 1962 after reading Vygotsky's comments on his work, felt that his use of the word 'egocentric' should be defined not in the sense of being centred on the self but more as a developmental inability to accommodate the views of others.) And rather than thought and speech being parallel processes, Vygotsky saw them as interdependent strands which regularly diverge (Vygotsky 1971). Where Piaget focused on the incremental stages of development, Vygotsky analysed developmental learning in social and cultural contexts.

Vygotsky's best known educational theory is his definition of the zone of proximal development, the level of skill achieved when working independently. He stated that a child could be moved beyond this stage of knowledge through interaction with someone, such as a teacher, with a greater level of knowledge. This translates in practice into a pedagogy which starts from what a learner already knows, moving thinking forward through challenge; prioritising how a learner learns rather than what is learnt; and using feedback from the learner to inform next steps in the teaching and learning process.

Critics of Vygotsky's work in practice suggest that unskilled facilitators could control, rather than guide learning, or conversely that they could unthinkingly provide support for a lazy or passive child who is quite capable of independent achievement.

Carl Rogers (1902–1987)

The American psychologist Carl Rogers was concerned with the definition of self. He believed that self was developed through interaction with the environment and that an individual was constantly reacting to changes in environmental experience. He argued that behaviour is best understood from within the internal framework of the individual; he believed that behaviour is usually consistent with self-belief and that behaviour which conformed, but which was not owned, would not be internalised. He also believed that a person should be accepted without any judgement of their worth.

Although he formed his theories through his work in adult therapy, he also applied his understanding to education. He believed that each student brought a unique knowledge to the classroom based on previous perceptions and experience, so the classroom environment needed to be learner, rather than teacher, centred. Relevance was vital, as he argued that the student would only genuinely learn those things which maintained or enhanced self. In addition, he stated that the self tends to resist any assimilation of experience which requires change, so open-mindedness in students should be encouraged and developed. He also observed that if the self felt threatened, learning could not take place. The classroom therefore needed to be a friendly and supportive environment.

In his text *On Becoming a Person: A Therapist's View of Psychotherapy* (1961) he defined a person who can function fully as being one who is open to experience; able to trust their own judgement and choose appropriate behaviour; and able to take responsibility for their own behaviour and choices without being reliant on external codes. For Rogers, learning and personal growth were interdependent.

Jerome Bruner (b. 1915)

Bruner made a significant contribution to educational theory and pedagogy through his work as a psychology professor at Harvard. He believed that learning was a social process in which new concepts were formed by the learner from existing constructs. During the 1940s, Bruner was involved in exploring how perception is influenced by motivation, need and expectation, before becoming involved in the 1950s with the MACOS (Man: A Course of Study) project, a large-scale curriculum project for American schools which sought to answer three questions about human nature and human culture through cross-curricular learning. The materials reflected Bruner's belief in enquiry-based learning, as they were divided into the categories of film and other visual aids, interactive resources such as games, and also written materials, all of which replaced more traditional text books.

Bruner is also credited with introducing the concept of 'scaffolding' into educational theory. He believed that the use of a temporary support frame at a specific point of learning would enable a child to grasp a concept. This can be verbal, with a teacher providing supportive questioning to lead a learner forward, or it can be more formal, such as the provision of a planning format for writing, conducting a science experiment or planning an investigation.

In 1960 he published his key text, *The Process of Education*, which outlined four themes: learning structure (the basic principles of each subject and connections between the various ideas inherent in the subject), learning readiness (what the learner already knows), learning motivation and analytical and intuitive thinking. He advocated a spiral curriculum, in which facts and techniques are regularly revisited and built on until concepts are understood and embedded in the learner's thinking. He believed that interest in the actual material being learnt was the principle motivator for children, in preference to the external motivation of grades or test scores. He also advised teachers to move from extrinsic reward such as praise, to the intrinsic reward inherent in problem solving or understanding new concepts. He believed that the intuitive thinking skills necessary for problem solving or forming hypotheses required self-confidence and he suggested that reward and sanction were likely to inhibit intuitive thinking and make pupils more risk averse in order to minimise mistakes. In 1996 he published *The Culture of Education,* in which he expounded the view that humans are shaped by their culture and it is through this that they make new meaning. The mind is not merely concerned with processing information, but also with constructing knowledge.

An evaluation of constructivist theory

The theory of constructivism, when translated into pedagogy, has many advantages for education as learners are actively engaged in their learning, leading to a development of higher level thinking than a model which only transmits information. Cross-curricular links are possible, problem-solving skills are developed and learning can be relevant to real-life contexts. Social skills are also developed through teamwork, collaborative problem solving and encounters with diverse perspectives. Constructivist theory suggests that the confidence of the learner grows and skills in self-management are fostered.

However, critics of the theory argue that it requires a greater depth of the teacher's subject knowledge, is time consuming to implement (it is essentially a theory of learning which must be translated into a theory of teaching), requires a level of interaction and self-management which many students lack, and that diversity of thought is not always a desirable outcome. Outcomes themselves are also unpredictable and time taken in teaching metacognitive skills is not always the best use of valuable classroom time. The inaccurate interpretation of constructivist practice in a pedagogy which lacks learning rigour also leaves the theory open to criticism of liberalism leading to lowered standards.

So, comparing behaviourist with constructivist theory, Skinner viewed society as a set of contingencies which shape and reinforce behaviour, culture as a force which controls the behaviour of organisms (Skinner 1972) and learning as a schedule of contingent reinforcements to build and strengthen knowledge (Skinner 1968). Constructivists view society and culture as contexts within which children, through the medium of language, develop a sense of self through transactions with their environment (Bandura 1997). Within a personal system of beliefs and values they both interpret and construct knowledge at observable developmental stages. In a behaviourist context, the role of the teacher is to plan and deliver learning schedules within which consistent praise and reward are contingent to success. In a constructivist context, the role of the teacher is to create an environment which stimulates self-directed learning and which mediates between the needs of children's differing socio-cultural experiences and learning behaviours. Contingent praise, rather than being a key to successful learning, could intrude into this personalised process.

Points for reflection

- How do you evaluate the knowledge of each student whom you teach? How does this support their learning?
- Discuss the extent to which problem solving, enquiry and the formation of hypotheses form part of your regular classroom practice.
- What do you perceive to be the strengths of constructivist theory? What are the weaknesses?

- According to the leading constructivist theorists, what role does praise have in the teaching and learning process? Consider this with particular reference to Rogers' self-theory.
- According to constructivist theory, how are learners motivated?
- How does constructivist theory align with your personal beliefs about learning?

Chapter 6

Constructivism contextualised – translating theory into practice

'Education is not the filling of a pail, but the lighting of a fire.' This quotation, attributed to William Butler Yeats, reflects the two sides of the behaviourist/constructivist debate. During the latter half of the twentieth century, the work of constructivist theorists significantly influenced the evolution of education, as researchers increasingly came to understand how people learn. But as national policy, school policy and the pedagogy of individual teachers evolved to reflect this view, a dichotomy emerged as behaviourist practices still continued to underpin the way that children were motivated to learn.

The constructivist paradigm evidenced in national policy

Constructivist thinking is embedded at every level of national policy relating to teaching, learning and curriculum design. The 1988 National Curriculum was built on Bruner's spiral model, with each subject designed to revisit skills and concepts regularly in order to develop a deeper understanding. In 2000, David Blunkett, the then Education Secretary, announced that he wanted to promote the teaching of higher order thinking skills, saying that he was impressed by a growing body of evidence that it raised standards at GCSE (General Certificate of Secondary Education), stating in a BBC interview that, 'This is not about some loosely defined or woolly approach to study skills. It is about the ability to analyse, make connections, to use knowledge effectively, to solve problems and to think creatively.' (BBC 2000). Thinking is now a core skill taught in many schools across the 4 to 19 curriculum.

This spiral model of learning has been encapsulated in all subsequent curriculum revisions, defining the knowledge, skills and understanding required at each key stage of learning. One example of this thinking is evidenced in national policy in the definition of personal, learning and thinking skills, as distinct from the functional skills needed to master individual subjects. It is threaded throughout the National Curriculum (DfES 2003a) from 11 to 16 and is comprised of six groups of skills: independent enquiry, creative thinking, reflective learning, teamwork, self management and effective participation. The Social and Emotional Aspects of Learning (SEAL) programme (a further example of spiral curriculum design), which has been extensively adopted in English schools since its inception (DfES 2005), outlines five key aspects of learning as self awareness, management of feelings, motivation, empathy and social skills divided into two subcategories of personal and interpersonal learning.

This is supported through Assessment for Learning, or AfL (DfES 2003a), which involves both teacher and learner in assessing how learning is taking place and how this information can be used to inform the next steps of the learning cycle. Prior knowledge is defined and ways of building new learning can be discussed, with pupils taking ownership of personal target setting and accountability for achieving targets. This then feeds into assessment of learning at the end of a unit of work, where achievement and knowledge are assessed against benchmarks to establish the level of a student. The current assessment structure Assessing Pupil Progress (APP) is an amalgam of AfL and benchmark assessment, defining skills and knowledge at each level, but also assessing the student's ability to use and apply that knowledge (DCSF 2010).

In May 2011, the Chief Executive of the Council for Learning Outside the Classroom, reporting to the Parliamentary Commons Select Committee on Science and Technology, demonstrated, through evidence-based research, that, 'Regular learning outside the classroom, including practical learning and experiments in the school grounds or field trips in the local community and beyond, raises attainment, improves behaviour and re-motivates children who do not respond well in the classroom environment' (Gardner 2011).

The following month, the Education Select Committee reported on behaviour. There is no mention of praise or reward as appropriate methods to deal with behaviour management, instead acknowledging that,

> The National Strategies have had beneficial effects; but a new, less prescriptive approach may succeed in giving a new stimulus to teachers in preparing and applying the curriculum in ways which engage children more and which reduce the risk of poor behaviour. Ministers should bear in mind, when developing proposals for the new National Curriculum, that if the future curriculum is to have a beneficial effect on standards of behaviour in the classroom, it will need to meet the needs of all pupils . . . while being differentiated and enjoyable. We heard in evidence that pupils who are positively engaged in learning are less likely to have behaviour problems.
>
> (Education Select Committee 2011)

The Committee further advised that a slimmed down National Curriculum would give schools the flexibility to design wider curricula which were contextual to the needs of their learning communities. This demonstrates a clear understanding that involving pupils in their own learning increases motivation and therefore lessens poor behaviour without the need to use reward systems.

The constructivist paradigm evidenced in school policy

Appendix B contains examples of a behaviour policy and a teaching and learning policy from schools which encompass constructivist theory in their thinking. They clearly demonstrate the view of the schools that good behaviour is a community matter, with everyone working in partnership to meet high expectations. There is no public reward for good behaviour. Expectations are reinforced in the classroom, but class contracts are similar to those outlined in Sue's classroom, in Chapter 1. The words chosen are related to the creation of a mutually supportive and inclusive learning space, in contrast to a list of rules to be followed. Staff and students believe that this encourages wider thinking about the consequences of poor behaviour choices, which in turn leads to the development of empathy.

The sample teaching and learning policy also epitomises a constructivist approach to teaching and learning, which is seen as an interactive partnership between staff, pupils and parents; a partnership in which everyone is accountable for their role and their own growth. Children are encouraged through praise which acknowledges effort, progress and resulting achievement. Because they are expected to take responsibility for their own learning in partnership with their teacher, there is no evidence of the use of contingent praise. The homework policy reflects the same approach to learning – tasks are related to curriculum content but often include open-ended enquiry or investigations based on real-life situations. Marking policies also demonstrate the concept of a learning partnership, incorporating self evaluation and peer evaluation, feedback comments from the teacher rather than a grade or level and pupil responses to the teacher's comments.

Professional Development and In Service Training (INSET) policies also mirror pupils' learning, advocating an enquiry and problem-solving approach which will engage staff in their own learning. In this school, the concept of a learning community is taken seriously with more than half of the staff involved either in Master's degrees or Master's-level research projects. Lesson observations are much less about box ticking on a clipboard for performance management categorisation and more about sharing strategies and techniques to support effective learning. There is less emphasis on individual targets and more focus on individual contribution to a collaborative process, through which everyone can learn. Staff may mentor or coach each other and training is also less about attending external courses and more about shared expertise and investigation in the context of the learning community.

In recent years, pupil voice has been widely debated, with the majority of schools forming pupil councils and also parent councils. In a school which genuinely engages in constructivist practice, the pupil council will have real influence in the decision making process and will know that its ideas are taken seriously. Some such schools also have pupil learning consultants who contribute to the teaching and learning process and work as peer mentors.

Constructivist theory also extends into curriculum design. Many Primary schools have developed creative curricula in the last few years, placing creativity at the heart of learning whilst ensuring that pedagogy supports rigorous learning. Often there is an increase in subject specialist teaching to support this. In 2007, the National College of School Leadership researched the impact of creative curricula. The final report, *Lifting the lid on the creative curriculum: How leaders have released creativity in their schools through curriculum ownership* (Burgess 2007), defined creativity as:

- connecting: seeing relationships and combining in new ways;
- risking: having the self-confidence and freedom to fail and keep trying;
- envisaging: being original and imaginative about what might be;
- analysing: asking critical and challenging questions;
- thinking: taking time for reflection and soft thinking;
- interacting: sharing ideas and collaborating;
- varying: testing options and trying in different ways;
- elaborating: exploring and fiddling and doing the unnecessary with love!

Schools that have followed this route have found a substantial increase in learning engagement (together with a corresponding drop in low-level classroom disruption), an increase in quantifiable standards and a stronger collaborative working environment. And personalised learning has to be part of this equation – accepting that education is about lighting the fire requires an understanding that some fires are initially tiny and need a lot of attention before they become established, while others burst into flame (and may be in danger of burning out very quickly if not constantly refuelled).

Various initiatives have developed around the increased understanding of learning behaviour. Some examples include the cognitive acceleration programme, which grew out of a King's College, London, research project designed to develop pupils' thinking from concrete to abstract. It combined the ideas of Piaget and Vygotsky, developing Thinking Maths, in which each student contributes to collaborative investigation according to their understanding of the concepts involved. Philosophy4Children aims to teach children explicit thinking skills with which to explore ideas, develop confidence in their own thinking and share suggestions without fear of getting the wrong answer.

The constructivist paradigm evidenced in classroom practice

It is at the level of classroom practice that the changes effected by constructivist thinking are most obvious. Not only is the classroom a more active place, with pupils grouped flexibly according to current learning need, but the style and quantity of talk contrasts sharply with a classroom modelled along behaviourist lines. Questions from the teacher are likely to initiate thinking, rather than scaffold or signpost an expected answer to demonstrate knowledge – questioning may even be reciprocal. Pupil talk will be more about learning and less about getting the right answer. It is less likely to be purely transactional and should, with well-trained pupils, be exploratory rather than cumulative (in which everyone agrees with what is said), presentational (one person taking over) or disputational (pupils competing and arguing). 'Exploratory talk', the outcome of the Thinking Together research team at the education faculty of the University of Cambridge (*http://thinkingtogether.educ.cam.ac.uk*), requires pupils to explicate their thinking and challenge each other for evidence and it is an invaluable tool in collaborative learning. It also enhances social learning – pupils can initially be reluctant to move into an area which they regard as 'teacher territory' and it takes time for them to become comfortable both with challenging and being challenged. This is discussed further in Chapter 14.

Seating, grouping and the way pupils move within the learning space are indicative of active learning. Jigsaws, snowballing and envoys are all outcomes of constructivist thinking, as are guided writing, reading and thinking sessions, all of which are scaffolded to support pupils as they move on in their thinking. There will be evidence of regular formative assessment and pupils may well build their own portfolios or maintain evidence of self-evaluation as part of their learning accountability. All of this must be underpinned by the building of strong trust, not only between teacher and pupil but also between pupils.

Perhaps the best known exponent of constructivist theory in practice is Maria Montessori (1870–1952) an Italian doctor who was drawn into teaching through her work with special needs children at the University of Rome's Psychiatric clinic. Now recognised worldwide, the Montessori method is based on a belief in the creative potential of every child as an individual. Inspired by the principles of Pestalozzi and Froebel, Montessori believed that education was a natural, spontaneous process acquired through transaction with the environment. The role of the teacher in a Montessori classroom is one of observer once tasks have been set up and the children are engaged. This is a strict principle, as Montessori herself wrote,

> If a child has a difficulty and the teacher interferes to show him how to deal with it, the child will leave the teacher with the work and go away. The interest of that child was not in the mere task but in conquering that difficulty. Praise, help or even noticing a child are often sufficient interruption to destroy activity.
>
> (Montessori 2009: 399)

In fact, contingent praise plays no part in a Montessori environment – teachers are trained in the difference between evaluative praise, which imposes adult values on a child's work, and descriptive praise, which scaffolds a child as they evaluate their own work and therefore become independent thinkers and learners.

Another example of constructivist practice can be seen in Reggio Emilia, a town in northern Italy; the Reggio Emilia Approach is world renowned. It was started after the Second World War by Loris Malaguzzi and the parents of the town and surrounding villages. The Approach emphasises active, exploratory learning in a supportive environment in which parents are fully involved. The community believes that emphasis should shift from teaching to learning, through a 'pedagogy of listening' (Rinaldi 2006), in order to better understand the learning of children through collaboration and constructive action.

Parents are genuine partners in their child's education; control is shared between teachers, children and parents (Edwards *et al.* 1998) and many parents support the values of the Approach in the way they interact with their children at home. Speaking at the Scottish Learning Festival in 2009, Carla Rinaldi, the former director of Reggio Emilia schools, challenged listeners to consider how they used questions. Did they teach children that there is an answer to every question, did they search for the answer with the children, or did they use the question to prompt even more questions?

The Approach, similarly to the Montessori Method, uses observation to learn about the actual learning processes of the children. Pictures, sound recordings and notes are all used for the teacher to observe, but also for each child to discuss and evaluate what has been learnt or what questions next need to be asked. Children are encouraged to record their thinking in whatever way they wish (described as The Hundred Languages of Children) – this could include drawing, acting, modelling, painting or sculpting. As Edwards *et al.* write in their book entitled *The Hundred Languages of Children*, 'In reliving earlier moments via photography and tape recording, children are deeply reinforced and validated for their efforts' (Edwards *et al.* 1998: 185). In extensive interview and lecture transcripts, Carla Rinaldi (2006) makes no reference to praise, concentrating entirely on the relationship with the child and the role of dialogue in constructing knowledge with a child through a comprehensive understanding of their socio-cultural contexts.

The constructivist paradigm evidenced in research literature

Although there is extensive research about the theory of constructivism and the pedagogies which have resulted from the theory, the issues of praise and motivation are rarely part of the research work. This is almost certainly because constructivist approaches, with their emphasis on how the learner learns, rather than what is learnt, obviate the need for the extrinsic motivation of reward. This is highlighted by Martin Covington (2000) a psychology professor at Berkeley, University of California, who, in using research papers to consider the effect of praise and reward on learning, concludes that intrinsic and extrinsic motivation are not necessarily antagonistic.

Conflictingly, Mark Young (2005) of Winona State University, in an article entitled *The Motivational Effects of the Classroom Environment in Facilitating Self-Regulated Learning*, which quotes pedagogical examples, concludes that performance-contingent rewards both undermine intrinsic motivation and encourage pupils to use social comparison as a means of self-assessment.

Paul Burnett (2002) of Charles Sturt University in Australia, considering the effect of teacher praise on student perceptions of the learning environment, found that students' perceptions of their relationship with their teacher and their classroom environment were not related to general teacher praise, although effort feedback impacted considerably on a teacher–pupil relationship.

Effie Maclellan (2005) of Strathclyde University, Scotland, argues that teachers should not take too simplistic a view of praise, stating that, 'Within a social-cognitive perspective . . . praise cannot be understood as a stand-alone application to be enacted solely through a set of procedures but has to recognize that the effects of praise are mediated by students' goal orientations' (Maclellan 2005: 198). She concludes that praise should be restricted to process, not person, particularly as evidence suggests that the former helps to foster resilient learners.

The work of Ann Shreeve, of the University of East Anglia (2002), working with a cross-school research group, was concerned with student perceptions of reward across a number of schools in Norwich, England, demonstrating that praise was most effective when consistently applied (usually in behaviour management) but was rendered ineffective where pupils considered its application to be inconsistent or unfair. However, the most successful schools in the study used little praise or reward, as the learners were well motivated through a rich curriculum and strong teacher–pupil relationships. Whilst most of the teachers in the study thought that praise was effective, less than half the students agreed, with particular comment about the unfairness of promising reward in exchange for good behaviour which should be seen as the norm.

Andy Miller *et al.* (1998) of the University of Nottingham, England, unusually considers the parental perspective on praise, asking children and parents to rank order ten aspects of praise. The results showed overwhelming agreement that informing parents about good work was seen as the most effective form of praise, even though the commonest reason for contacting home was to complain about poor behaviour. The form of praise which was most valued in this study was informative, or descriptive praise, acknowledging effort and achievement after the event, rather than offering rewards which were contingent on task completion.

The constructivist paradigm evaluated

Evaluating constructivist practice is tricky, as the term is something of an umbrella which covers practice from an 'everything goes' approach in which children are given freedom without rigour, to carefully and precisely planned learning programmes within both cognitive and socio-constructivist contexts. There is no doubt that children enjoy active learning in preference to passive transmission learning. Students are given ownership of their learning and feel empowered. There is also evidence that thinking skills are transferred across the curriculum, enhancing all of a student's learning. Social skills and the ability to empathise are also significantly enhanced.

However, the application of constructivist theory to education pedagogy has attracted significant criticism. There is some evidence that the model develops higher order thinking skills at the expense of basic skills and knowledge and this has an effect on test outcomes – what is learnt is not compatible with what is tested. It could also be argued that concern with how learning is occurring rather than what is learnt leads to the avoidance of account-ability for standards. There is also a criticism that active and exploratory learning favours more competent and more articulate children, immediately creating an advantage for those children who arrive at school with a high level of learning readiness. In addition, a socio-constructivist environment is likely to lead to domination by a few individuals if preparation for collaborative learning has not been carefully made.

The role of a teacher's subject knowledge in a spiral learning environment has also been considered. Some concepts which are introduced during Primary schooling can demand specialist knowledge in order to guide learning effectively, as pupils may formulate ques-tions which are beyond generalist knowledge. Some critics also observe that whilst explora-tory learning works with younger children, who learn through play in the early years of life, it is not a model which is appropriate to older students who need to engage with the disci-plines inherent in each subject. Young children are motivated by curiosity and they learn from their environment. But can this motivating curiosity and the time needed for investi-gative learning be extended beyond Early Years education?

Curriculum changes can also raise parental concern if different ways of learning are intro-duced, particularly when parents have not been involved in the decision making process. Whilst children feel empowered by investigative learning tasks for homework, many parents who want to ensure that homework is 'right' before it is given in, feel correspondingly disempowered. They also feel that without regular test scores being available, they no longer know how well their child is doing at school. Information about thinking skills does little to allay their fears of rampant liberalism.

Whilst the debate about pedagogy, effective teaching and learning models is ongoing, one theme which recurs through most debates is the effectiveness of any model in moti-vating learners. What actually makes pupils learn: extrinsic or intrinsic motivation? And how do we develop a sense of self – can self be taught or is it through transactions with our envi-ronment and experience that we develop those aspects of self which are vital to our growth: self-awareness, self-esteem, self-confidence, self-reliance and self-control?

Points for reflection

- How many of the strategies and approaches to learning outlined in this chapter do you use in your classroom?
- What are the particular challenges to a teacher who wants to develop a constructivist model of teaching and learning?
- How can a constructivist model of teaching offer equal access to learning?
- How far should a child's freedom in learning be extended?
- Genuinely collaborative learning requires a high level of trust between teachers and pupils. How can this be achieved?

- Discuss the differences between contingent praise, evaluative praise and descriptive praise. What does each type of praise say about the relationship of the person giving praise and the recipient?
- What types of praise do you use in your classroom? In what ways is your use of praise consistent with your beliefs? Is there any dissonance?

Chapter 7

Praise, motivation and positive psychology

> If we really stop to think about praise . . . we will see [it does] not have the least importance . . . The only important thing is that we have a pure motivation . . . When people praise us and we glow with delight, it is because we think that being praised is beneficial. But that is like thinking that there is some substance to a rainbow or a dream. However much benefit appears to accrue from praise and acclaim, actually there's none at all.
>
> (The Dalai Lama, from *http://www.buddhaquotes.co.uk*)

The development of self and the role of praise in motivation

The debate surrounding the function of praise and reward hinges on motivation, but even though this is the central tenet of the discussion, the debate ranges divisively, with stance depending on individual viewpoint. Supporters of praise and reward, generally working within a behaviourist paradigm, ask what more they can do to motivate learners. But is praise merely ephemeral, as the above quotation suggests? Constructivists, who believe that they should work with students rather than do something to them, ask how they can create an environment in which learners motivate themselves. Alongside the development of behaviourist and constructivist theories in the twentieth century, a quite different set of humanistic theories developed which widened the debate still further. In 1998, the American psychologist Martin Seligman further defined a paradigm of positive psychology, which is concerned with how people, families and communities thrive. Motivation and self-theories play a significant part in the research work of the positive psychologists. So how has the debate moved forward?

Harry Harlow (1905–1981)

Until the 1940s, it was generally accepted that motivation was driven by external factors, such as the need to eat and drink, or to gain reward or avoid punishment. But in 1949, the American psychologist Harry Harlow observed that a group of rhesus monkeys with which he was working started investigating a puzzle spontaneously, out of curiosity. There was no reward for solving the puzzle. Until this point, it had been accepted that reward was a necessary motivation for learning, but Harlow was observing a different phenomenon. Over time, the monkeys not only continued to solve the puzzle but they did so more quickly, still without reward. Harlow concluded that he was seeing a form of learning motivation which was internal to the monkeys, who were gaining satisfaction from what they were doing as an end in itself. He termed this 'intrinsic motivation', observing that this force was as strong as other motivational forces and that it could be a way to facilitate learning.

Edward Deci and Richard Ryan

The concept of intrinsic motivation was not accepted by behaviourist theorists and it was largely ignored until Edward Deci, now of the University of Rochester, New York, started to consider Harlow's findings in 1969 whilst searching for a dissertation focus. He devised an experiment using a Soma cube, a seven-piece puzzle block which can be constructed into various different shapes. Participants were divided into two groups, both of which were asked to use the blocks to build shapes which matched given images. There were also magazines on the table. Deci remained in the room to give instructions. In the first session, neither group was rewarded and showed similar results in their level of engagement with the task. In the second session, the people in one group were told that they would be paid for each shape that they constructed. Not surprisingly, they initially worked with more concentration than the unpaid group. However, when Deci left the room, allegedly to enter data into the computer but actually to observe, he found that the unpaid group persisted in the task for much longer than the paid group before starting to thumb through the magazines. On the third session, neither group was paid. But whilst the engagement of the unpaid group remained consistent with the previous sessions, the paid group showed markedly less engagement from the outset. So although payment initially motivated harder work, once the reward was removed, the participants generally lost interest in the task altogether, their intrinsic motivation vanishing along with the reward. They did not recover the level of engagement which they had shown in the first session, suggesting that the reward had stifled their desire to engage in the task for its own sake.

Other experiments have given the same result, showing that in the short term, extrinsic motivation produces better performance, but once the reward is removed, performance noticeably declines. Earlier intrinsic motivation for the task is never fully recovered.

In the following years Deci, working in partnership with Richard Ryan, showed that intrinsic motivation is not just about the inherent value or interest in the task itself. Intrinsic motivation is not even a single entity – there are actually various factors at work when a person is intrinsically motivated. They named this 'self-determination theory', which states that there are three factors which produce the most effective form of intrinsic motivation – competence, relatedness and autonomy.

Competence is about feelings of confidence in any situation. As applied to the classroom, pupils need to feel that they are not only at ease in the environment but that they are able to use it to their own advantage, both practically and socially. Learners also feel competence when they meet a task which is challenging, but which they can achieve. When the goal is achieved, there is a perceived shift in competence in the mind of the learner. Deci's work also showed that specific positive feedback increases feelings of competence, lessening the need for extrinsic motivation.

Relatedness is about reciprocal care and respect within a group to which an individual belongs. In young children, this will centre around carers, it will widen to include friends and social groups during Junior school years and will shift to peer approval during teenage years. So while young children will be motivated by the pleasure of parents and wider family, teenagers will tend to form social groups within which values or interests are shared.

Abraham Maslow (1908–1970)

In 1943, Abraham Maslow, who studied with Harry Harlow in the 1940s, proposed a hierarchy of needs in his paper *A Theory of Human Motivation*. A person's motivation, or in the case of education a pupil's level of readiness to engage with learning, is determined by the level at which needs are met. The physical needs of sleep, nutrition and hydration are at the lowest level of the needs pyramid, followed by both physical and emotional safety, a sense of belonging within a family and friendship group, and confidence and reciprocal respect within a social group. Only when all of these needs are met, Maslow argues, can a person fulfil needs at the top of the pyramid, which relate to being creative, ready to meet challenge and open minded to accepting facts.

Self-determination theory also postulates that human beings are averse to being controlled and that autonomy, or personal control over the environment, is key to intrinsic motivation. The role of autonomy in motivation was seen to be so important that Deci and Ryan coined the phrase 'autonomous motivation' (as opposed to extrinsic, or controlled motivation). In the context of a classroom, this could involve allowing students to set their own goals, decide how to complete a task or contribute to curriculum content.

However, the level of autonomy a pupil feels depends on the reason for performing a task. A pupil might learn tables as an extrinsically motivated task, because he understands that it is a necessary part of becoming a mathematician, or he may learn tables to avoid punishment if he fails a test the following day. Both motivations are extrinsic, but complying by choice for one's own later good is a form of self-determined extrinsic motivation. In fact, many choices that we make in our lives are both intrinsically and extrinsically motivated: we work to earn money and also, if we are fortunate, because we enjoy our work. Few people would continue to work if a salary was not part of the equation. There is also a suggestion that feelings of autonomy increase when people understand the reason for a task. So in the context of education, for students who are given the big picture of learning, both as an objective for a lesson and for a complete unit of work, motivation is likely to increase.

In 2007, when researching teacher autonomy, Guy Roth and a group of researchers at the University of Ben-Gurion in Israel, hypothesised that,

> Autonomous motivation for teaching was predicted to be associated positively with teachers' sense of personal accomplishment and negatively with emotional exhaustion. Most important, teachers' self-reported autonomous motivation for teaching was expected to promote students' self-reported autonomous motivation for learning by enhancing teachers' autonomy-supportive behaviour.
>
> (Roth *et al.* 2007)

In other words, they suggested that teachers who experience autonomy are not only likely to feel a greater sense of achievement but they are also more likely to give their students autonomy, thus increasing learning engagement. They concluded from their research, which involved both teachers and their students, that teachers' motivation followed the autonomy continuum suggested by self-determination theory (this is considered in more detail in Chapter 8).

Some externally motivated teachers worked to avoid parental complaint, to avoid drawing undue attention to themselves from school Principals or to minimise behaviour problems during lessons. Some teachers worked effectively so that they would not feel guilty. Others wanted to keep up with current developments or wanted to feel that they were helping their students. The final group, which was intrinsically motivated, tried to find new ways to challenge students, explored creative ideas for their own sake and enjoyed connecting with their students. The research suggested that the further along the autonomy continuum a teacher was, the more likely their students were to experience autonomy and higher levels of learning motivation. The report also found that the more autonomy teachers were given the less emotional exhaustion they reported – the impact of high-stakes testing and imposed control on teacher autonomy (and therefore, by implication on pupil motivation), was also noted.

To explore the significance of autonomy in a classroom context, look back to Chapter 1 and consider the level of autonomy which Sue's pupils experienced in their classroom – but this all went wrong one day when Sue was out of school. Whilst she was going through the day's work with the cover teacher (who was unknown to the school), she was asked where the stars or stickers were – this seemed to be more of a preoccupation with the supply teacher than the lesson content. Sue showed her where they were, but explained that in their school, children were expected to show high standards of behaviour without rewards.

When Sue arrived home later that afternoon, she found her inbox bulging with emails from parents (the first sent just minutes after the end of the school day) complaining about the supply teacher. Worse was to follow on her return to school the following morning – her in-tray was overflowing with internal memos with complaints from parents via phone calls. When she finally made it to the classroom she found a note from the supply teacher which started, 'This is the rudest class that I have ever taught'. What could have gone so badly wrong?

When the pupils arrived, their mood was one of caution until Sue embarked on a discussion about how disappointed she had been to read the supply teacher's note. There was a sudden wave of frustration, from which various facts emerged. The supply teacher had started the day by promising a star to everyone who sat in silence throughout the register – the class always did this anyway so they reckoned that collecting stars (which added to house point totals) for something they always did was quite a good game to play with a teacher who clearly did not know the system.

It started to go wrong when one pupil reached for his water bottle, only to be told to put it down and not touch it again without permission. When the pupil tried to explain that they were allowed to drink whenever they wanted to, they were told that children with water bottles looked like babies with dummies. They were made to put their water bottles on the floor and only drink when given permission – this would be withheld so that lessons would not need to be disrupted by visits to the toilet.

Next, a child got up from her chair to change a reading book, only to be scolded for moving without asking. Then an habitual fidget was made to sit with her hands on her head, at which point the class rebelled. But being a feisty bunch, they rebelled by all putting their hands on their heads and refusing to remove them even when they were offered more stars than they would normally collect in a week. The day went from bad to worse – for the teacher. During breaks, the class planned their resistance activities with military precision, sometimes all sitting on their hands, sometimes all sucking their thumbs and sometimes all putting their hands up to answer a question at the same time. And then, to round off their day, they all went home and pressed just the right buttons with their parents to trigger complaints, by saying that they had not had a drink all day, were not allowed to go to the toilet, had been called babies and had not been allowed to ask for help when they did not understand their work.

So what had happened? The class had reacted to overt control when their customary autonomy in the classroom was under threat; rewards and sanctions had been offered simultaneously in an attempt to establish control and the children had quickly decided to reject the bribes and risk the sanctions (which they were confident their teacher would not enforce on her return to school) in order to demonstrate resistance to the removal of their autonomy. There had also been a significant lack of relatedness between the class and the teacher; one which only served to strengthen the relatedness of the children to each other as they united against a common irritant. They expected to be given reasons for decisions, to be able to explain their needs and to be respected by the adult working with them. Rejecting the stars, pupils told Sue, was easy because they were just bits of coloured paper. What they were really saying, of course, was that the value which they attached to a star was dependent on the respect they had for its donor. The discussion ended in laughter when one child said, 'She treated us as if we were children'. When Sue pointed out that they were, in fact, children, she was told, 'But you treat us like people.' Her relationship with her class was based on mutual trust and respect. Within that relationship, her praise was valued.

A.S. Neill (1883–1973)

Student autonomy is nowhere better exemplified than the world renowned Summerhill School, a co-educational boarding school in Suffolk, England. Its founder, A.S. Neill, believed that inner compulsion and absolute freedom were principles which should be enshrined in education. In 1921, after teaching for some time, he started his own school, embodying his ideas. In addition to a structured timetable, pupils have free access to other activities such as art and computers. Attendance at lessons is optional, but each child is supported individually in their chosen learning path. Recreation is not organised, as pupils choose and create their own leisure activities. The Meeting demonstrates democracy in action as pupils and teachers vote equally on issues which affect the community, defining expectations for conduct. Academic achievement is not seen as an indicator of success, as the school aims to create an environment in which each child can find out who they are for themselves; in his definitive book, *Summerhill – a radical approach to child rearing* (cited on the school website, *http://www.summerhillschool.co.uk/pages/school_policies.html*) Neill wrote, 'Children, like adults, learn what they want to learn. All the prize-giving and marks and exams side-track proper personality development.'

Summerhill, which is now led by Neill's daughter, has remained consistent to its principles for 90 years. In 1949, a Ministry of Education Inspectors' Report stated that, 'What cannot be doubted is that a piece of fascinating and invaluable educational research is going on here it would do all educationalists good to see.' But by 1990 the Department of Education and Science was voicing 'significant concerns' and in 1999 the Department for Education and Employment issued a notice of complaint after Inspectors noted that standards, particularly in core curriculum, were unacceptably low and that pupils were, 'allowed to mistake the pursuit of idleness for the exercise of personal liberty.' In 2000, threatened by this external attempt to control their community, staff and pupils won a court case defending their freedom and autonomy over their own learning.

In October 2011, a book about Summerhill alumni, titled *After Summerhill: What Happened to the Pupils of Britain's Most Radical School?* (Lucas 2011) was reviewed by Sarah Cassidy in the *Independent* newspaper. The article quotes Neill as saying that he 'would rather Summerhill produced a happy street cleaner than a neurotic Prime Minister' and the book asks the question about what actually happens to people when they leave Summerhill (Cassidy 2011). The fifteen contributors to the book, some of whom pursued academic careers and some of whom did not, all speak positively about their education and the effect which it had on shaping them as people. One former pupil talks about the school encouraging a sense of spontaneity and fun and a 'fundamental sense of well-being'. Another contributor describes the school as fostering a 'childlike thirst for knowledge'. The only cautionary note appears to be an observation that a Summerhill education does not prepare you for the 'hierarchical and petty nature' of many workplaces. The book's author, Hussein Lucas, assesses it thus:

> The key feature that sums up the distinctive nature of the Summerhill experience is the virtual absence of fear: fear of failure; fear of authority; fear of social ostracism; fear of life and the consequent failure to engage with it with a feeling of optimism and a positive outlook.
>
> (Lucas 2011)

A further example of total autonomy over learning is offered by Sudbury Valley School in Framingham, Massachusetts which was founded in 1968. Similarly to Summerhill, the School Meeting is the democratic forum within which decisions are made, but unlike Summerhill, there is no structured curriculum. Students learn what they wish, when they wish. Supporters of the Sudbury system argue that traditional education was designed for the Industrial Age and we should now be preparing children and young people for the Information Age in which they source their own self-motivated learning. They further argue that the move to personalised learning programmes and self-directed learning within a traditional structure is still a controlling structure dictated by adults which merely appears to offer autonomy.

Whatever one's view of the level of freedom in the Sudbury schools and Summerhill, there is no doubt that pupils value the experience, talking about developing self-confidence, the ability to think and speak for themselves and the confidence to manage their own lives. Praise and reward form no part of a democratic school, as any aspect of adult control would contradict a central principle of the community.

Carol Dweck (b. 1946)

Carol Dweck, a Stanford psychology professor, has researched and written widely on the role of motivation and self theories in learning. She describes learners as falling into two distinct categories – entity theorists who believe that their intelligence is fixed and cannot be changed through effort or determination (these learners have a fixed mindset) and incremental theorists who believe that intelligence can be developed through effort and persistence (these learners show a growth mindset). Learners may not have fixed mindsets in every context of their lives; they may believe that they can grow in one area of learning but not another, but a mindset will determine learning motivation. Dweck's work (2009) with Seventh Grade pupils showed that fixed mindset learners thought it was important to demonstrate how good they were whilst growth mindset learners valued learning over achievement. But even though growth mindset learners valued learning, the gap in achievement widened continually, with growth mindset learners consistently achieving higher grades. Focusing on the purpose of learning rather than performance still leads to higher achievement.

In 2006, Dweck involved fixed and growth mindset learners in an experiment in which they were asked difficult questions and their brainwaves were measured as they responded. After 1.5 seconds, the computer told them if they were right or wrong. A further 1.5 seconds later, the computer told them the correct answer. The fixed mindset learners all paid attention to the first piece of information then disengaged. Growth mindset learners, however, continued to pay attention until they discovered what the right answer was. Even when their answer was right, they continued to pay attention to gain further knowledge. In the next stage of the experiment, the computer repeated the questions which students had got wrong the first time. The growth mindset learners achieved significantly higher scores. The researchers concluded from this that people with a growth mindset want to learn, whereas fixed mindset people just want to get it right.

The difference between these two groups of people, whom Dweck also describes as learners and non-learners, shows most noticeably when they encounter failure.

Entity theorists are performance and achievement oriented, and so they personalise failure, blaming their own lack of ability. In future, their mindsets say, avoid any situation in which you might fail, as you will no longer look clever. They will therefore become risk-averse in their learning, choosing options which are easily attainable so that they can continue to define themselves as clever. Failure undermines motivation for these students and achievement-related praise will only reinforce this self-view.

In contrast, Dweck states that incremental theorists, with a growth mindset, will use the dissonance created by failure as a challenge to try harder, learn a skill which will help to solve the problem, or return to the issue at a later date – failure motivates them. Their approach is encapsulated in the words of the playwright, Samuel Beckett, 'Ever tried? Ever failed? No matter. Try again. Fail again. Fail better' (Gruen 1969: 210). Often, growth mindset children who fail at a task do not attribute it to any particular factor, accepting that sometimes failure just happens. They appear to interpret success and failure as equally useful sources of information (Deci 1975). Performance-related praise is irrelevant, although effort-related praise will be consistent with their self-theory. Dweck argues that these learners will be more persistent, set more challenging goals for themselves and take more risks. Deci (1975) also adds that such children feel more competent in relation to their learning environment. These theories were substantiated by the work of Richard Robins of the University of California and Jennifer Pals of Northwestern University (2002) when they formulated and tested a number of hypotheses from Dweck's work.

In the 2009 Scottish Learning Festival keynote speech, Carol Dweck outlined research which she pursued with two groups of students who were both showing a decline in learning. One group was taught a set of study skills and taught about growth mindset. The other group was taught just the study skills. Their teachers were not told which students were in which group. In spite of the study skills, the standards of those in the second group continued to decline, whilst the standards of those being taught mindset theory started to increase. At the end of the project, teachers were asked about the motivation of their students – they defined three times as many students in the growth mindset group whose motivation had improved as the fixed mindset group, offering as evidence completed homework from students who previously had often failed to hand in any homework and at least one student who voluntarily sought teacher feedback. The encouragement from this evidence is that growth mindset can be taught – learners need not be locked into fixed mindsets unless they choose to remain so.

Mihaly Csikszentmihalyi (b. 1934)

Another significant contributor to the field of motivation research is the positive psychologist, Mihaly Csikszentmihalyi. Through his research on play, Csikszentmihalyi defined the concept of autotelic experience, one in which a person is fully engrossed in an activity which is its own reward. He later described this as a state of flow and he has spent many years researching this, which he describes as the most optimal form of intrinsic motivation possible: when concentration is such that a person is totally absorbed in what they are doing. For flow to occur, there must be an equilibrium between the challenge of the task and the skill level of the performer of the task. During a state of flow, goals are set with immediate self-feedback, a sense of time is lost and the experience is self-rewarding. Flow is demonstrated perfectly by gaming participants. Firstly, the activity provokes curiosity and triggers involvement. Then an individual skill level is chosen and the player has control over the tactics and strategies which are used. Imagination is sparked by the fantasy element of the game, feedback is immediate if a goal is not reached and the participant has complete autonomy over movement through skill levels based on achieved goals.

Daniel Pink (b. 1964)

The writer Daniel Pink, in his book *Drive*, applies much of the thinking and theorising of the positive psychologists. He outlines two categories of task – algorithmic tasks, which follow single lines of instruction to task completion, and heuristic tasks, which require creative solutions. There may be several ways of performing heuristic tasks, which are rapidly replacing algorithmic tasks in the twenty-first century workplace. So society needs workers who are essentially intrinsically motivated and Pink argues that anything other than specific task-related praise will stifle this motivation. This prompts a question – are current education practices adapting fast enough to meet this change? Or are parents and teachers so convinced of the value of praise and reward that they are preparing children for a lifetime of algorithmic task performance?

Pink acknowledges that praise has a role to play in the performance of algorithmic tasks, such as working on a production line or stacking supermarket shelves. Because these tasks are essentially routine, he argues that financial reward in this context is actually a positive step as workers are required to perform functions, not to think creatively. But does this translate to a classroom context? Many schools praise or reward students for performing routine tasks such as attending school in the correct uniform, handing in work on time, returning registers to the Office, running errands and keeping classrooms, cloakrooms and locker areas tidy. Is this helping or harming?

Various models of teaching and learning have emerged from behaviourist, constructivist and positive psychological theories, some of which are mutually exclusive. The praise, reward and sanction model, which was formulated from behaviourist theory and has now become embedded at every level of our thinking, has been described as a product of an Industrial Age when workplace compliance was the norm and education systems were shaped to support this need. A constructivist approach, which acknowledges the need to adapt education to a changing world in which creativity and problem-solving are key skills, now shapes policy and pedagogy in most schools. However, many of these schools are still overlaid with praise and reward systems which inhibit intrinsic motivation in favour of the quick results which extrinsic motivation appear to offer. Finally, the work of positive psychologists has moved our understanding of the role of motivation in learning so far from control through reward that it should no longer be an issue.

Points for reflection

- How much autonomy do you feel that you have in a) your classroom and b) the wider learning community?
- How does this affect your sense of achievement and purpose?
- Think of an area of your own competence. How have you achieved this? How does this relate to your professional practice, in particular your expectations of your pupils' resilience and determination?
- Think of a time when you experienced flow. What were you doing? What circumstances caused flow to occur? How could this relate to the students that you teach?
- Think about how you react to failure. Are you a fixed or growth mindset person? How do you know?
- Identify two pupils with fixed mindsets. How could you help them to change their mindsets?
- How is your school adapting to meet the needs of a twenty-first century workplace?

Chapter 8

Praise – help or harm?

In October 2011, Noreen Malone, Assistant Editor of *New York* magazine, wrote a detailed article considering the effect of a shrinking economy on American twenty-somethings. Firstly, Malone comments on the effect of the praise culture on self-esteem, writing,

> . . . our parents tried to see how much self-confidence they could pack into us, like so many overstuffed microfiber love seats, and accordingly we were awarded clip-art Certificates of Participation just for showing up. Self-esteem among young people in America has been rising since the seventies, but it's now so dramatically high that social scientists are considering whether they need to find a different measurement system – we've broken the scale. Since we are not in fact all perfect, this means that the endless praise we got growing up, win or lose, must have really sunk in.
>
> (Malone 2011)

But the article then goes on to describe the feelings of these young adults who are unable to access the successful careers that they were expecting. One person commented, 'The worst thing is that I've always gotten self-worth from performance, especially good grades. But now that I can't get a job, I feel worthless' (ibid.). This feeling is a direct outcome of performance related praise which means that the speaker attributes her failure to herself, rather than the state of the economy. The author goes on to observe that,

> It's part of the American way to get a lot of self-worth from your job. Meanwhile, one of the reasons there aren't enough of those jobs out there is that America no longer makes enough stuff. Young people feel that void, intrinsically. Making stuff is what got us smiles from our parents . . . And since we are, as a generation, more addicted to positive reinforcement than any before us, and because we have learned firsthand the futility of finding that affirmation through our employers, we have returned to our stuff-making ways . . . this is a golden age for creativity and knowledge for their own sakes. Our pastimes have become our expressions of mastery.
>
> (ibid.)

In titling the article *The Kids Are Actually Sort of Alright*, Malone is saying that a generation of young American adults has found a new set of values, based on the mastery of skills which were once merely seen as a route to self-advancement in the workplace.

So, does praise help or harm? The answer to this question is far from straightforward. There are some forms of praise which clearly harm the learning process, but there are other forms of praise which can foster motivation and support learning. And there is no simple formula or answer even within a single context, as the role of praise in motivation is dependent on a range of factors which combine differently in each individual and within each separate relationship.

Optimal learning is, of course, achieved through intrinsic motivation. From birth, humans learn most effectively through exploration, investigation and activity, without incentives of any kind. Young children are curious, acting on their own interests as, through play, they develop socially, cognitively and physically. But whilst the level of intrinsic motivation defined by Csikszentmihalyi's theory of flow is the desired optimum state for creative learning, it is unlikely to be regularly achieved in a learning context once the early years of childhood have passed and formal education begins. As children grow, they will often be expected to engage in routine tasks which they do not find immediately interesting. Hours of detailed, repetitive work are necessary to build skills and achieve mastery. At home, too, as part of a mutually supportive social group, they will be required to do chores such as tidying their rooms or taking out the rubbish.

So the issue becomes how teachers, parents and carers can support children as they learn to internalise the social values and develop the sense of personal responsibility which leads to effective social and cognitive growth. It's a crucial issue, because the alternative is alienation or even a state of amotivation which has been described as learned helplessness.

Seligman and learned helplessness

This state was first described by Martin Seligman, the founder of the positive psychology movement. In 1965, while Seligman was using Pavlov's methodology to research the link between fear and learning, he discovered a phenomenon which had not been previously observed. If, instead of ringing a bell, he delivered a mild shock to a restrained dog, Seligman hypothesised that the dog would run away when the shock was administered and it was no longer restrained. What actually happened was quite different. The dog, instead of reacting to the shock, eventually became completely immobile. He concluded that if there was no way to act to avoid a situation which was painful, the dog would not act at all, perceiving that it was unable to succeed with any chosen action. The inability to act in an adverse situation created an inability to act at all, even when the dog was able to in a future situation.

Extending this to human reaction, Seligman concluded that this was the root of depression. However, the theory of learned helplessness did not explain why two people would react to similar circumstances in different ways, one person becoming helpless whilst the other did not. He then included the concept of attribution theory in his considerations. Attribution theory, or explanation theory, says that we attribute why things happen to external or internal factors. For example, whilst some children would blame a poor test result on poor teaching, other children would consider themselves to be at fault due to lack of intelligence. Each time a child attributes something, it redefines the child's self-theory and determines future behaviour.

Schunk and attribution theory

Attribution theory was explored by Dale Schunk, of the University of North Carolina, in 1982. He hypothesised that children's self-perception of achievement would be improved if they were given effort attributional feedback. He wanted to contrast achievement perception when external factors were attributed, for example task difficulty, ability or luck, with effort attribution, a factor which is within the control of the individual. Schunk divided 40 children aged between seven and ten years old into four groups. All the children had been defined by their teachers as lacking understanding of subtraction skills. After all receiving the same didactically taught lessons on subtraction skills, the children pursued the development of these skills independently. One group was told that their progress was due to the effort they had made, one group was told that they needed to make more effort in future, one group was monitored without feedback and the fourth group was not monitored.

Over time, the past-effort group not only made significantly more progress than the other groups, but they also began to perceive as moderately difficult tasks which the future-effort group was perceiving as very difficult, even though the tasks were identical. Schunk suggests (1982) that this is because past-effort feedback brought about changes in self-efficacy, whereas the future-effort group, having been told that they needed to work harder, possibly started by perceiving that they needed to make more effort because they lacked ability, and eventually started to attribute their lack of competence to their perception of task difficulty. Schunk concludes that effort feedback which comments on past effort has a significant effect on learning behaviour and self-efficacy. He observes that future research should consider the effect of praise, reward and punishment on feelings of competence.

However, the following year he conducted a similar research project, but this time the four groups of children were given ability attributional feedback, ability plus effort feedback, effort only feedback and no feedback. He found that the most significant achievement was made by those children who received ability praise as they showed increased self-efficacy and skill. Those children who received ability and effort praise actually attributed this negatively, interpreting low ability as the need for their effort to be praised. Schunk (1983) did note that the finding about the ability feedback group was limited by the fact that they did not have to meet unexpected challenges in the maths tasks so no conclusion could be drawn about the effect of ability attribution on dealing with failure. Interestingly, he also noted differences in attribution dependent on age. Younger children tend to view effort and ability as synonymous but around the age of nine, children start to differentiate the concepts. The efficacy of ability versus effort feedback would therefore be dependent on the age of the recipient.

A further example of the value of attribution theory in shaping social behaviour is given by Steve Booth-Butterfield, a Professor at the University of West Virginia. He illustrates a solution to a common classroom problem, that of dropping litter. He describes a class where the children were given wrapped sweets and the number of wrappers dropped on the floor was compared with those put in the bin – not surprisingly, there were more wrappers on the floor. Over the next few days, the children were told by their teacher and the school Principal that they were really tidy children. A parallel class was given tidiness training, together with an explanation about why keeping the classroom tidy was important. The second time wrapped sweets were distributed, considerably more wrappers were binned in the attribution classroom. There had been no modelling by adults, no reinforcement and no praise or reward for binning the wrappers. Quite simply, the children had internalised the tidiness attribution and shaped their behaviour accordingly – they believed they were tidy children, so they adjusted their actions to align with their self-view.

Dweck and self-theory

Carol Dweck also describes the phenomenon of learned helplessness, which she noticed in her work with pre-school children, in her book *Self-Theories*. Whilst researching feelings of goodness and badness in children, she discovered that significant numbers of the three-year-old children with whom she worked experienced self-blame when something went wrong. She gave a group of pre-school children four jigsaw puzzles, three of which could not be solved in an allowed time and one of which could. After celebrating the completion of the fourth puzzle, the children were told that they had some more time and so they could choose which puzzle they wanted to return to. Thirty-seven per cent of the children returned to the easiest puzzle and reworked it, whilst the remainder of the children chose an unsolved puzzle. This choice pattern was also repeated at a second opportunity. The children who returned to the easiest puzzle were clear that the other puzzles were too hard for them to solve.

Dweck then asked each child to pretend to speak to their father on the phone, in role as their mother. The non-persistent children discussed punishments for failing to complete three of the puzzles. The persistent children not only made task-specific praise comments about how hard they had tried or how well they had done, they also offered some advice about how to react to the three incomplete puzzles, such as trying again after lunch or having another go. Dweck concludes that since it is unlikely that a child would be punished for not finishing a puzzle, these children were already, by the age of three, defining failure as something for which they were to blame and for which they deserved punishment – they were already making performance-related judgements about themselves which encompassed their value as people.

The phenomenon of children's self-concepts of goodness and badness which were dependent on performance was noted as early as 1959 by John Holt, who wondered why so many of his pupils appeared frightened of failure and so avoided risk. He wrote in his field notes, 'May there not be altogether too much praise for good work in the lower grades? If, when Johnny does good work, we make him feel "good", may we not . . . be making him feel "bad" when he does "bad" work?' (Holt 1987: 79). In contrast, consider the following self-view. Speaking in 2010, the great basketball player Michael Jordan said this about himself,

> I've missed more than nine thousand shots in my career. I've lost almost three hundred games. Twenty-six times, I've been trusted to take the game-winning shot and missed. I've failed over and over and over again in my life and that is why I succeed.
>
> (Jordan 2010)

To Michael Jordan, as to all successful people, failure was information and a reason to persist.

Dweck (who suggests that we have created a generation of learners who are unable to make it through a day without praise) observes that adults have a significant role to play in the creation of these mindsets, remarking on the focus which many parents and educators have on self-esteem. In one survey, she found that 85 per cent of American parents firmly believed that praising talents and abilities as much as possible created self-esteem. They also believed that any form of negative comment could harm self-esteem. But whilst praising ability and performance may enhance self-esteem, it is a form of self-esteem which promotes a sense of entitlement; this does not prepare a child to deal with setback or failure. In fact, the effect of failure on self-esteem has less to do with the act of failing as with the context of the failure and the quality of any feedback. Attribution of reasons for failure, which is a uniquely individual experience, will raise or lower self-esteem regardless of external praise.

Self-esteem, a construct defined by Maslow in 1954 and which was the focus of the work of Nathaniel Brandon, a member of the Ayn Rand group, can be a contentious issue to discuss. Everybody would agree that helping children to have a positive view of themselves is good, although only if positive self-esteem is an outcome of academic or social success. However, the equation that praise equals high self-esteem may be a faulty one. In addition, it is not a commodity which can be quantified, as self-esteem assessments depend entirely on the participant's view of themselves. As Alfie Kohn points out in an article entitled *The Truth About Self Esteem* (2011), there is little empirical evidence that self-esteem levels and prosocial or antisocial behaviour are linked. Young people who act antisocially may well enjoy feelings of high self-esteem amongst their like-minded peers and have little regard for the views of society. Conversely, prosocial teenagers whose actions meet with approval may have low self-esteem. It is the same with self-esteem and academic performance. Whilst research data suggests that there is a link between academic performance and high self-esteem, it only demonstrates a link; it does not prove cause and effect. He argues that it cannot be assumed that high self-esteem leads to academic success; the reverse may equally be true, or other factors may be at work.

As Dweck suggests, self-esteem is not something which can be given by an external agent, it is something that a person experiences for themselves, within their own set of beliefs and values. The role of teachers and parents is to create the conditions in which self-esteem can be developed. In fact, as with every question surrounding motivation in learning, there is no single answer. But as Kohn says, 'to the extent we as educators want to help children feel good about themselves, we would do better to treat them with respect than to shower them with praise' (Kohn 2011).

So, attribution builds or damages self-esteem and adults can have a significant effect on this by the comments that they make and the type of support and praise which they offer, particularly when a student is experiencing failure. However, even before the point of feedback is reached, teachers often need pupils to engage in tasks which are not obviously enjoyable, and so they must find ways to encourage engagement. Tangible reward can be used and this will ensure a certain level of compliance if the reward is deemed worth the effort by the recipient. But extrinsic and intrinsic motivation need not be considered as mutually exclusive entities.

Deci and Ryan and a continuum of motivation

In addition to Deci and Ryan defining the three separate components of intrinsic motivation as competence, relatedness and autonomy, they also defined separable strands of extrinsic motivation, creating a taxonomy of motivation which is actually a continuum from control and compliance to complete autonomy and competence. They described the first strand of extrinsic motivation, in which praise, reward and punishment are used to control learners, as an impersonal form of external regulation. Not only does this inhibit the development of intrinsic motivation, evidence suggests that it can stifle it even when it previously existed in children at play. This is described as the overjustification effect.

In 1973, just a few years after Deci's Soma cube experiment, David Greene (University of Michigan) and Mark Lepper (Stanford University, California) divided a class of nursery children who loved drawing with felt pens into three groups. The first group was told that they could be awarded a 'Good Player' certificate if they drew with the pens. The second group was awarded the certificate as a surprise at the end of the activity and the third group played and drew with the pens as before. Observations of the children playing some time later showed that the rewarded group had lost interest in the pens which they had previously loved to draw with, thus showing that external intervention, even if only with a certificate, can inhibit the intrinsic enjoyment of the task for its own sake.

Other studies also reached the conclusion that tangible reward which is made contingent on task outcome undermines intrinsic motivation. In fact it is not only external regulation through contingent reward that causes aversion, but factors which are perceived as controllers of behaviour such as deadlines, competition, directives and threats. So harmful praise offers praise or reward contingent on engagement ('if you start work you can have . . .'), contingent on completion ('you can have a merit if it's finished by break') or provokes competition ('the first four to finish will get their work put up on display').

In fact, so many studies have concluded that contingent reward is harmful, that it is surprising that schools still choose to adopt such schemes, in particular those which involve considerable financial or material reward. However, one research project in the United States has collected data to analyse the effect of financial reward on learning amongst those children who are destined to drop out of education without graduating high school.

Fryer and financial rewards

Roland Fryer, whose own life story is a case study in motivation, is a Harvard economist who adopts a research and design approach to finding out why certain children fall behind and eventually drop out of education altogether. One line of research which Fryer pursued involved paying students for a range of activities. This proved to be a highly contentious form of research, but Fryer, whilst not necessarily expecting payment to result in raised performance, did point out that he was conducting an empirical study from which evidence-based conclusions could be drawn.

The experiment, known as the Capital Gains Project, ran in Chicago and New York, where students were paid for test performance, whilst in Dallas and Washington, students were paid for task engagement, for example $2 was paid for each book a student read. The outcome of the experiment showed that paying for test performance yielded no improvement in standardised test results. Paying for the input task of reading produced a statistically significant increase in reading comprehension but without any significant increase in vocabulary or language use. Payment for attendance, wearing uniform, good behaviour and handing in homework produced marginal increases in achievement which were not considered significant enough to draw conclusions with any confidence. When the incentives were withdrawn, the fade-out effect was no worse than in other incentive programmes such as smaller classes or a high quality teacher for one year.

In addition, Fryer concluded that there was no empirical evidence that incentives decreased motivation. Boys benefitted more than girls, the gains were similar for students on free school meals and students who were not, and there seemed to be more gain with input incentives for Hispanic male students than Asian or white students. Possibly the most positive evidence to emerge from the study was the fact that in one city, paying second grade pupils to read, not only increased reading comprehension but pupils continued to read after the incentives were withdrawn.

The conclusion was that incentives alone did not close the achievement gap. But there were some other more significant observations, including the fact that students could not maximise their earning potential because they did not know how to learn or that they lacked the self-control to learn effectively. The possibility that students were too risk averse to engage with the project was also suggested, together with the possibility that other factors were involved which were out of the students' control, such as parental support, quality of teaching or curriculum content. Although students, and often their parents, were keen to earn more, they just did not appear to have the necessary learning skills to do so. This research is pertinent to current UK practice in which material reward is used, as Fryer's research shows that there is a short, but very effective, gain in meeting goals on algorithmic tasks, but this has no impact on the mastery of those skills necessary for long-term effective learning.

KIPP schools, Duckworth and the Grit Scale

Another school network which pays pupils to attend is the Knowledge Is Power Program (KIPP) in America. In these schools, pupils are paid for actions over which they have autonomous control such as attendance, behaviour, in-class participation and positive attitude. One of the founders of the KIPP movement states that the long-term aim is to encourage intrinsic motivation in their students. But although KIPP students showed significantly improved scores (almost all of one cohort which achieved high grades also graduated high school and 80% went on to college), the dropout rate of former KIPP students started to rise rapidly throughout college (Tough 2011).

It was noticed that the students who did persist were not necessarily those who achieved the most academically during their school careers. After considerable reflection and consultation and a meeting with Martin Seligman, programme leaders concluded that their alumni lacked the persistence needed to pursue a degree course and that their school careers had not prepared them to meet this challenge. As a result, KIPP defined a list of character-defining traits which were identified in successful students and the development of which they now include in their programmes. This included determination, self-control, social intelligence and curiosity. It resulted from the work of Angela Duckworth of the University of Pennsylvania, who devised the Grit Scale, a way of measuring determination. The Scale contains seventeen questions, the answers to which can be evaluated to assess an individual's ambition, consistency of interest and perseverance of effort. Duckworth has proved, through her research, that the Grit Scale is a more effective indicator of long term outcomes than academic performance.

So, as these examples show, the extrinsic motivation of payment does produce compliance in the behaviour being rewarded, but there are many other factors at play in the fostering of the long-term persistence and determination which are needed to achieve effective learning. However, in 2000, Martin Covington, a psychologist working at Berkeley, California, suggested that the relationship between extrinsic and intrinsic motivation was reconcilable. He examined the assertion that 'the will to learn for its own sake is inhibited or even destroyed by the offering of extrinsic rewards and incentives like school grades' (Covington 2000). He felt that it was important to redefine the issue more clearly, as there is evidence to suggest that offering tangible rewards can actually increase learning where a task is perceived as lacking enjoyment or as a chore. 'Rather,' he argues, 'the issue is whether offering rewards focuses undue attention on the tangible payoffs, thereby decreasing students' appreciation of what they are learning' (ibid.).

Covington's research, which centred on grades as the form of external regulation, concluded that students offset the negative aspects of performance-related reward by looking for interesting topics with which to engage with the necessary tasks. Students offered various plausible reasons why concern about reward might be overstated, if not actually without foundation. They reported feelings of pride and other positive emotions which prompted further engagement with learning.

Others suggested that seeing good performance in the form of a grade minimised the fear of future failure and some said that success with a good grade prompted them to study more. They reported that the more they studied, the more interesting the material actually became. This suggests that although the issue of grading work is controversial in that it creates competition, hierarchies and lowered intrinsic motivation, students are engaging with a form of extrinsic motivation which is stimulating task engagement. This contradicts Deci and Ryan's assertion (2002) that the more external regulation is evident, the less effort and interest students demonstrate and the more likely they are to blame teachers for negative outcomes. It would appear that some students are able to negotiate around the issue of control by creating their own areas of autonomy which are also consistent with the external requirements.

It is possible that these contradictions can be explained by looking further at Deci and Ryan's subdivisions of extrinsic motivation (represented diagrammatically in Figure 1), the understanding of which is necessary for teachers in order to engage pupils in effective learning when intrinsic motivation is not evident. Deci and Ryan defined the continuum step adjacent to external regulation as introjected regulation. In this form of regulation, a person accepts the necessity for a particular action without assimilating its value or the need to align the value of the action with a self-view. Hence the person acts on a type of internal coercion to gain approval either from oneself or those around. So, for example, a student may wear the correct uniform merely to stop himself feeling guilty and may demonstrate a grudging compliance. In the learning context, this motivates the student to expend effort out of an accepted necessity, although such students often show higher levels of anxiety and less coping strategies than those further along the continuum.

Identified regulation, the next step, is something of an internal motivational force in that an individual accepts the value of an activity, aligns it with the self-view and so acts with a higher level of personal commitment. This is a personal choice and so, in a learning context it is more likely to lead to greater enjoyment of learning and a more positive approach to coping with, and learning from, failure.

Integrated regulation is the most autonomous form of extrinsic motivation because the student accepts that the value of an activity correlates with their personal values, but it differs from intrinsic motivation because goal achievement is for extrinsic reasons. So, for example, a student may work willingly at tasks which will lead to success in a test or an exam. The outcome is extrinsic, but because the outcome is valued, the need to achieve it is internally embraced by the learner.

Kohn and the purpose of praise

The purpose and effect of praise in education has been the subject of extensive reflection by the American psychologist and teacher, Alfie Kohn. His book, *Punished by Rewards*, is a

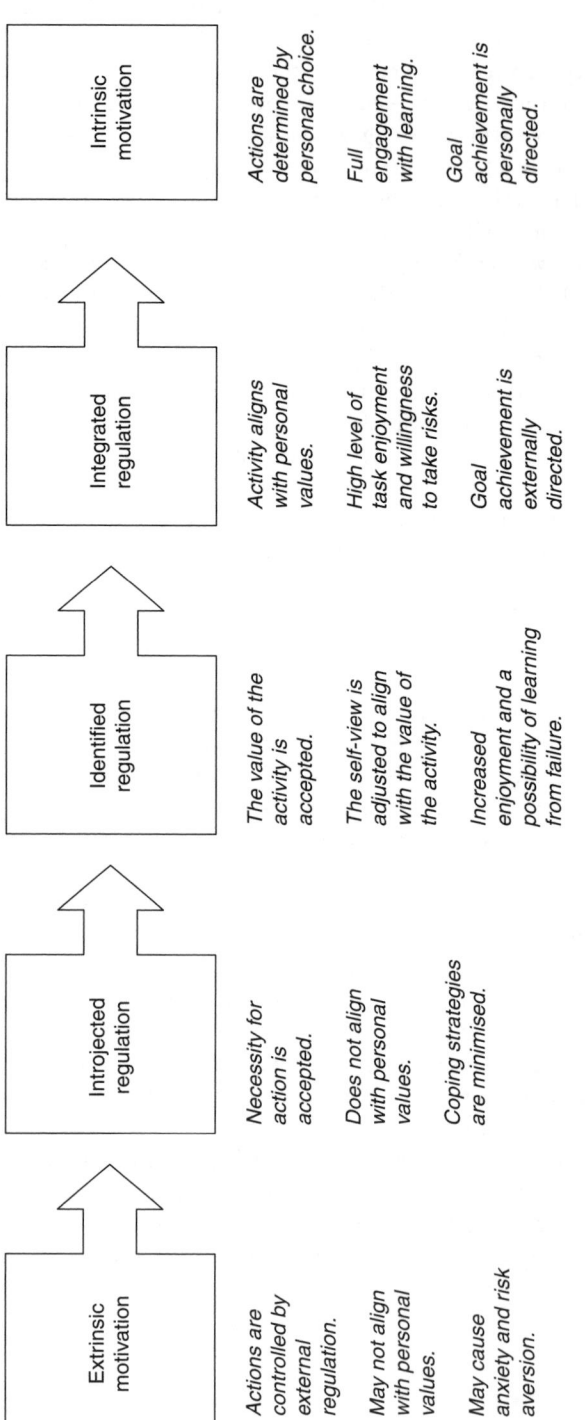

Figure 1 A motivation continuum as defined by Deci and Ryan.

comprehensive consideration of the purpose of praise. Even the common act of giving a child a sticker for being quiet, he says, is not as simple as it seems. As Kohn asserts, the action 'embodies distinct assumptions about the nature of knowledge, the possibility of choice and what it means to be a human being' (Kohn 1999: 10). It assumes that the teacher and the child have shared values and that the recipient wants to conform to those values. He considers the moral acceptability of praise and reward, questioning whether the intention of people offering rewards is to 'teach a skill, promote a value, boost self-esteem or are we mostly interested in making someone do what we want?' (ibid.: 31). Each intention, of course, has a different impact on the recipient. He observes that praise can create competitive hierarchies – the ubiquitous star chart in the Primary classroom being a pertinent example.

Further, even traditional celebration assemblies, the intention of which is a corporate reinforcement of community values, is still harmful, as creating 20 certificate winners in a school of 300 pupils immediately creates 280 losers, many of whom would have been hoping to be chosen. There is a point of view which states that celebration assemblies are nothing more than a display of power, in which the members of a community are publicly reminded of the nature of the compliance which is expected in order to fully belong. It is a form of selective recognition with criteria decided by the adults in charge. If the purpose is to let the recipient know that she has done good work, this could be done privately and with more immediacy than waiting for a weekly assembly. If the purpose is to encourage others to work, there needs to be some consideration of the resentment that this could cause and the effect of that on peer relationships. The only alternative is to reward everyone at some point, which then immediately devalues the reward.

Kohn also reflects on the view that praise and rewards are a positive alternative to punishment – he argues that rewards are, in fact, still a form of punishment because failure to gain a reward has the same effect as punishment. He suggests that because a culture of praise is divisive, it must therefore be disruptive to pupil–teacher relationships (even a positive judgement is still a judgement) and damaging to collaborative peer relationships. Kohn also comments on the popular view of 'catching children being good' in order to praise them, which is only marginally better than the previous method of catching them being bad in order to punish them. In both cases, children are being used as examples to the rest of the community and in either case, the adult is in control and children are regularly reminded of where the power lies. He quotes a comment from a typical school day in which a teacher remarks on how one particular child is sitting nicely and quietly. The teacher's overt intention is to highlight and praise good behaviour although the implicit intention is to manipulate the behaviour of everyone else by highlighting one child. The outcome is to immediately create a class competition to be nicer and quieter than the praised child. His credibility with his peers is not likely to be helped by being singled out and set against them competitively in this way.

One of the most persuasive reasons against the use of praise and reward to shape behaviour is the fact that behaviour has a cause which a behaviourist methodology ignores – in fact, often behaviour has several causes and merely praising prosocial behaviour does nothing to look at the causes of antisocial behaviour (or understand the reason that most people make prosocial choices). As Kohn says, if a young child consistently gets out of bed during the evening, offering a treat for staying in bed (or a punishment for getting out of it again) might control the undesirable behaviour but it does nothing to understand the cause. It could be boredom, discomfort, loneliness or playfulness, and the one-size-fits-all approach of the praise or punish method fails to consider the child's primary purpose; it just assumes that the child will fit the adult's chosen methodology for solving the problem.

Kohn's suggested alternative to praise is pupil autonomy, active learning, the acknowledgement of curiosity as a powerful motivator when designing curricula and opportunities for collaborative learning – in other words, a constructivist classroom. These issues are considered further in Chapter 12.

In 2006, a group of researchers led by Jennifer Corpus of Reed College, Portland, published a report on the effects on intrinsic motivation of social comparison praise compared with mastery praise. They gave groups of children different feedback after completing a set of puzzles. One group was given social comparison praise, one group was given mastery praise and one group was given no feedback. Although initially the social comparison group showed greater self-efficacy and motivation, this changed when they were given no feedback after a second task. At this point, the mastery group showed greater levels of intrinsic motivation. The researchers concluded that although the first group of children was more motivated when experiencing normative superiority, this disappeared when they no longer perceived themselves as superior to their peers. Intrinsic motivation was also diminished once the principal reason to act, i.e. to be the best, was removed. The outcomes also showed gender differences – females were more adversely affected by social comparison praise than males. Although social comparison praise offered a short-term boost to the self-view, in the long term those praised for their mastery of the task were more intrinsically motivated.

One of the current concerns of educationalists and government departments alike is how to solve the problem of low achievement, which in the minds of many theorists is linked with poverty as its principal cause. But while the data shows quite clearly that children living in poverty or deprivation are generally low achievers, these are two factors in the lives of underachieving children, neither one of which is necessarily causal. This case against such a reductionist view is argued by David Brooks in his book *The Social Animal*. He describes emergence theory which states that, 'Emergent systems exist when different elements come together and produce something that is greater than the sum of their parts' (Brooks 2011). He argues that because it is virtually impossible to find a root cause in an emergent system, every aspect of poverty and underachievement has to be tackled at the same time in order to have any effect.

Dopamine and the brain's reward centre

A more concerning possibility of praise causing harm has been observed from the research of Brian Knutson of Stanford University (2001), who found that the anticipation of increasing rewards led to reports of increased feelings of happiness from the participants which was linked to the release of dopamine into the brain. This was also the focus of research by Wolfram Schultz of the University of Fribourg, and in 2002 he wrote a paper entitled *Getting Formal with Dopamine and Reward* in which he describes the location of a reward centre in the brain which responds to reward by the release of dopamine. These dopamine neurons become depressed when an expected reward is not delivered. But further, neurons are not activated if an expected level of reward is achieved and become active again when the reward is either unexpected or better than expected. He states that, 'Reinforcers occurring better than predicted induce learning, fully predicted reinforcers do not contribute to learning, and reinforcers that are worse than predicted, or omitted reinforcers, lead to extinction of learned behaviour' (Schultz 2002: 143).

So, ever-increasing levels of reward are needed in order to create the feel-good factor of reward, a mechanism which Daniel Pink suggests, in his book *Drive*, is identical to the brain chemistry of addiction. So, arguably, it is quite possible to become addicted to reward. Kohn was quite right when he asserted, 'Do rewards motivate people? Absolutely. They motivate people to get rewards' (Kohn 1999: 67) – his assertion is supported by empirical evidence.

Cheating

Another outcome of the effect of performance praise has been described by students themselves, with Dweck reporting that students openly said that they would cheat on tests in order to make themselves look better than they actually are and enhance their reputation with their peers. Cheating concealed their deficiencies but also hampered the ability of the teacher to match tasks effectively to the learner. But in a praise dominated culture, people will take the quickest possible route to achieving the goal which makes them look smarter than everyone else.

This becomes particularly corrosive when adopted as formal policy for teachers. In July 2011, several American papers reported an allegation that 178 teachers and school principals were involved in a systematic attempt to change pupils' answers on standardised test papers in Atlanta, Georgia. In some schools, it is alleged that teachers even organised 'changing parties'. In the *Christian Science Monitor* on July 5, the Mayor of Atlanta was reported as saying, 'There is no doubt that systemic cheating occurred on a widespread basis in the school system'. It is suggested that this is also just the first of many cases reported across the US. When challenged, many of the teachers blamed a system in which their jobs are dependent on target achievement. In order to meet targets and keep their jobs, they cheated.

Critics of the system agree that making high-stakes testing the central pillar on which to build school improvement both rewards and punishes students, teachers and school principals. A spokesperson for the National Center for Fair and Open Testing is quoted as saying, 'When test scores are all that matter, some educators feel pressured to get the scores they need by hook or by crook. The higher the stakes, the greater the incentive to manipulate, to cheat'. The paper reports that ten US states currently use test scores as the main criterion for teacher evaluation. Other states reward teachers who achieve high scores with bonuses of up to $25,000. In an article written in 1991, Edward Deci observed that teachers who were externally controlled by performance criteria and test results were more likely to externally control their pupils. One can only imagine the level of extrinsic motivation that teachers exercise when their very jobs are contingent on end of year test scores.

Does praise help or harm?

Returning to the key question around which these considerations are based, does praise help pupils or harm them? The evidence is by no means clear – whilst contingent reward stifles intrinsic motivation, it would appear that children who are motivated to learn operate a form of offset by creating their own autonomies within the restrictions of the task. And as Deci and Ryan suggest, extrinsic motivation is not a single entity – their research leads them to conclude that motivation is actually a continuum. The Capital Gains Project showed that reward definitely works, but only to achieve compliance with the given criteria. Clearly effective learning involves more than conforming to rules – students need to be taught how to learn. Can praise help to achieve this?

Research does appear to suggest that using praise privately in certain specific contexts can help. As Deci (1975) points out, praise usually has a dual function – to inform and to control. The effect of the praise is entirely dependent on which of these is the salient function. Informative praise is the only form of praise which is proven to support sustainable learning as it does not interfere with the learner's feeling of autonomy and it increases self-efficacy due to perception of increased competence. This could include praising effort, persistence in the face of setback, choices of strategy or selection of challenging tasks rather than easy ones, or evidence of learning and improvement.

Perhaps the questions should be less about whether praise and rewards are good or bad, but how and why they are being used. As this chapter has shown, different kinds of praise and reward have different effects, depending on the perception of the recipient. And whilst all educators would wish for their students to be intrinsically motivated, they are also pragmatic enough to know that as students get older, there will be more need for them to make extrinsically motivated choices about learning. Rather than, 'Do praise and reward help or harm?' the key consideration is whether, or how, praise and reward can play a part in the creation of an effective learning community.

Points for reflection

- Compare Fryer's Capital Gains research project with KIPP schools. Why did Fryer's project fail to produce any worthwhile gains in test performance whilst KIPP schools demonstrated significantly raised performance? What other factors must be involved?
- Think of specific examples of how you use praise or reward in your classroom. What is your intention in choosing to do this? What effect does it have? How can you be sure?
- How important is the teacher/student relationship in the effective use of praise? How could this be affected by the age of your students?
- Which is more important, ability or grit? How does this shape your view on the use of praise and reward?
- What are the advantages of rewarding pupils for performing routine tasks? What are the disadvantages?
- How do you teach your pupils to learn? Can praise play a role in this?
- How do you personally react to positive comments and praise from others?
- Think about a recent success. To what do you attribute it?

Chapter 9

Praise – what do young children think?

Praise and age-related self-perception

In the course of the research for this book, it became clear that there are two broad, often entrenched, categories of thinking around the issue of praise and reward. Avid supporters feel passionate about the fact that 'it works' even though the evidence shows that this is too simplistic an answer. Does praise work? That really depends on what you are hoping to achieve.

Although children and young people have participated in a wide range of studies, these have all involved collecting evidence in consideration of specific hypotheses. This chapter takes a different angle. Starting without any hypothesis, children were given different opportunities to express their views quite openly about their experience and the effects of praise and reward in their schools – what they liked, how they felt and what they perceived praise to be about. This evidence was then analysed in line with the major theories outlined in previous chapters.

The youngest pupils to contribute to this project were 31 five- and six-year-olds in a school where praise is clearly defined as informative and is given for specific reasons. Praise is minimal in its use, with many aspects of behaviour and learning attitude which are rewarded in most schools simply woven into the ethos and expectations of the community. Seven interviews were conducted, lasting just over 50 minutes in total. In conversation, the children described praise as being positive comments from their teachers when they had worked hard and done well (these two factors were cause-and-effect linked in all of their minds), a Class Reward and the Achievement Book. Class Rewards were interpreted by the children as being given by teachers to acknowledge prosocial and positive learning behaviours. Good friendships and achievement were expected outcomes of such choices. Rewards cannot be worked for as contingent praise; they are given both unexpectedly and for specific reasons. Class Rewards are un-named, so the whole class works together to achieve extra Golden Time or a treat when the Class Rewards card is full. The Achievement Book, which is for exceptional learning or social behaviour, is read out in assembly. Children are also invited to tea with the Head, but again this is not contingent on any particular achievement or behaviour and the reason for it is specific.

The first question that children were asked was about reasons for praising them.

Teacher: Why do you think that teachers, parents and grown-ups praise you for doing things?
Ellie: Maybe if you've done really well, to let you know.
Gemma: If you've done something good.

James: To say thank you.

Teacher: Do you know, for yourself, if you've done something well?

All: No. Not always.

Teacher: So how does your teacher let you know?

Ellie: Sometimes they do a ginormous tick or you get a smiley face or an alien face, or something.

Teacher: Why do you think that grown-ups give children praise?

Rosie: To tell you that you've done good things and then you'll do more good things.

Teacher: So it's a way of telling you . . .

Maddie: And they punish you so that you don't do it again.

Teacher: So as well as praise for good things, we need punishment for bad things?

All: Yes.

Teacher: And it helps us to know the difference between good things and bad things?

All: Yes.

Teacher: Why do teachers say, 'Well done' or put you in Achievement Book or give you a Class Reward? Why do they do that?

Aaron: It's hard to do stuff that they ask you, like . . . you've got a *really* hard piece of work . . . it might be, like . . . really tricky for you, and if you do it you go in Achievement Book or something.

Teacher: So it would be a way for a grown-up to say, 'You've tried your best and I've noticed that. Well done'?

All: Yes.

It is clear that the children view praise as a source of information, particularly when they are unsure for themselves about the quality of their work. One group raised the issue of punishment, discussing at some length the need for both praise and punishment as part of the process of learning the difference between good and bad. The final extract also shows the link between challenge and praise. Two boys discussed in considerable detail the fact that they often found work hard, but they persisted. At various points in the discussion, Aaron seemed at pains, both in his spoken and body language, for the interviewer to understand just how hard learning can often be. Both boys were able to identify for themselves that hard work led to achievement, but praise served an important function in encouraging them. The second question concerned the effect of praise on learning and future attitude to work. The interview with Aaron's group about this issue continued as follows:

Teacher: So your teacher says, 'Well done.' How does that make you feel next time you,'re given a piece of work that's quite tricky or challenging?

Harry: Well, you feel quite worried, but once you've done half of it you think, 'That was quite easy.'

Teacher: So you look at the piece of work and you think, 'This is hard,' then you try it and you get it done because you've worked hard and you've thought carefully, and you get a Class Reward . . .

Aaron: You feel really happy.

Teacher: So next time, you come to the next day and you think, 'Oh, this is hard', do you think differently about it because the day before an adult noticed and said, 'Well done'? How does it make you feel about doing difficult things next time?

Harry: I just have a go.

Molly: But you look forward to it because it might be quite easy or it might be quite hard. When it's something hard . . . um . . . I think, 'I've just got to do it.' But the next day I try to do the same.

Teacher: So if the day before your teacher notices, does it make you think, 'Well, maybe I can do this today then'?

All: *(nodding)* Yes. Yes it does.

This interview, in particular, demonstrates the virtuous learning circle and feelings of competence that these children have already established through informative praise. They are willing to accept 'tricky' challenges because past experience has taught them that their teacher knows what they are capable of, that persistence leads to achievement and that their teacher will not only support them all the way, but also celebrate their achievement with them when the task is complete. The whole group was in total agreement that being noticed and encouraged with praise created a positive attitude to future persistence, even when the work was still viewed as hard.

Other responses to the question, 'How does praise help you to learn?' are represented in the following extract:

Beth: You kind of . . . know that you've done really well and we could make Achievement Book *again* if you do really well again.

Laura: If we like that feeling of being proud and everything . . . um . . . we would try and work our best again to try and get that feeling again.

Teacher: So every time you get something which says that you've done well, it makes you feel good inside and that makes you want to try harder next time?

All: Yes.

Pupils all described praise as making them feel good about themselves as well as encouraging them to persist in future learning. One child also spontaneously raised the issue of parental pleasure at the end of the day. This, together with the responses to the first question, suggest that young children need information about the outcomes of their work and that informative praise not only helps them to develop the ability to evaluate their own achievements but is also a significant factor in the development of feelings about 'self'.

Next, the children were asked about private and public praise. Their answers were generally reflective of personality, with some preferring all praise to be private, some enjoying public celebration without reserve and the majority enjoying both, although with considerable comment about the embarrassment of public praise, even whilst it was being enjoyed. Children are invited to bring certificates and achievements from outside of school to be presented in assembly – some children commented that they found this too embarrassing and so kept their achievements private. In all cases, praise was seen as very personal and just for the individual, even when it was publicly celebrated.

Finally, children were asked about their preferences for how they were praised.

Teacher: Do you have a favourite way of being praised?

Ben: Having a treat at home.

Flora: I like class rewards best 'cos we get extra play and we can make stuff in our den.

Teacher:	When you get a Class Reward, how does it make you feel to know that you are helping everyone in your class to get a treat?
Flora:	Really happy.
Craig:	I like Achievement Book 'cos you get read out in Assembly and everyone goes, 'Well done'.
Teacher:	How do you feel when you've done something so good that you're sent to the Head?
Elise:	Well, I feel a little bit nervous but I quite like it. Sometimes you get to be invited to tea with her, and I've been, like, waiting on Fridays for me to go to tea. When I go in the Achievement Book I think, 'Oh, I'm only going in the Achievement Book' . . . but still, it's a really good thing.
Teacher:	Why do you like going to tea?
Elise:	You get to go with your friends and you can have a really good talk with her and you get cakes and doughnuts . . . well, it's not only about the food.

Opinions were fairly evenly divided between Achievement Book and Class Reward as favourite ways of being praised, but being invited to tea with the Head was seen by all children as the most desirable recognition of achievement. There was also evidence from the conversations that unexpected praise has significant impact. One pupil had been invited to tea with the Head (which is viewed by the children as the ultimate form of praise) after generously giving her chocolate mousse pudding to a fellow pupil who had forgotten to collect her own one at lunchtime. Several children, in addition to the two involved, discussed this with great enthusiasm. It had been a spontaneous act of kindness from one child to another, but the resulting praise left a considerable impression on everyone.

So for younger children, who are inexperienced in self-evaluation, praise fulfils an important role in helping them to understand good work and behaviour from bad. Relationships are critical – these children trusted their teachers' judgements, which freed them to take risks, meet challenges and then celebrate the resulting achievement. Evidence suggests that they expect hard work to lead to success and they are developing robustness as learners and as social beings without a steady flow of contingent praise. At the age of five, they are already showing a clear understanding of effort-based achievement and self-determination.

Praise Posters and public praise

The next group of pupils to participate used a set of Praise Posters (Appendix C) designed by Paul Dix of Pivotal Education. After some discussion with the class of nine-year-olds, it became clear that although they were able to list the rewards they were given in school, such as stars and certificates, they needed some time to reflect on the concept of praise and locate evidence of it in their everyday experience. Even when discussing how they were praised at home, they were very focused on the treats and rewards that they were given for 'being good' without really being aware of what prompted the reward. Probing what was meant by 'being good' led to 'doing good work' and 'doing as you're told' but there was no obvious understanding of what constituted 'good' work beyond it being work that your teacher liked and for which you were given stars. They did not seem to be able to self-evaluate their work or behaviour beyond categorising it as 'good' or 'bad' and they relied heavily on adult information to make their judgements. Verbal praise was certainly not something which they were aware of, either in the context of school or home.

The Praise Posters define different aspects of praise, what it sounds like and what it aims to achieve. Because of the age of the children, the posters were introduced and discussed one at a time and the children were asked to spot as many examples of that type of praise as possible. When this became embedded, the next poster was introduced.

The first poster was titled 'Wallpaper Praise', which describes general praise that is given to the whole class, such as thanking them for settling quietly, lining up and moving around the school sensibly, or words like, 'Amazing work' when the class has worked really hard at something together. The phrase, 'You must be the best class in the school' was considered by the class not to be praise, as their teacher told them this on a regular basis so in their view, it was a fact. (When this activity was repeated with eleven-year-olds, they suspected that their teacher told her class that every year.)

Each child kept a tally chart to record the number of instances of each type of praise that they heard, but it became apparent quite quickly that although the children's physical actions were demonstrating positive responses to comments like, 'Well done, Class 5, thank you for settling down so quickly', few of them consciously noticed this and so failed to record it on their tally chart. So, although Lee Canter (1992) advocates meticulously planning this type of praise, it would appear that it does not function as praise at all to the children, merely as a form of verbal cuing. Canter also asserts that it creates a positive classroom atmosphere and it should be a constant feature of teacher/pupil inter-action. Although in discussion the children commented on the calm atmosphere and positive feelings it created, their tally charts seemed to indicate that they were unaware that they were being praised. Possibly, they were responding to other environmental factors and there is a false assumption that it is the praise per se which is responsible for their actions.

This latter view was reinforced in discussion, when children told their teacher that not only did they not perceive or value it as praise, but that, as she always cued them in from a particular spot in the classroom in a particular tone of voice, they acted as much on visual and auditory as verbal cuing, when they needed to be ready to listen. It appeared that wall-paper praise was part of the social glue of the class, but once the initial focus had passed and children had stopped consciously noticing what was said, it seemed to be little more than white noise in the soundscape of the classroom. In feedback, most of the children did not rate it highly as a useful form of praise, saying that it 'wasn't amazing' or 'not my favourite praise'. Just five children commented positively, saying that it made them feel good because everyone had done something good, they felt proud of helping to contribute to whole class success and it was good because everyone got praised at the same time. A couple of children commented that although they quite liked it, they preferred getting stars because that was more personal.

'Directed Praise', described on the second poster as being designed to notice good behav-iour choices, was met with two different responses. Firstly, several children described this as embarrassing, particularly if an individual name was attached to the comment. On these occasions, one child said, others had called her a 'goody-goody' when a teacher had publicly thanked her for helping. This would support Kohn's view that the effect of public praise comments is to manipulate behaviour by highlighting what is acceptable. Whatever the teacher's intention, children clearly interpret a positive comment made publicly to one child as an indictment on the rest of those within earshot. Most of the children who discussed this expressed a wish for comments to be made privately unless the whole class was included, in which case, they thought, it would be wallpaper praise.

In a conversation with a group of girls about praising good behaviour, the children appeared genuinely puzzled about the question. The majority of the children were well mannered, loved to help and were proud of their own behaviour when they were representing their school on trips, sports and music activities. Although they were able to identify past experiences where teachers had rewarded them for 'good' behaviour, they had no clear view of intention. As the following transcript shows, they eventually created a scenario where it was satisfactory to reward behaviour which involved a real effort to change but this was very personalised, with perceived effort being rewarded, not actions. This would appear to be contrary to a behaviourist view of behaviour management, although it could possibly also be argued that the behaviour of the children in this conversation had clearly been so well reinforced early in their lives, that rewarding it was no longer an issue. The children certainly seemed to be suggesting that good behaviour was about expectation and agreed (not imposed) social rules, within which the courtesy of saying, 'Thank you' was a reward in itself.

Teacher: Is it important that we praise you or give you rewards for behaving well?
Jodie: *(long pause)* I wouldn't do that, like, if I was a teacher because it's just being good, really . . .
Lucy: . . . but if someone was really naughty, say in the morning and then . . . they were good all afternoon, not talking, maybe you'd get one 'cos you'd really changed.
Teacher: So are you saying, then, that it's OK to be rewarded for making an effort to change, but because you're all very polite girls, *you* wouldn't expect to be rewarded?
All: Yes . . . It would be a bit odd . . . You should do it anyway.
Lucy: *(thoughtfully)* . . . but 'Thank you' is a kind of praise.

For those children who always made prosocial choices, praise was clearly an unnecessary reinforcement. However, these girls were in a class with two pupils whose classroom behaviour was disruptive and whose playground behaviour could quickly become physically aggressive. Both pupils were supported with target charts containing achievable targets which built towards extra computer time each day – the reward which the pupils themselves had chosen. But a conversation with one of them about the effect of praise told quite a different story.

Teacher: Is it important that we praise you and give you rewards for behaving well?
Joe: It doesn't make any difference.
Teacher: Do you like having your extra computer time when you've met all of your targets for the day?
Joe: Yeah, but if I don't get it, it doesn't matter.
Teacher: When you're making a bad choice, do you think that you're going to lose some computer time?
Joe: Sometimes.
Teacher: And does it make you stop and think about making a better choice?
Joe: No.
Teacher: Why not?
Joe: 'Cos if I wanna do something, I'll do it. It's only a computer.

This conversation showed two things. Firstly, using a target chart to support adaptive behaviour development only worked as long as the child chose to comply. Secondly, the methodology used was behaviourism in its purest form and the child was being controlled. He was not involved in the original decision to use the target chart, which was presented to the child and his parents as a positive way to encourage good choices. Other conversations with him showed that he hated the chart – it made him feel different from everyone else, he felt powerless against the combined forces of his parents and his teacher and he clearly did not see it as a positive support mechanism. As Lepper asserts (2002), 'In general, praise that is not given spontaneously but rather to reinforce or manipulate behavior may appear contrived to the recipient and will therefore be ineffective.'

The child's responses also support Alfie Kohn's assertion that this form of adult control and manipulation actually does nothing to find the root cause of the child's antisocial behaviour choices (which were not only severely affecting his own academic progress but also disrupting the learning of others in his class). On the occasions when he chose to do something which he knew to be wrong, he valued his own choice above that of his teacher, even though it would mean the loss of an activity which he enjoyed. And although he had chosen the reward activity himself, there was no genuine autonomy in this situation. It is entirely possible that on occasions he chose to behave antisocially just to retain some autonomy in a situation where he would otherwise be completely powerless.

Next, the children turned their attention to the issue of 'Public Praise', opening the discussion with the issue of work on display. All but two of the children who commented said that seeing their work on display made them feel proud of themselves, they felt acknowledged and they enjoyed bringing parents into school to see the work. One child appeared to value the impersonality of it, saying that, 'I like having my work on display because I feel I've worked really hard and I'm proud of myself. I wouldn't show my work to the class or anyone, so I would rather it was just on the wall for people to see.' For this child, public praise which could be given without causing her embarrassment was an obvious preference. One child admitted to feeling disappointed if a piece of work which she felt was good was not displayed, but also felt happy for her friends when their work was chosen, adding pragmatically, 'I suppose there isn't room for everything'. But one child told his teacher that when a new display went up and his work was not chosen, 'it makes me feel like my work isn't good enough'. The way children attributed the failure of their work to be chosen differs, but it is clear that this child (together possibly with those children who chose not to comment at all) was attributing his failure to make it onto the display board to the comparative 'badness' of his work.

Visiting the Head Teacher with work was universally deemed to be 'scary' and some children said that they declined the offer when asked by their teacher. One child said that it, 'makes me nervous but when I'm there it's OK' adding further that, 'it makes me feel special and different from everyone else, but in a good way. I feel good for the rest of the day'.

Teacher: Your comments about going to the Head are all positive even though some of you said it wasn't such a good idea. Why is that?

Zac: It's scary, especially if you go on your own, but she's the Head so showing your work to her means that your work is really good and it's much more . . . special.

Teacher: Is the sticker that she gives you important, or is it what it means that's important?

Zac: Everyone can see that you've been to the Head, so your work is really special. It means something. Not many people get them.

Robert: Yeah, everyone knows.

The social value of wearing a Head Teacher's sticker, which everyone could see for the rest of the day, usually overcame reluctance about making the visit. It was also a spontaneous, not contingent, reward which was not given to everyone, so it was afforded a high status in the community.

Taking work to another class was so universally disliked that the class, through their Class Council, asked their teacher to stop doing it. They said that although, 'it's nice when they all clap,' it was horrible when the whole class looked at them when they went into the room, they felt embarrassed and one child commented that he preferred his work to be private.

The children also discussed the weekly celebration assembly when certificates were awarded. They appreciated this and enjoyed seeing their friends getting certificates and standing at the front of the Hall. They described feeling proud that the Head, all the staff and all of their peers knew what they had done when they were chosen and the pleasure of their parents when they took the certificates home.

The 'Personal Praise' poster was the one which provoked the most discussion and it was also the form of praise which, according to the tally charts, was most often noticed. These are some of the comments that were made to the teacher:

- I like getting a little private comment.
- It's something the teacher likes about my work.
- I like to keep it to myself.
- I like it because only me and the teacher knows.
- It makes me special.
- I like having a private comment because it's just you.
- It feels good because you know me best.
- I love getting praised by you because it means you're recognising me.
- I like having happy comments. It makes me feel like I've done something good.

Children also wanted to comment on the change to the star system which had been made during the previous year. To prevent unfavourable comparisons, a change was made to the star chart display at parental request. Names of the children were removed so that only the team totals were publicly displayed. Parents had commented that the children were competitive about the star charts, sometimes accusing each other of cheating and using the chart as a means of comparative assessment. Although the parents felt strongly about this on behalf of their children, there was also plenty of anecdotal evidence that parents were conducting comparative assessments at the school gate, wrongly interpreting the star chart as an indicator of performance.

The children universally approved of the removal of names from their star chart. A typically representative comment was, 'I like how the stars are now because I can keep them private to myself.' Pupils also liked the fact that they had private cards but at the same time they were contributing to corporate rewards for their teams. Several comments acknowledged the competitive element of the named charts, which had included name-calling of those children who won the most stars. This had disappeared since the names had been removed.

The school also awarded praise notes which were sent home. These were universally popular with both parents and pupils. Parents valued them because they were individualised and they were reliable evidence of something good which had been achieved. One girl liked it because it was 'secret' and nobody else could comment and many children said that they were rewarded again at home, so it was of double benefit. Personal pride and the ability to make members of their families proud was mentioned consistently. Also, several children commented on the purpose of praise notes, perceiving them to be a way of their teacher letting them know that they had been appreciated. Particular reinforcement of the value of praise being personal came when the teacher was so impressed with everyone in the class that she gave them all a praise note. To save writing out 30 copies, she printed them, signing and naming them individually. At the end of the day several children unusually left their notes on their tables and one child threw his praise note in the bin. When questioned he said, 'It's only special if it's got a good thing that *I* did. It's not very nice. They're all the same.' This particular form of praise was very much valued for its personalisation.

The final poster was titled 'Reflective Praise' and it encouraged children to evaluate what they had achieved for themselves. They found this concept quite difficult to engage with as the school had only recently introduced feedback marking and the children were still learning to respond. Parents and children alike initially felt that the teachers were not doing their jobs properly by asking questions and prompting further thinking, rather than marking work right or wrong. Verbal prompts to encourage reflection were part of the children's classroom experience but they did not view this as praise. The amount of discussion that this final poster provoked confirmed that the children still had some way to travel before becoming reflective learners.

After all the posters had been considered, the children held an open discussion about praise. Pupils said that it made them feel good, that they liked feeling special and important and that, 'It makes me like my teacher more', which touched on the importance of relationship. Although they most valued notes and certificates which they could share at home, the majority of children also appeared to value all verbal praise comments from teachers and praise from their friends. When asked why teachers praised children, their answers all centred around the effect that praise had on them, rather than why it was given. It would be reasonable to assume that as young children, the approval of parents, adult carers and teachers was shaping their self-view. Because praise from these people was still important to them, the issue of intention had never been considered.

One final consideration prompted by the use of the praise posters was the value of praise and reward to those children who were unable to engage with these issues at all. They chose not to join in with the discussions, which usually formed part of the weekly circle time and they also struggled to respond to their teacher's questions when she talked to them individually, sometimes side tracking the conversation into areas where they felt comfortable, as this transcript shows.

Teacher: What do you think about praise notes?
Aimee: Children could take them home to tell parents, then some days you could have bad notes when children have been bad . . .
Teacher: *(child clicking fingers)* I don't give bad notes, Aimee.
Aimee: Well, you could. Then children could take them home and show their Dads and Mums and they would know they've been bad.
Teacher: Do you ever work . . .
Aimee: *(singing and whistling)*
Teacher: *(singing continues)* Aimee, could you help me with this? We're talking about stars. Would you like to join in?

Aimee: By the way, could we, maybe, one day, could we make Father's Day cards?

Teacher: We don't usually make Father's Day cards, because some children in our class don't have a Dad to give a card to.

Aimee: Have I told you about our horses?

Teacher: Yes, you have. Do you like collecting stars, Aimee?

Aimee: I never get any. By the way, could we make . . . one day . . . like choose a day . . . for Brother's and Sister's Day? Or Grandad's day or Granny day. We could make pop-up cards.

In fact, Aimee was regularly given stars by support staff and her class teacher, but she lost them and had her chart replaced on a regular basis because of weak organisational skills. She needed constant support to complete tasks and a lot of adult mediation to determine what constituted a successful piece of work. Praise as it was used in her classroom experience did not motivate her to learn, because she had a less than robust understanding of the purpose or process of learning itself. Most of her school day, including the collection of stars and praise notes, was an enigma to her.

So the children in this study had clear views about the role of praise and reward in their experience and they knew when they were being personally praised. They overwhelmingly preferred private forms of praise to public ones because it made them feel special (this word was used repeatedly) but they also enjoyed corporate celebration assemblies. Their comments about display work showed more clearly than any other discussion the extent to which attribution affected self-view, with one child accepting that there was not enough space for her work, whilst another child attributed it to the quality of his work. This is consistent with Carol Dweck's mindset theory. The final category of reflective praise also gave insight into the children's view of the role of praise as being for information about, or celebration of, a positive outcome. The concept of praise being an ongoing part of learning was novel and although teachers had committed a great deal of time and effort to reflective learning, the children still remained attached to what was described as 'right answer syndrome' with some pupils still following teachers around the room asking questions such as, 'Have I done enough yet?'

It is clear from discussions with these nine-year-olds that children not only value praise, but that they actually need it to inform their judgements about progress and the quality of their work. It is less clear whether this is the case with behaviour; most children know how to behave prosocially so praise is not needed for informative purposes. However, the fact that children were able to express a personal view of their work when it did not appear to align with the teacher's view (for example, when work was overlooked for display) suggests that the skill of self-evaluation was latent, or possibly, due to the age of the children, emergent.

Points for reflection

- In what ways might children's perceptions of, and need for, praise change as they mature?
- Review the types of praise described in the Praise Posters and discuss the intention of each form of praise.
- Compare these different types of praise with your own context. What are the intended outcomes?

- How do you know what effect any praise strategies which you use are actually having?
- How can children for whom school structures are an enigma be supported?
- What effect does the age of your students have on your use of praise?
- What is the role of relationship in the use of praise? In what ways is this affected by the age of the children you teach?

Chapter 10

Praise – discerning intention and defining value

Reward hierarchies

Following on from the previous chapter which considered younger children's views of praise, this chapter conducts a detailed exploration of the deeper issues, such as the effect of praise on the motivation of learning and social behaviours. A group of eleven-year-olds were involved in this study as they were more able to reflect on, and articulate, the effect of praise on their behaviours. By the time the study ended, all the children were preparing for transition to Secondary school and so were beginning to compare their Primary school experience with a new context and a change in culture.

The context for this study was a fairly typical Primary school in the way that praise was used. Merits added up to certificates and also functioned as House points, two children from each class were awarded certificates in Gold Book assembly each week and children were given Good News notes which were taken home to parents. The school was in the process of designing a creative curriculum, Assessment for Learning principles were embedded and active, investigative learning was the norm. Teachers expressed concern about pupil passivity, particularly when it came to self-evaluation, but this was, at least in part, seen to be due to external factors such as the effect of a prescriptive National Curriculum which had shaped the children's early experiences as learners, and the effect of a standards-driven agenda which dominated the final year of Primary school. Whilst the first factor would eventually become irrelevant, the dissonance created by an active learning programme which became dominated during the last year by the need to achieve targets in Standard Assessment Tests (SATs) was unlikely to be resolved while high stakes testing was national policy.

In order to create an environment for the enquiry, the study started with the children making Mind Maps® on the theme of praise and reward. Children were familiar with this form of recording their thoughts, and chose various ways of organising their initial thinking around the topic – from place (e.g. school, home, friends' homes), to person (e.g. teachers, parents, families, friends) or reason (e.g. who, what, when, why, where). The two maps in Figure 2 show a typical mix of comments, merits and certificates in school, and comments, treats and sweets at home. They demonstrated a range of purpose and process in reward, but a common theme throughout was their perception that reward was about acknowledgement and celebration with people whose opinion they (presumably) valued.

Then children were asked to think of as many forms of in-school praise as they could and list them hierarchically. They chose 14 praise categories, although interestingly there

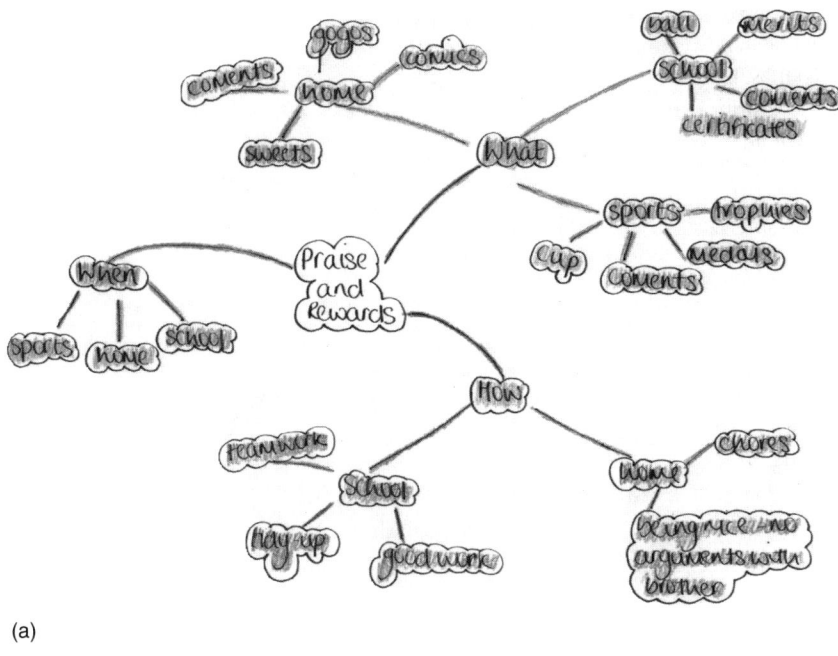

(a)

(b)

Figure 2 Mind Maps®.

were a further three forms of praise which they failed to include. Two Lunchtime Certificates were awarded in the weekly celebration assembly for good playground behaviour, which were decided by the lunchtime staff. There was also a Top Table award, again selected by the lunchtime staff, for good manners and helpful behaviour in the Hall during lunch. Every week one award winner from each year group would choose a friend to join them at a special lunch table, which was laid with a cloth and different plates and cutlery. A teacher or Governor joined them at the Top Table with a food treat to share, and they were waited on by children from other classes. There was also a Tidy Cloakroom award, which had been created in an attempt to deal with perennially untidy cloakrooms.

The lists were then scored 1 to 14, the points were added up for each category and the total subtracted from a possible maximum total of 434 to represent the categories hierarchically for the whole class. The results are recorded in Figure 3. The outcome was broadly in line with the views of the group of children in the previous study in that there appeared to be a preference for personal praise and reward. Some forms of praise were clearly disliked.

There was some discussion with the children about their exclusion of the Top Table, Lunchtime and Tidy Cloakroom awards, particularly the latter, which had been the solution suggested by the School Council when the issue had been referred to the Council by the Head Teacher. Remarks showed quite clear evidence of attribution – tidy people were tidy and untidy people were untidy. Children felt that little could be done to make untidy people tidy and a certificate would certainly make no difference.

They were unable to explain why they had forgotten about the lunchtime awards, which also remained unmentioned during several hours of interview. In later, informal class discussion there was a suggestion that hierarchical relationships were significant. All of the lunch staff were the mothers of their friends and therefore lacked the perceived status of the teaching and support staff. In the same conversation, the Top Table award for good behaviour in the lunch hall was universally and scathingly dismissed as lacking value because everybody got chosen eventually, regardless of the consistency of their manners. So, they

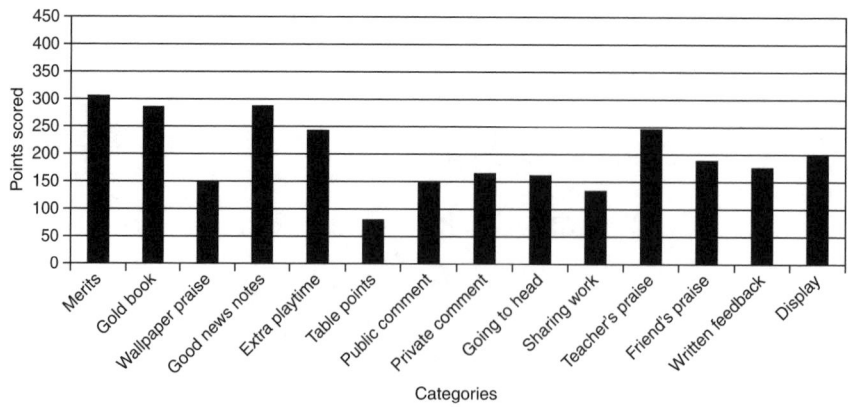

Figure 3 Reward hierarchies.

decided it was just a case of showing good manners until they got their invitation, after which it was no longer relevant.

They did appreciate receiving a Top Table invitation, but only because it allowed them to go into lunch first and because they enjoyed making the waiters do their bidding. Clearly, this was not the intention of the reward at its inception, but it does demonstrate how rewards can be distorted by children and used for their own amusement whilst appearing to comply with the adults' rules. It also created friendship issues, as the child with the invitation suddenly became the most socially desirable commodity in the room because they held a ticket to first lunch sitting and a waitress service. (Some teachers also became more desirable hosts than others, the reason for which apparently depended on how broadly the teacher interpreted the words 'healthy food treat'.) Any possible chance that this reward would effect long-term change was completely negated by the decision that every child had to receive an invitation once during the school year – a Dodo bird verdict which children were quick to see through. In fact, this phrase, which was coined in 1936 by the psychologist Samuel Rosenzweig, is an apt description of many examples of praise and reward. In Lewis Carroll's classic story, *Alice In Wonderland* (Carroll, 1997), some of the characters decide to run around the lake in order to dry off. Without any consideration of distance covered or the length of time each person had run, the Dodo, when asked who had won, answered after consideration, 'Everybody has won and all must have prizes'. Remembering your manners once a year might get you a prize, but it does not nurture adaptive behaviour.

Alongside the 14 selected categories, children were invited to comment either verbally or in writing. There were two distinct categories of comment: first, reaction comments related to feelings about getting certain sorts of praise, which, it is reasonable to assume, were also the ones which they valued most highly. The other category could be described as preference comments and there were almost exclusively negative observations about the forms of praise and reward which children disliked or chose not to participate with. Children were then invited to form groups of three or four if they wished to join in with interviews about praise. Of the 33 children in the class, 30 opted to join in and they formed groups largely based on friendship. About five hours of wide-ranging discussion was recorded.

The single category that attracted the most comments was the use of table points. Although their current class teacher did not use this strategy, it was much loved by some staff, so all of the children would have experienced it at some point in their journey through the school. Although all other forms of praise had both their supporters and their critics, the use of table points was universally disliked and with considerable passion. These are just a few of the representative comments:

- I think table points are pointless because people show off.
- Pointless.
- When people win they brag about it.
- Everyone just gets competitive.
- Bad idea.
- I don't like table points.
- Everyone blames it on one person and there are arguments.
- There's no point and it ends up in tears.
- I don't really like this because it starts arguments.
- They make everyone upset if you don't get a table point.
- I don't like picking on people.

A more detailed conversation about table points also yielded the following perception:

Teacher: Nobody seems to like rewards that depend on group behaviour, like table points. Why?

George: Because it's unfair. We used to have them and it was . . . like . . . people who could tidy up the quickest.

Teacher: So why do some teachers use table points?

Harry: *(all laughing)* To get us to do what they want.

Pupils understood that this form of praise was about coercion and there was significant strength of feeling about the unfairness of it. Since, in classrooms where this system operated, one untidy or disruptive child was seated on a table with hard-working peers, the intention was presumably to influence poor behaviour. What actually happened was that in order to win whatever was on offer, such as extra play, extra golden time or extra computer time, compliant children had to do more than their fair share of the work to cover for their non-compliant peers, if they were to stand any chance of winning. This meant that when they did win the extra treat, the non-compliant child on the table had got something for doing absolutely nothing. The competitiveness that this provoked was also disliked. Inevitably, if one table won, all the others lost, which the children said prompted blame, arguments and ultimately, tears. And children who are already struggling socially are unlikely to benefit from the blame culture which surrounds them when their harder working peers hold them, usually justifiably, responsible for the loss. It is difficult to see why, when even children can see the injustice and divisiveness of it, that this form of praise is still so widely used.

Contingent praise

The school where this study was conducted was also typical in that, although the Feedback and Learning Policy stated that praise and reward were given for effort as much as achievement (and only rarely for ability), the system was still overlaid with contingent reward where social behaviour was concerned. This is what the children had to say:

Teacher: Some of you chose extra playtime as being a good reward. To get extra playtime you would have to, maybe, stop talking ten times . . .

Ruth: *(interrupting)* That's never going to happen *(giggles)*.

Teacher: *(laughing)* . . . I think you're right, I don't think it is . . . so is extra playtime the same as merits and certificates? Is there a difference between saying, 'You've put a lot of effort into this. Well done', and saying, 'If you do this, you can get that'?

Alice: But sometimes you feel really good, like when sports coaches are here you get praise from someone you don't know and that's really good because you aren't expecting it.

Ruth: Playtime's . . . like . . . you've got to do it . . . but playtime doesn't really mean anything . . . rewards mean more because you choose to do it.

Teacher: So if you'd had extra playtime for not talking, what would happen when you came back into the classroom?

Ruth: *(giggling)* We'd start talking again . . .

Teacher: And how about getting extra playtime for keeping the cloakrooms tidy. Why hasn't that happened?

Alice: We only did it once because School Council stopped checking.
Ruth: And it's not fair, 'cos some people don't bother so nobody gets extra play. I'm always picking up things that aren't mine.

This conversation demonstrates the children's understanding of contingent praise. They had been offered extra playtime if they won the Tidy Cloakroom award. Although in their brief one-line comments children said that they liked the idea of extra playtime because playing with their friends was more fun than being in the classroom, they did see it for what it was – a short-term fix which did not cause any long-term change. Ruth understood that they would start talking again as soon as the reward had been achieved and she also perceived that a reward based on something she had to do (stop talking to get extra playtime) was not worth anything compared with rewards which were gained through autonomous choice. Alice also highlighted another issue with contingent reward – cloakrooms only remained tidy whilst they were being policed. As soon as the monitoring stopped, the tidying stopped. In addition, Alice further highlights the unfairness of either losing the reward because some people did not bother, or picking up other people's things so that everyone could gain extra playtime through her hard work. She did, however, value unexpected comment, which is consistent with Deci's view that spontaneous praise is an effective way to use praise informatively.

Praise and reward such as table points, Tidy Cloakroom and all other rewards that rely on the prosocial choices of the majority covering for the antisocial choices of the non-compliant few, merely coerce the majority into compliance, so that those who 'don't bother' can benefit at their expense. What these latter children are learning is not how to respect other people's right to a positive working environment; rather they are being taught that if they wait long enough, somebody else will do the work and they can enjoy the benefits.

Students' perceptions of the reasons for praise

There were two clear strands of praise in evidence in the school – contingent praise of social behaviour and praise which was largely informative of learning behaviour. The interviewer also wanted to probe the children's understanding of why they were praised for their work. Each of the following conversations began with the question, 'Why do teachers praise you?' They defined six main reasons.

Effort

Teacher: Do you get praised for achievement or for the effort you put in?
Emily: Well . . . both really.
Bethany: Yeah, both really, because if you put a lot of effort in, your work is really good . . .
Jane: . . . and then your teacher's really proud of you. . . . then you think, 'Yes, I've done it'.

Concentration

Teacher: Why do teachers praise you?
Zac: In PE if you're told to make a game and you make a good one you'd be rewarded.
Teacher: And why do you think you're being praised?

Robert: Because you've listened, which is why it's really good.
Teacher: So you think teachers praise you for listening?
Robert: Yes . . .
Joe: . . . and it's kind of like . . . um . . . if it's concentrating and listening . . . um . . . if it's impressed the teacher.

Encouragement

Teacher: Why do you think that teachers praise you?
Naomi: To encourage you. It shows that they appreciate what you've done.
Sarah: To let you know that you've done good work and encourage you to keep going. It's like, 'Well done'.
Teacher: And do teachers reward you for the effort you put in?
All: Yes.
Naomi: Yeah, because if they didn't give it to you, your work would stop going up and you wouldn't get anything out of it so there wouldn't be any point in trying any more . . . like a dog, if you're training it, you tell it to do something and give it a treat if it does it.

Building confidence

Teacher: Why do teachers praise you?
Susanna: . . . if you do something and you're not very confident on it . . . if you write a story and you don't think it's very good and the teacher thinks it's good, it gives you confidence.
Teacher: So a merit in your book is your teacher saying to you, 'You've done really well and I know you can do this again'? It's about boosting your confidence?
Both: Yes.

Feedback

Teacher: When a teacher gives you a merit, what are they telling you?
Charis: They're telling me that I've achieved something, so it makes me want to put more effort in again next time.
Emma: Nothing really. They're not amazing. They're just sticky bits of paper. I value the work more than the merits. But I do like them adding up to the House Party . . . it's something the whole school can do without it getting really competitive.
Teacher: So do you value the *meaning* of the bit of sticky paper; it says that I've noticed?
Emma: Oh, yeah. I get the meaning of merits.

These children also talked about outcomes as being synonymous with teacher intention. They perceived that praise was used to encourage them and build confidence and they used the information to adjust their self-perception. This may contradict the views of Piaget regarding the role of praise and adult intervention in the development of self-esteem or it may prove that appropriate challenge which is supported and encouraged with praise, leads to enhanced self-efficacy. Most of the girls were certainly ready to assimilate and interpret the view of a trusted adult in their self-view. Naomi's comments, though, demonstrate the firmly fixed mindset of a pupil who is totally dependent on praise and reward, even likening her education to the behaviourist method of dog training in accordance with Skinnerian theory. Presumably she would also blame herself rather than external factors for any perceived failure and would feel that unrewarded work was necessarily bad.

She was gifted and capable of much deeper interaction with her own learning than she was willing to engage with – this comment reveals why she was a risk-averse learner. Even within her fixed mindset, she still performed at the highest level necessary to retain her position as one of the brightest pupils in the class, but she always remained within her comfort zone as a learner. Coping with failure was never, therefore, an issue.

Challenge

Sarah: In my last school we didn't have merits or rewards.
Teacher: And did you mind?
Sarah: Well the work was really easy so I just did it and went home.
Teacher: So have you changed your attitude as a learner now that you've come to a school where we have merits?
Sarah: Yes. The work was so easy I was bored. Now it's like . . . thinking of building . . . it you're building up a technique and you get praised for it, you need to build on that . . . it's like your strength . . . now I get praised for working hard and learning things.
Teacher: So are you saying that in our school, praise is tied in to challenge in your work? So we set you a challenge and praise you when you put in effort and achieve it?
Sarah: *(nodding)* Yes.

These children perceived praise from teachers as encompassing some form of positive teacher–child communication. There was no suggestion that rewards were used as incentives. The ethos of this school was concerned with supporting children as they built self-awareness, self-confidence, self-control and self-motivation without incentivisation. Positive relationships were placed at the core of the school's beliefs and these conversations suggest that practice aligned with policy.

An analysis of Gold Book certificates for the year (Table 1), shows that rewards were made for effort and attitude in relation to achievement on a ratio of about 2:1. The achievement certificates usually related to specific work targets which had been met, although in the case of PE this was almost exclusively ability based. Research suggests that this support of process rather than outcome is one which is likely to produce resilient learners. The children's comments show that they understand this, together with the cause-and-effect link between effort and achievement as an outcome. Since the children perceive intention as being communication within a supportive partnership with their teacher, this would appear to negate Skinner's view that for effective teaching to take place, absolute power needs to rest with the teacher and effective learning is contingent on reinforcement.

One word was used repeatedly – 'noticed'. Effort was the most frequently stated factor. This could suggest that the blanket application of praise such as recommended by Lee Canter (1992) or the Steer Report (2005), merely skates over the surface of the children's consciousness. They see the intention of teacher praise as being focused, personal comment

Table 1 Certificate analysis table

AUTUMN TERM

ACHIEVEMENTS											
ENG	MA	SCI	PE	ART	DT	TOPIC	RE	ICT	MU	MFL	
33	3	1	4	7	1	4	1	0	6	0	
TOTAL											60

ATTITUDE				EFFORT	BEHAVIOUR
LEARNING		SOCIAL			
SPECIFIC	GENERAL	SPECIFIC	GENERAL		
51	23	28	23	51	9
74		51			
125					
				51	9

SPRING TERM

ACHIEVEMENTS											
ENG	MA	SCI	PE	ART	DT	TOPIC	RE	ICT	MU	MFL	
25	4	3	3	4	4	2	0	0	4	0	
TOTAL											49

ATTITUDE				EFFORT	BEHAVIOUR
LEARNING		SOCIAL			
SPECIFIC	GENERAL	SPECIFIC	GENERAL		
47	18	20	17	28	12
65		37			
102					
				28	12

SUMMER TERM

ACHIEVEMENTS											
ENG	MA	SCI	PE	ART	DT	TOPIC	RE	ICT	MU	MFL	
34	1	3	4	7	1	1	2	4	2	1	
TOTAL											60

ATTITUDE				EFFORT	BEHAVIOUR
LEARNING		SOCIAL			
SPECIFIC	GENERAL	SPECIFIC	GENERAL		
35	13	22	19	21	4
48		41			
89					
				21	4

which aims to support, rather than control. This intense personalisation of the praise process would also support the view that children develop a sense of self when they are ready, in a process which cannot be controlled by an adult. There is certainly no evidence that these children viewed their teacher's praise as a form of judgement; rather, they viewed it as acknowledgement.

One section of each interview aimed to discover whether praise had any definable effect on learning motivation, including the children's reasons for working and their view of themselves as learners.

Learning behaviour

Teacher: So do you work to get praised, or do you work anyway and then enjoy getting rewards?

George: I enjoy working . . . if I find something difficult I will basically . . . have a go.

Harry: But sometimes you don't get what you were hoping to . . . you feel frustrated because you don't get anything.

Teacher: Do you feel frustrated because you need your teacher to tell you that it's good, or do you feel frustrated because she didn't notice?

Harry: Because I like her to notice and I'd feel frustrated if she didn't notice that I'd done my best.

Teacher: So you know what good work is; you can decide that for yourselves, but you like your teacher to say that she's noticed that you've worked really hard.

All: Yes.

Teacher: If you didn't get anything, would you think you were a bad learner?

Noah: No, not always.

Teacher: Might you think that the teacher just didn't notice?

Noah: Yeah, probably.

Teacher: Are merits fair?

Daniel: (*slowly*) Most of the time . . . sometimes you work just as hard as someone else and they get a merit and you don't. That's really . . . um . . . frustrating.

Motivation

Teacher: Do you ever start a piece of work thinking, 'Oh, I might get something for this'?

Richard: No. When I've finished it . . .

Matthew: Yes, same. When I finish it and I look at it and think it's good, I wonder if I might get a merit.

Richard: I get bored if I think it's not very good. I don't really enjoy it.

Teacher: But do you enjoy doing it if you expect to get a reward? Or do you enjoy it and then hope to get something?

Matthew: Yeah. I enjoy doing it, *then* I wonder.

Teacher: So if I said to you, 'Get this piece of work done in 20 minutes and you can have a merit', would the merit matter to you?

Richard: No. I wouldn't like it . . . because it doesn't matter if the work is good or bad, so you haven't really worked for it. You just work fast, which means it's not very good.

Teacher: So would you rather have a reward for something that you've worked really hard at?

Ben: *(all nodding)* Yeah. 'Cos you've done all that effort. And you put your heart and soul into it.

This transcript was taken from a conversation which became very focused at this point, with all the boys' posture and eye contact showing full engagement, suggesting that they wanted a shared view understood. Ben stated that he would rather be rewarded for something that he has put his 'heart and soul into', showing that he values his work and the effort he has made to achieve it, for itself, and there was a lot of nodding from the others. They perceived the lack of value in contingent reward and the negative effect that it would have on learning, thus supporting the view that contingent reward does stifle motivation. This would also support Deci's assertion that praise used to inform or provide positive feedback strengthens the recipient's perception of confidence; a view supported by other comments which said that praise made them feel 'useful', 'appreciated' and 'important'.

Richard is clear that his enjoyment of work is unaffected by possible reward. Boredom arises when he feels that the work is not very good (he does not define whether this is contingent on task, mood or external factors) and he appears to suggest that he does not consider the possibility of reward unless he has enjoyed the work and therefore, presumably, is confident to make his own judgement. He is clearly not being externally regulated and so negates Skinner's theory of the need for reward to be applied as a form of operant conditioning. These boys' motivation appears to be enjoyment of task, completion to their own satisfaction and pride in achievement; this form of regulation places them on the most integrated step of Deci's motivation continuum, just one step short of intrinsic motivation.

Self-evaluation

Teacher: If we had no rewards, would you stop work?

Simon: No, because you'd know that you'd still get praised by the teacher saying, 'Well done'.

Teacher: Supposing I didn't even say that. Suppose, instead of saying 'Well done' I said, 'What do you think?' Would you be able to say whether you were good at learning?

All: Mostly. Yes.

Jake: If I did a good piece of work, I would say I was proud of it, but if we didn't have any merits or anything it wouldn't actually do anything.

Teacher: Whose opinion matters, yours or mine?

Jake: Well . . . partly . . . kind of both.

Teacher: But it's your work and your opinion . . .

Simon: But it's your task.

Teacher: OK. Alright.

Philip: It's nice if I think it's good and you agree.

Teacher: Would you think it's bad if I didn't agree?

Philip: No.

Teacher: You'd think . . .?

Philip: Maybe you didn't concentrate as much when you were marking because you were doing other jobs.

When asked, Jake is clear that nothing would happen if he was not rewarded, thus demonstrating that his behaviours are driven by something other than reward – possibly the pride which he takes in his work when he thinks it's good and his confidence in his own opinion. Again, this is evidence of integrated regulation within an effective teacher–pupil partnership. Philip's final comment also demonstrates growth mindset theory in operation – he is happy, as were many pupils, to attribute the lack of a merit or praise comment to his teacher's busy life, rather than poor work.

This conversation also gave an insight into the importance of relationship, so demonstrating the complexity of learning behaviour. Although the boys were capable of discerning effective learning and felt that their opinions were more important than their teacher's, Philip was happiest when his judgement and hers coincided. A reward in this situation served merely to confirm his judgement, so the reward could not have been the motivator. Their relationship with their teacher was inextricably linked to what happened in the learning process – they were keen for the teacher to understand that because she had set the task and they had done the work, they had a shared role in an assessment of the outcome. This would suggest that they valued partnership with their teacher above reward. Other comments were imbued with acknowledgement of relationship both with their teacher and communication of the teacher's view with their parents.

Self-esteem

Teacher: You said sometimes you're not very good at something and you get a merit or you're in Gold Book. Does that make you feel better?

Charlotte: Yeah.

Teacher: So having any kind of reward, what effect does it have on you?

Susanna: It makes you feel like, oh, I'm quite good at that now.

Charlotte: Yeah, it makes you happy and the next time you do it you might feel a bit, like, happier about it.

Teacher: When you get a reward, does it change the way you think about yourself?

Bethany: Yeah . . . because I feel really proud and think that I've tried really hard and that I can do harder work.

This transcript demonstrated an interesting response to the question, 'When you get a reward does it change the way you think about yourself?' The intention of this probe was to discover if reward influenced the girls' self-confidence as learners, but Bethany's response about feeling proud of her achievement confirms that they view reward as a reinforcement of their own view, rather than a shaping of it. These conversations show that none of these children worked merely for rewards, regarding them as a positive by-product of hard work. They also seemed to be using merits to gauge progress, either confirming self-assessment, or for adult support at that point in their learning. Again, they mostly chose to talk about merits rather than other forms of praise and conversations were limited to academic rather than social behaviour, by the children's choice of response.

However, as the following transcript shows, the relationship between praise and motivation is a complex one. Simon is ambivalent about the role of reward in building his confidence, saying that sometimes it does and sometimes it does not:

Teacher:	Simon, would you rather have a merit for working hard at writing, which you don't enjoy so much, or would you rather have a merit for winning a race, because you run really fast?
Simon:	Ummm . . . (*long pause*)
Teacher:	Which would mean more to you?
Simon:	Doing the writing. I'd like both, but I know I'm not very good at English so if I could have the same reward I think I would rather have it for English than running.
Teacher:	You find writing really hard, don't you? You have to make a real commitment to it, whereas running fast is natural for you. Would a reward for writing mean the same as a reward for running, even if it was the same reward?
Simon:	Not really.
Teacher:	Why?
Simon:	Because of the effort. But sometimes I get really confident about writing and I think I can do it again, but I never can.
Teacher:	And how about your Mum? What would she think?
Simon:	She'd prefer the English. She knows I'm a good runner.

A further part of the conversation showed that when Simon was confident about his ability and performance (in art and PE, both of which he excelled at and loved) an adult opinion might be welcome, but did not affect his judgement. He was less self-confident when it came to writing, which he did not enjoy even though he was able to write with sensitivity. He was praised equally for art, PE and writing, so it is reasonable to conclude that reward had no effect on his motivation when he was confident in his own skills, but he used praise and reward, even verbal comment, to boost his confidence when he was not secure in his own judgement when writing. Even so, his confidence as a writer suffered constant setbacks in a way that his confidence as an artist and sportsman did not, in spite of his teacher's support. Peer opinion would also have contributed to self-view, as Simon was much in demand when sports teams were chosen, always represented his House on sports day and was acknowledged by the whole class as a fine artist and a person to look to for advice during art lessons.

However, whilst most conversations clearly showed that the children in this study were learning effectively and that praise was intended and interpreted as supportive and informative, some children did raise the issue of demotivation when expected praise did not materialise – the majority of children expressed frustration, but freely attributed it to rushed marking or lapses in concentration. Harry (cf. 'Learning behaviour' transcript above) was clear that he did not need the teacher's opinion but was frustrated about not being noticed. Two other representative comments made were, 'Sometimes even if I just get a small, vocal praise I still know inside that I've actually achieved something,' and 'I feel sad when I know I have done a good piece of work but I don't get a merit, but I am pleased with myself anyway.'

Although most of these children displayed growth mindsets and they were quick to attribute their failure to secure merits and praise to external factors, they did still express feelings of frustration and disappointment. This raised the issue of consistency – although pupils realised that with a class of 33 there might be occasions when their teacher would miss the work which they valued, they were still tangibly disappointed, especially if they compared their work with their peers.

This is consistent with Dweck's definition of a growth mindset learner, who will blame external factors for failure, in this case the achievement of a merit. Their self-confidence is unshaken. However, the reaction of the fixed mindset pupils, who blame themselves for perceived failure, is concerning. There are a few such comments: one boy used the word 'rubbish' to define his work, when he was not chosen for Gold Book and one child attributed it directly to poor quality of work, even though he knew that only two children were chosen from each class. And although these represent a minority of views, it suggests that these children are, indeed, punished by others' rewards and their attribution is shaping a permanent self-view.

The views of the children in this study showed their frustration with the use of contingent reward where the aim was to bribe the community into compliance. They saw it for exactly what it was and they were able to discern intention with clarity. The interviews also confirmed Dweck's theory with regard to mindsets and Deci with regard to the existence of a motivation continuum. The children were motivated to learn and usually used praise as a means of measuring their performance and achievement against their teacher's view. Generally, where the teacher's view did not align with theirs, they attributed a lack of agreement to external factors. There was evidence that her comments could support the growth of self-confidence where those comments were interpreted through a growth mindset. However, there were also a significant number of observations about the disappointment of failing to secure praise and this was brought more sharply into focus where pupils compared their work.

There were also some very significant comments made by the children after the interviews were completed. The school, as part of the creative curriculum design, had included theme days and activity trips either as hooks into themes or to review learning at the conclusion of a theme. These were extremely popular with the children; they were anticipated for weeks before the event and were mentioned constantly in reviews of learning, feedback to parents and whenever pupils showed prospective parents around the school. At the beginning of the year, children talked about witnessing their siblings' involvement in theme days and they became highlights in the school calendar. Praise became redundant on these occasions – although the interviewer did not raise the issue, the children's comments included:

- I feel that we don't need merits for a theme day because we're being treated already.
- On theme days you don't need rewards as the day seems like your reward.
- When we have a fun day at school it just feels like we have been rewarded.
- I feel more encouraged to learn if the day is fun.

Often, these days, which were talked about long after the students moved on to Secondary school, were examples of genuinely intrinsic motivation. Children also talked enthusiastically about the curriculum exhibitions which arose from the creative curriculum, when everyone's work was displayed for parents, Governors and the rest of the school. This was felt to be an exciting and fair way of everyone being able to make autonomous choices about what work to display without the teacher having to make difficult decisions.

Of course, school cannot always be intrinsically motivating, but the staff and children in this study had certainly formulated a methodology for learning which combined intrinsic motivation and integrated motivation where praise was used to inform, support and motivate further learning. Reactions to praise depend on a complex set of relationship and cultural issues, but in interview children showed that they were able to discern intention, define value and, in the case of contingent praise to reinforce prosocial choices, divert purpose.

Using social networking sites to praise children

In order to praise prosocial behaviour, some schools are starting to use blogging and social media sites; as a result, they have seen significant improvements in behaviour choices. On the surface this appears to be a positive move – good behaviour is available for a very public audience to see, especially where Twitter is also used to share examples of good behaviour. Pupils are keen to be caught working hard so that they can be blogged. However, whilst the pupils are engaging enthusiastically, the motivation for their engagement has not been considered, which leaves several questions unasked. Are pupils making positive choices for the good of their communities, or to be blogged? If the latter, then behaviour will deteriorate as soon as the reward is removed. According to pupils, public praise often creates competition, back-biting and even name-calling. Is this any different if praise is blogged? What about children who prefer private to public comments? Does it exclude pupils who cannot be blogged? Using a pseudonym simultaneously emphasises your difference and negates the point of publicly celebrating you as a person. Does it merely play to a very contemporary desire for celebrity status – the X Factor of behaviour management?

Before assuming that this is an effective way to nurture adaptive behaviour, it is necessary to examine whether it is still just behaviourism dressed in technological costume. It is still an 'if/then' form of contingent praise.

The views of teachers

In August 2011, a UKedchat on Twitter asked the question, 'How can we deal with the mindset amongst children that it is not cool to do well at school?' About 50 teachers took part from a range of Primary and Secondary schools. The session was hosted by Chris Leach, a teacher at Winchester House School in Brackley, Northamptonshire. He opened the discussion with some personal thoughts, which included the following,

> How do we as teachers celebrate a pupil's achievement without making them resent the praise? . . . Is the person giving the praise the problem? . . . How are achievements celebrated in your school? I have seen assemblies where children are called to the front to receive Commendations – some children love this public display and others hate it.

> (Leach 2011)

He goes on to describe his enthusiasm and passion for his subject (Information and Communication Technology – ICT) saying,

> I hope that by showing them that I really care about the subject and the work they do that they will engage in the subject more. I use displays in the classroom to celebrate the subject and provide role models for the children as well as provoke questions and discussion. Hopefully by demonstrating a love of the subject, it may rub off on the children and they will be more willing to achieve.

> (ibid.)

Many of the views expressed in the following chat also reflected similar thoughts and concerns about the use of praise in motivating pupils to learn.

The issue of fairness was raised by several teachers, in particular noting the injustice of praising children who are regularly rewarded for small efforts when the persistent hard work of other children goes unnoticed:

- [They] see an imbalance in praise. They work hard, and it doesn't get noted, whereas others get praise thrown on them whenever!
- There is always the perceived injustice with praise – some children get it all the time, and some for what seems to be nothing. Naughty kids get praised when they're better than normal but good kids don't get anything.
- Rewarding children who eat some veg at lunchtime is perceived as unfair by children who always eat it.

The need for praise to be fair and honest was mentioned, as students can 'spot fake praise and are rightly contemptuous' while, 'receiving genuine praise from staff the kids respect is a good one: same as adults, hollow praise means nothing'. There was some discussion about external versus internal motivation, with some teachers feeling that as an external motivator, praise was a barrier to learning, and some responses suggesting that external and internal motivators are necessary. One teacher suggested that there is a dissonance between teachers' and students' definitions of success, questioning, 'What do they see as success? Celebrity? Work avoidance? An easy life? Academic achievement? Wealth?'. The value that children place on the rewards they receive was also questioned by one teacher, who asked, 'How many certificates have you found in trays weeks later?'.

There was considerable discussion about the need for positive models of praise and the importance of relationships in the effective use of praise:

- Enjoyment comes from success and empathy.
- Praise that involves communicating achievements with parents or allows children to show something to parents.
- It's about teaching children to work hard for themselves not to gain praise from others; that inner self-confidence.
- Personal acknowledgement is as important as praise.
- Getting families to value school achievement is crucial.
- Research with my class showed they really want praise from friends and family, not teachers. Blogging helped them get that.
- Having inspiring learning happening will engage the students. They will then be motivated and the prizes, etc., are a bonus.
- So what is the best method of praising children? Experts take 10,000 hours to create. Praise effort and tenacity.

The teachers involved in this discussion were a small sample and not therefore representative. It is also possible that teachers who share their thoughts in social networking CPD (continuing professional development) sessions may well be like-minded, but these comments do show much thought about the role of praise in motivation, together with views which are very similar to the children who participated in this study.

Points for reflection

- Several children in these interviews raised the issue of consistency. How could this be overcome so that everyone can see that praise is given fairly?
- What did the children in the study feel about the use of contingent reward to deal with social issues? What alternative strategies could be used to keep communal areas tidy or reduce disruptive classroom noise?
- In what ways could Kohn be correct in asserting that rewards actually punish students?
- Discuss the importance of relatedness and teacher–pupil relationship in learning.
- What factors in the use of praise might harm teacher–pupil or peer relationships?
- Think about the students whom you teach. How do you use praise to support and enhance learning experiences?
- What other factors, in addition to praise, are needed for the most effective learning to take place?

Chapter 11

Praise – privacy and preference

Students' views and preferences

When talking to younger children, it quickly became clear that many of them preferred praise to be private rather than public, so part of the interviews with the eleven-year-olds sought to establish whether this remained the case as children grew towards the end of their Primary school lives. They were also asked whether some forms of praise were preferable to others. Younger children, when considering the Praise Posters, showed considerable preference for those forms of praise which they could take home and share with parents.

Although research suggests that most children prefer private to public praise, it seemed from talking to the children that this was, at least in part, dependent on personalities. While most children concurred with a comment that being singled out in a class context was embarrassing, they were more divided over celebration assemblies and school-wide situations in which they were praised. Several children talked about feeling proud of themselves, happy to have been noticed and proud that the Head and the whole school could hear about their achievements. Others felt uncomfortable – the following transcript reflects both points of view.

Gold Book

Teacher:	We have different ways of praising you. Some of them are private. Some are public. Do you prefer one type to another?
Charis:	It's nice to get Gold Book because you stand up in front of the whole school and it's something bigger and more special. You feel happy and cared for.
Teacher:	What do you like about it?
Emma:	Because they call your name out and you feel really chuffed and everyone knows what you've done 'cos they read it out.
Amy:	I like getting Gold Book because I feel the special one. But I don't like going up in assembly 'cos I get embarrassed. If everyone's staring at you, you just want to laugh.
Teacher:	So how would you like to be given a certificate?
Amy:	I'd rather just get it from the teacher and not to share it with anyone else. I still feel special though, because someone's said, 'Well done'.
Jodie:	It feels really good when you're chosen 'cos everyone is looking at you and clapping. When you get home and you show your Mum or Dad they're really proud of you.

Children clearly enjoyed the celebratory aspects of the weekly assembly and loved being chosen. There is some evidence in two transcripts in the following section ('Certificates' and 'Merits') of attributing a failure to be chosen to lack of work quality, and several children commented on the frustration of not being noticed. A solution which the children themselves suggested to this is discussed in more detail in the following section of this chapter.

Good News notes

Teacher: Do you think I should give more Good News notes?
All: (*emphatically*) Yes.
Teacher: Why?
Amelia: It makes you feel really good and proud. I like feeling special around my friends and you don't have to share it with people and with the whole school.
Bethany: Yeah. You can keep them forever.
Emily: I like it because nobody else gets it, like . . . it's usually just there, like, in your place and nobody else is seeing them, otherwise they would think, 'Oh, I thought I did that better than them', or . . .
Teacher: Do other people think 'I did that better than you? How come you got something and I didn't?'
Emily: Yeah. They go off and talk about it and then say you didn't really deserve that.

This discussion highlighted the children's concern with competition and back-biting which is consistent with Kohn's view (1999) that public rewards create hierarchies – several conversations included details of the sort of critical conversations which followed Gold Book. Although children liked to be publicly acknowledged and were willing to accept the embarrassment as part of the process of public celebration, they also valued Good News notes which were entirely private. They even seemed to enjoy the intense, personal moment of finding such a note on their table or tucked into a book. Most children also mentioned the value of a Good News note as currency with parents, who seemed to value notes above Gold Book certificates. On average, a child only received two certificates each academic year, but there was no limit on Good News notes, so parents viewed these as a more consistent picture of their children's achievements.

Some children also commented that their parents trusted a Good News note, which was signed by a teacher, as more valid than their own comments. They observed that while they would be treated by their parents for a Good News note, nothing happened if they expressed their own verbal recount of praise or a personal opinion about good work which they had done. In this respect, parents are reinforcing the view that a teacher's judgement about work matters more than that of the child who produced it. Just one child of those interviewed expressed a non-committal opinion of certificates and notes saying, 'I'm happy that we get encouraged for doing good things but I'm not really too bothered about it. It's only some paper. When I get home Mum reads it and says well done but then just puts it in the recycling bin.'

Interviews then considered praise in marking. The children were familiar with feedback marking, expecting comments from their teacher which they described as, 'nice to see when you open your book' and 'nice to know that teachers have something to say about my work'. However, nearly all children accepted the teachers' perception that they looked for merits first, and only then read the comments. Although a great deal of effort had been made by teachers to encourage children to act on their comments, there was limited response. Time was allowed at the beginning of each lesson, but consistently, instead of acting on the comment, children would either ignore it, or respond by closing the situation down. So, for example, when a teacher wrote, 'Go back through this problem and work out where the calculation went wrong,' the pupil would write, 'I don't know'. The impression the interviews seemed to give was that a finished piece of work was exactly that and nothing would persuade pupils to return to it. As this transcript shows, several children felt quite resentful about feedback marking. They were used to Two Stars and a Wish, in which the marker (a teacher or a peer) would comment on two strengths of the work and one area which needed development.

Feedback marking

Teacher: How about Two Stars and a Wish?
Naomi: It's really annoying because you work really hard and then the teacher tells you to improve it.
Hayley: It's a bit negative.
Teacher: So are the Two Stars praise?
Hayley: Yeah, but there's always a comment. Like . . . you've done this now, so next do that. It feels like you've never finished.
Teacher: So would you prefer the comments to just say, 'Well done' or 'Brilliant, you've achieved this'?
Jo: But when you just write 'Well done', I wonder if you've really read it or you're in a rush.
Teacher: So how might next steps comments help you move on?
Hayley: Next steps make you feel like you're never good enough.
Sarah: But I don't think you should look at it like that. I kind of like them, 'cos it's ideas for next time.

This transcript, which is representative of the majority of the children's views on feedback marking, is particularly significant given the amount of time which the school had invested in this as part of embedding Assessment for Learning principles in the classroom. According to research, informative praise is the most effective form of praise, but most of the children disliked it when it involved them in further development of a piece of work. They felt that the Wish was negative and negated the benefit of the Two Stars, even when the comments were accurate. Interestingly, they were too keen to talk about the negativity of the Wish to engage with their teacher's comment that Two Stars were a form of praise.

This is consistent with a wider school experience of children's reluctance to self-evaluate work or revisit it to develop their ideas further and reward had no effect on this, even when teachers tried to encourage response to feedback with Gold Book certificates and Good News notes. The comments of these girls would suggest that they want detailed feedback, but only about the strengths of their work. Their reluctance to engage with suggestions for development indicate a lack of learning resilience.

One clue to the children's views about feedback marking might be found in the fact that the first thing children always did when their books were returned was to look for merits. It is possible that this was sending mixed messages about marking to the pupils. If they had obtained a merit, then feedback comments were disregarded, as the merit indicated that the work was completed to the teacher's satisfaction. If there was no merit, then pupils reacted with frustration about not being noticed, or they assumed that the teacher was too busy to notice or they attributed it to the quality of the work. Whatever their reaction, the absence of a merit created enough negativity for these children to also ignore the feedback comments. One solution to this would be to stop awarding merits as part of the marking process, in order to spotlight the feedback comments in the minds of the children.

The value of praise from peers in the form of peer review was also raised by some children. They accepted that they were experienced enough in the use of the system to have moved beyond saying nice things just to their friends, or taking the comments as personal criticism, although these comments demonstrated that praise from friends could be a two-edged sword:

- Praise from a friend makes them feel like a really good friend.
- I think my friends' point of view is very important.
- Not very good because we're friends so they might just say it.
- You never know if they're lying or not because they're your friends.
- Sometimes they lie to make me feel better.

In addition to the consideration of private praise, the views of the children about preference were sought. Younger children showed clear preference for personal rewards that were specifically related to their own learning or effort. Was this also the case with older children? The issue of certificates for Gold Book was considered.

Certificates

Teacher: You mentioned about taking certificates and things home. Is it important?
All: Yes. Because Mum's really happy . . . you feel really proud . . . you might get another treat at home.
Teacher: So it's a bit like getting rewarded twice?
All: Yeah.
Teacher: Do you like getting group certificates, for good behaviour when we've been out on a trip?
Ben: Not really. I feel better when it's personal . . . It's not a surprise . . . we kind of expect it.
Philip: And we behave.
Jake: Because the trips are really good fun.
Teacher: Thinking about Gold Book, it's only two people a week, so every week 31 people are disappointed. Does that matter?
Ben: No, because you still did work hard and you can think, 'I did really well in that' and just be happy for other people.
Jake: Sometimes, I feel I've let myself down. Like I've done a really good piece of work and I wait until Friday and go into Assembly thinking it's one of my best pieces of work, then when it isn't I feel I've let myself down.
Teacher: Sometimes there might be six people I want to put in Gold Book and then other weeks, nobody really stands out. How could we make it fairer?
Philip: *(long silence)* That's a really hard question.

This conversation probed the issue of fairness. Whilst children accepted that only two children each week could be rewarded through this form of assembly, they still expressed disappointment, frustration and negativity about their own work when they were not chosen. And although at that point they were unable to suggest any way of overcoming the problem of Gold Book creating instant losers, they did readily accept that the system is fair in that everyone's contribution is celebrated at some time during each term. They are therefore not only happy to wait their turn, but also enjoy seeing their friends being rewarded.

After this interview concluded, children discussed the issue and decided that a Proud Book would work well and would be fairer. This was an available book in which any child could write things which they had done and which they were proud of – this could be learning or social behaviours. It was felt that this was a fairer way of celebrating everyone's achievements, including those which had not been noticed by the teachers. Within a couple of days, allegations were being made about false claims and arguments then broke out. The Proud Book lived a short life, so the teacher discussed it with a group from the class:

Proud Book

Teacher: When I started using the Proud Book, a couple of people wrote in it regularly. I was going to choose Gold Book from it because you had identified something that you were proud of, but people didn't seem bothered. Why?

Emily: Well . . . I think it's better with you choosing otherwise . . . it's just a bit . . . like you're asking to go in Gold Book . . .

Bethany: And people write things that they haven't really done.

Jane: And I want teachers to notice that I'm good, not say that I'm good for myself.

Teacher: So are you saying it's fairer if I choose?

All: *(nodding)* Yes.

Jane: And it's better if it's a surprise.

This showed the children's explicit acknowledgement of the mediating role which a teacher plays in ensuring fairness. There were several complaints naming children who had written things that they had not done in order to get the teacher's attention. Children also acknowledged that the element of anticipation and surprise played an important part in their enjoyment of Gold Book, even if it ultimately led to disappointment. It is possible that the Proud Book did not work as the children had hoped because they were still too dependent on teacher praise to validate their own judgements, or maybe, after reflection, they were happy for the status quo to be maintained. It certainly demonstrated that some children acted prosocially to be noticed rather than for the better good of the class community, which suggests that the use of praise can distort motives for some children.

Merits

Teacher: What do you think about the way we award merits?

Daniel: Sometimes it's unfair because if you haven't got many, everyone knows and they say, 'Oh, I've got more than you' . . .

Chris: . . . and people get teased.

Teacher: We've tried to work on that. Do you think we've got it about right, now?

Daniel: Mmm. I find school quite hard and I put a lot of effort into it. So if I got a lot of merits people might think I'm really smart when I'm not. So it's right . . .

Chris: And if I got loads of merits I'd think, 'So why am I here then if I've done everything and I'm getting all these merits?'

Daniel: And I'd think, 'What's the point?'

Teacher: So you all agree that you like rewards given carefully because it means a teacher's noticed . . . *(nods of agreement)* But what happens when you've put effort in and nobody notices?

Chris: It annoys me . . . I think *(sarcastically)* 'Thanks very much'.

Noah: I think I must be rubbish at it . . .

Daniel: I get annoyed.

As with most conversations, the issue of not being noticed was raised; although the general fairness was accepted, even when the teacher failed to notice. So whilst some researchers have suggested that inconsistency rendered praise ineffective (Shreeve *et al.* 2002), these children seem tolerant of inconsistency due to teacher error. This issue was also widely discussed by the class after the completion of the interviews and they suggested that they should indicate for themselves when a merit was deserved. The idea was met with approval and tried in the classroom. This, too, had a short life as complaints started of children awarding themselves merits when they had allegedly done nothing and comparisons of work became the norm as children tried to prove their worthiness to self-award merits. The tried and tested method of teacher mediation was soon restored at the children's request.

How praise is valued

There was also an acknowledgement from some children that they occasionally received praise which they did not feel was deserved. When discussing how they felt about this they said:

- I love being praised. But sometimes people just say it to make you happy, like when you know it's not a great piece of work . . . and sometimes it makes you feel worse.
- Being praised makes me feel important. Sometimes I don't think I deserve it and feel a bit guilty.

The first comment shows the need for sincerity when praising children – saying something just to make them feel better actually has the adverse affect. As Henderlong and Lepper write,

> The perceived sincerity of praise may be dependent on the quality of the relationship between the evaluator and the recipient of the praise. One might imagine that, in the context of a close and caring teacher–child relationship, praise will be perceived as genuine and helpful. In contrast, the same praise statement given in the context of a more conflict-ridden or less-secure relationship may be perceived as manipulative, controlling, or as a sign that that the teacher feels sorry for the student.
>
> (Henderlong and Lepper 2002)

Insincere praise could also harm the quality of the teacher–pupil relationship. Undeserved praise may be harmful, but some children were also able to evaluate teacher praise (or the lack of it) against their self-view, saying:

- Praise makes me feel happy even if I don't think it is very good. But I think it is really my decision if it is good or not.
- My opinion matters the most whether I get praise for my work or not.

Minimal use of reward was also valued – Chris and Daniel appear to suggest that since they used praise as a gauge of progress, it should be given carefully. Over-reward would become meaningless in a context where praise is interpreted as a feedback mechanism. And although merits were given privately, Daniel expressed concern that if he was given too many merits, people might develop a false view of his ability, when he was clear that his achievements were due to hard work. This demonstrates that even though merits and Good News notes were given privately, children were still using the information to create hierarchies of perceived ability. And even though Daniel interpreted the praise he received as acknowledgement of effort and achievement, there was still an assumption on his part that others would use the information to judge his ability.

There was wide approval of the House system and the accumulation of merits for their House was popular with most children. It is reasonable to assume that relatedness to their House, within a wider school community, was the reason for this, even though House rewards were not personalised. This would support the view of Ryan *et al.* (1994) who found that pupil and parent relatedness 'was associated with greater internalization of school-related behavioral regulations'. Behaviour in this school was generally very good and the children also felt a strong sense of relatedness with the community.

The only negative comment about the House system was that the termly House Cup and House Party were rigged by the teachers to ensure that every House got a turn. They were quite correct in this assertion – although House Captains counted merits weekly, the final total was always done by a member of staff – sometimes with quite surprising shifts of total within the last week of term. But even though the older children saw this for what it was, they still enjoyed belonging to, and representing, a House. They were also quite correct in observing that the Sports Cup, for performance on Sports Day, was never fixed, which meant that one House could win for consecutive years. This forms an interesting link with the Gold Book analysis which showed that certificates were used almost exclusively to reward ability in sport, rather than effort or achievement. It suggests that in this school (and probably in many others) it is acceptable to praise and acknowledge ability and performance in sport even when this runs counter to the ethos of every other aspect of the school.

The value of reward as a means of communication was a significant issue in the children's thinking. Although the frequency of praise and reward had fallen noticeably since the inception of a creative curriculum (this would be consistent with Shreeve *et al.*'s findings 2002: that schools with rich curricula and strong teacher–pupil relationships made little or no use of reward), pupils were still well motivated learners within a successful community. In fact, enjoyment of learning had increased noticeably as a result of curriculum changes; this was regularly commented on by parents.

Interestingly, throughout all of the interviews, children talked about praise in an almost exclusively personal way. Although open questions about praise were asked, all the conversations quickly focused on personal praise, specialness and the pleasure of sharing something with someone that cared about them. This would suggest that children see the intention of praise as being a personal communication with them. Perhaps the commonest response had little to do with motivation, as the words 'happy' and 'proud' were those most often used. However, the reasons for feeling happy were various, including sharing rewards at home, pleasing parents, creating a sense of achievement and personal and corporate celebration. Although a direct correlation cannot be made between praise and outcome, there is no doubt that it played some part in the complex layers which define these children's view of success.

Private versus public praise

As with the issues discussed in the previous chapter, teachers' comments mirrored those of the children. One teacher said that her own six-year-old got upset by public praise, which showed that a one-size-fits-all approach is not always appropriate, while another teacher said that his seven-year-old really loved public praise and was disappointed when he did not receive any during the week. One teacher also discussed a four-year-old who hated receiving positive comments, and another who remarked, 'I've seen children tear down work from displays and be in tears when called out in assembly.'

The role of praise in Secondary schools was particularly interesting – one contributor asked their own 15-year-old son about praise and he declined to comment saying that 'being quoted on UKedchat would be worse than public praise'. Other teachers commented that secondary students actually went out of their way to avoid collecting House points, one student because he thought it was stupid and another because, 'The thought of getting praise makes some people not want to do well when they are capable.' This last comment is a clear indication of the use of praise actually inhibiting the learning process. The student is implying that rewards are used as a means of peer categorisation, and in a school where learning is not 'cool', students will avoid anything which creates a public perception of ability or competence which may draw undue attention to them. The change of attitude towards the end of Junior school was noted, along with students' ability in diverting the purpose of rewards – one teacher described a school where the top 40 House point achievers in the school were rewarded with a trip. The students developed a healthy black market trade in House points.

So, both teachers and students agree that praise is best given privately and that there is a considerable change in attitude towards praise and reward as pupils get older. One teacher observed that the culture of the school was important – where the majority of students valued praise, there were less issues with self-conscious responses. This does, of course, raise the question of why, if praise has this effect, is it used at all in a Secondary school context? Are there other ways of motivating students and acknowledging those things which are valued in each school community?

Points for reflection

- In what ways can praise be used by students (and parents) to create hierarchies?
- How can a teacher ensure fairness in the use of praise strategies?
- What characteristics define resilient learners?
- How can praise play a role in the growth of resilient learning?
- How do the teacher–pupil, parent–child and pupil–pupil relationships change as children mature?
- How might the use of praise change to reflect these differences?
- Is it possible to educate children without the use of praise?

Chapter 12

Praise and motivation in a cultural context

Amy Chua

At the beginning of 2011, a newly published book called *The Battle Hymn of the Tiger Mother* caused something of a media storm. The Chinese-American author, Amy Chua, is a Law Professor at Yale Law School and the book was intended as the story of her family's journey within two cultures: Chua was brought up in America by Chinese immigrant parents. She is grateful for the typically Chinese upbringing which she was given and she remains close to her parents. But when she started to bring up her own two daughters in the same way, she discovered a significant cultural dissonance between Eastern and Western parenting styles. Whatever one's view of the controversy which surrounded the publication of the book, it does highlight some significant issues about cultural differences in the use of praise.

The expectations of Chinese parents are very high. Children are expected to work hard and use feedback to improve future performance. Praise does not form part of this process until there is an achievement to praise and it is done in private. Ability is never part of the consideration of performance. In an article in the Wall Street Journal in 2011, Chua contextualised the contrast as follows:

> . . . if a child comes home with an A-minus on a test, a Western parent will most likely praise the child. The Chinese mother will gasp in horror and ask what went wrong. If the child comes home with a B on the test, some Western parents will still praise the child. Other Western parents will sit their child down and express disapproval, but they will be careful not to make their child feel inadequate or insecure . . . If a Chinese child gets a B . . . the devastated Chinese mother would then get dozens, maybe hundreds of practice tests and work through them with her child for as long as it takes to get the grade up to an A.
>
> (Chua 2011)

She goes on to explain that while a Chinese parent attributes poor grades to lack of work, a Western parent would start to question teaching competence, curriculum content or lack of aptitude, rather than effort. She attributes this to a Western focus on the development of self-esteem, observing that a Western child would be praised for work or performance that is actually mediocre, where a Chinese child would be told the truth about the quality of their work and told how to improve it in future.

The view of Chinese parents is that children are sturdy enough to accept accurate appraisal and that mastery is a route to enjoyment of learning. Chua argues that the Chinese parenting model creates a virtuous circle, once children start to see mastery of their own making. Praise plays a part in this, but for effort-related achievement, not for each incremental step along the way. As she says,

> Once a child starts to excel at something – whether it's math, piano, pitching or ballet – he or she gets praise, admiration and satisfaction. This builds confidence and makes the once not-fun activity fun. This in turn makes it easier for the parent to get the child to work even more.

> (ibid.)

The Chinese parenting and education model understands the hours of committed work necessary for the mastery of any skill. But it is also based on a difference in parent–child relationships. Chinese children are expected to be obedient and make their parents proud, and that is a lifelong expectation. Because of this, Chinese children take a different view of achievement and do not expect affirmation of their skills and abilities on a regular basis. Chua offers evidence for her views, saying that studies have shown that Chinese parents spend about ten times as long as Western parents supporting their children with academic work such as homework. Also, in a study of 50 American mothers and 48 Chinese immigrant mothers, almost 70 per cent of the American mothers did not think that stressing academic success with their children was a good thing and they felt that parents should encourage their children to consider learning as fun. The Chinese mothers not only all believed that their children could be the best students, they also believed that anything less reflected badly on them as parents.

Cross-cultural studies

The role of praise in this cultural view of effort and ability was noted as early as 1986 by a German research team led by Wulf-Uwe Meyer, working at the University of Bielefeld in Germany. They found that praise and blame from a teacher shaped a learner's self-view in an unexpectedly paradoxical way. In their study, one group of students was praised and one group was not. Students who were not praised were assumed to have higher abilities than those who were praised, because both sets of students were successful, therefore it was assumed by the participants that the praised students must have worked harder. A repeated study in 1992 reached the same conclusion – that praising students led to an assumption that there was an ability deficit.

In 1994, Farideh Salili and Kit-Tai Hau of the University of Hong Kong addressed the question of the ability–effort relationship in a collectivist culture. They found that although older Chinese students tended to think that non-praised students had higher ability than praised students, this view was reversed with younger students. Although this correlated with the Western view, there was a contrast in that Eastern students always correlated their perceptions of effort and ability. In a second part of the study, Chinese students were given a maths test which resulted in identical outcomes, some students being praised and others receiving no feedback. Regardless of the nature of the feedback, students were able to evaluate their own effort and ability.

As the researchers noted, 'for Chinese students, people working hard have high ability and those who have high ability must have worked hard' (Salili and Hau 1994: 233). In a further study in 1996, Salili noted that praise is rarely given in Chinese and Japanese cultures;

'Praise, when given, is seldom done publicly and only for exceptional achievement or other virtues. In such an environment, praise or reward has a highly motivating effect' (Salili 1996: 61). Where learners are unable to attribute their learning and social behaviours to adult control, children appear more willing to take personal responsibility for what they do.

Speaking at the Third Hawaii International Conference on Education in 2005, Tsui Cheng-Fang, an Assistant Professor at Taiwan's National Chengchi University, presented his research into the achievement beliefs of three cultural groups. His findings suggest that Chua's observations are correct. He worked with three groups of college students, Caucasian-American, Chinese-American and Taiwanese. Previous studies had shown that Chinese parents were generally less satisfied with their children's performance than American parents at all stages of education and he wanted to know how, or whether, this cultural difference affected attribution. Another study had shown that Chinese parents would blame poor performance on lack of effort, American parents would blame a range of factors, including ability, and Chinese-American parents tended to show similar expectations to Chinese parents with slightly less emphasis on effort.

Yet another study, comparing the views of 1440 children from 20 classes in each of the cities of Minneapolis (US), Taipei (Taiwan) and Sendai (Japan), showed that whilst all the children agreed that something could be done to help improve poor performance, the American children did not agree with the statement that 'the best students always work harder'. The research also showed inextricable links with parental relationship as Taiwanese mothers demonstrated higher levels of parental control than immigrant Chinese mothers in the US, who in turn exhibited higher levels of control than Caucasian-American mothers.

Chinese and Japanese mothers showed through interview that academic achievement was their highest priority once their children started school and the resources of the home environment of these children were mobilised in order to give the most effective support possible. American mothers expressed more interest in cognitive development and activities in the home were organised to nurture cognitive growth. It was also found that Chinese and Japanese mothers had realistic views of their children's academic achievements whereas American mothers tended to overestimate expected achievement. The latter group emphasised innate ability over effort and tended to praise achievement and ability in way that Chinese and Japanese parents did not.

Working with 285 students to explore this cultural difference, Tsui Cheng-Fang used a persistence task which contained some unsolvable problems, followed by interviews with 15 participants. Analysis of the data with regard to attribution showed that the Caucasian-Americans expressed quite clear views that they achieved well because of natural ability, all explaining how they found school work easy, succeeding without much work where others failed even with days of studying. Only one student attributed her success to her parents' involvement, encouragement and expectation. There was a clear correlation with lack of persistence in the problem-solving exercise for some of these students.

The Chinese-American group all seemed to view effort and ability as necessary factors for success, although they did not think that ability without effort would yield success. This, too, was reflected in their persistence at the task. The Taiwanese students all attributed their success to effort, with one student suggesting that achievement was ultimately determined by effort. One Taiwanese student also discussed norm referencing, saying that the competition that this promoted actually made her a better student as she was more determined to achieve.

International differences in socio-cultural expectations

In 2001, a group of researchers from Croatia, Finland and Japan (Niemivirta *et al.* 2001) examined the effect of socio-cultural expectations on learning motivation. Some factors are constant across a range of cultures, but these researchers wanted to know to what effect achievement behaviour was shaped by the differences in cultural expectation. They started from the premise of previous research which showed that Western cultures tend to attribute failure to external factors and success to internal factors, whereas Eastern cultures tend to blame lack of effort for failure and attribute success to a range of situational factors. This led them to express the motivational contrast as 'a case of self-enhancement versus self-improvement' (Niemivirta *et al.* 2001: 163). They found that although the understanding of the concepts of ability and effort were similar in Western and Eastern children, their attribution was shaped by cultural belief. Where Western children generally believed that ability was an immutable entity, Eastern children believed that ability was a malleable entity which could be extended through effort. The trust relationship of Eastern children with adults was also shaped by this belief; as the authors of the article point out, 'if and when one is expected to act on potential imperfections, one must also be confident that the identification of such weakness is correct' (ibid.: 165).

It is this relationship between effort and ability which is key in shaping students' beliefs about learning. If a student believes that achievement is the outcome of effort and that ability increases through this, then effort is seen as a positive action. For students who believe that ability is an immutable entity, effort serves only to demonstrate an ability deficit – the less effort one makes to achieve, the greater one's innate ability. This, in turn, will shape both learning motivation and the relationship of teachers, learners and parents. Further, where the power to influence achievement through effort is in evidence, praise appears to have little effect on self-perception.

However, the relationship between praise and motivation is not solely of academic interest. Writing in the *New Yorker* early in 2011, the journalist Elizabeth Kolbert noted that whilst Western countries emphasised creativity and flexibility in the education of their children, international data (the Programme for International Student Assessment, or PISA) show that East Asian countries are out-performing Western countries in every area of education assessed by the data. She observes that parents are told to encourage their children, stating,

> This, the theory goes, will improve their self-esteem and this, in turn, will help them to learn. After a generation or so of applying this theory, we have the results. Just about the only category in which American students outperform the competition is self-regard.
>
> (Kolbert 2011)

Implications for the future

In the UK, there are also immediate economic considerations. Speaking at the Conservative Party Conference in the autumn of 2010, the Education Secretary, Michael Gove, commented that the performance of children in receipt of free school meals (a key measure of deprivation) was a 'reproach'. But this does not tell the whole story. In February 2011, writing in *The Guardian* newspaper, the education journalist Warwick Mansell observed that in the case of UK Chinese students in receipt of free school meals (FSM), GCSE (General Certificate of Secondary Education, the UK national benchmark testing for 16-year-olds) data shows that they outperformed the national average for all pupils, regardless of economic status (Mansell 2011). In 2009, 71 per cent of Chinese FSM students passed five GCSEs including maths and English. The figure for non-FSM Chinese students was 72 per cent. The gap in all other ethnic groups varied between 10 per cent and 32 per cent. National benchmark testing of 11-year-olds (Standard Achievement Tests – SATs) showed the same pattern, with Chinese FSM pupils even outperforming non-FSM Chinese pupils.

So Michael Gove's statement needs some qualification, as poverty clearly does not have the same impact on learning across all ethnic groups. There is, apparently, very little research into the reasons why Chinese children are such successful learners. Mansell (2011) quotes Becky Francis, a visiting professor at King's College, London who has been involved in researching this question as saying, 'Our main argument is that families of Chinese heritage see taking education seriously as a fundamental pillar of their Chinese identity, and a way of differentiating themselves not just within their own group, but from other ethnic groups as well.'

There will, of course, be many factors involved in the under-achievement of children, not least a heritage of low expectation and unemployment reaching back over two or three generations. But it is also clear that more research is needed into a phenomenon in the Chinese culture which has such significant impact on achievement regardless of socio-economic status. The issue goes beyond how praise is used in classrooms across the world. There are clear differences in the use of praise in Eastern and Western education systems and the socio-cultural expectations of each nation shapes the learning behaviour, self-view and motivation of its people. But whatever position one takes, it is beyond dispute that Eastern countries, in particular China, are emerging as world economic powers. Perhaps it is necessary to consider why this is happening and what can be learnt which might inform the preparation which Western children are given to meet the challenges of their futures.

A further issue which underlines the complexity of learning motivation in a socio-cultural context was raised by Adolph Cameron, head of the Jamaican Teacher's Association when addressing an event in Bristol, England, in 2011, aimed at promoting the educational achievement of black boys. He stated that in Jamaica, boys lagged at least 10 per cent behind girls in national test results, while in the UK, African-Caribbean boys were 18 per cent below the national average in achieving five good GCSEs, including English and maths. He attributed this to a cultural view amongst African-Caribbean males that academic success is a feminine issue. In an interview with the BBC, he said,

> Education . . . takes second place to notions of entrepreneurship as, predominantly our young men, get involved in the informality of what the University of the West Indies academics, Witter and Gayle, have called a 'hustle culture' . . . Boys are more interested in hustling, which is a quick way of making a living, rather than making the commitment to study. This is supposed to be a street thing which is a male thing.
>
> (Richardson 2011)

Whilst there is no research into this specific issue amongst African-Caribbean boys in the UK, it is, according to data, one of the lowest performing groups in the country and Adolph Cameron raises the possibility that this may be due to the same expectations of peer conformity in other countries than Jamaica.

It is clear from extant research into the achievements of different ethnic groups that family expectations and peer conformity have a far greater effect on learning motivation than simple praise and in-school incentives. There is a persuasive argument to be made that contingent praise as a peculiarly Western phenomenon is of no cultural relevance to many children currently being educated in British schools.

Points for reflection

- How many different cultures are represented in your classroom? Discuss your understanding of how praise is used in the homes of these children.
- How does the use of praise in other cultures align with a Western view?
- How do expectations differ according to socio-cultural background?
- What impact might this have on a) the motivation of children from other cultures b) the ability of those children to integrate?
- Which do you believe is more important – ability or effort? Explain why you believe this.
- Discuss your reaction to research which shows that praising a child's effort may lead them to assume that they have an ability deficit.
- What are the implications for your classroom of the studies described in this chapter?

Chapter 13

Creating a culture of compliance

In Chapter 1, three different teachers were profiled and the question was asked, 'What's wrong with these pictures?' Although all three teachers, and the schools in which they work, share the same wish to provide the best education possible for their pupils, research evidence suggests that this may not be what is actually happening; that at least one of the schools may be limiting pupils' real development by creating a culture of compliance.

In his 1991 article *Motivation and Education: The Self-Determination Perspective*, Deci wrote that 'praising [children] for doing what they "should" have done or what you told them to do is likely to lead to their feeling controlled, which in turn would reduce intrinsic motivation and strengthen non-autonomous forms of extrinsic motivation.' In a controlling environment, controlled forms of extrinsic motivation are much more likely to be in evidence. This is why the issue of how praise and reward is used in a classroom goes beyond the simple consideration of star charts, House points or certificates. Chapter 1 ended with the statement, 'So why the concern with praise and reward? Because a school's position on this together with sanction (the opposite side of the same coin), is an effective indicator of its place on the behaviourist–constructivist spectrum.'

In fact, the issue goes even deeper than the positioning of a school or an individual educator on an ideological spectrum. A school's use of praise and reward goes to the very effectiveness of the education which is given. And whilst it is unsettling to consider that classroom practice might be having negative consequences for the children who are being educated, even when intention is positive, it is still necessary to reflect on the impact of praise on learning motivation.

Jack – a case study

Consider the case of Jack. In his school, praise was the essential strategy for motivating children to learn and there were lots of rewards, awards and certificates that children could earn. Teachers were firmly in control of their classrooms and poor behaviour was dealt with efficiently, with star charts, contingent reward and positive reinforcement of good choices. The school was chosen by his parents mainly because of its reputation for the overt direction of learning and behaviour which resulted in excellent SATs (Standard Assessment Tests) results. Unfortunately, compliance, which was very much the ethos of the school, was not on Jack's agenda.

Jack arrived at school from his Nursery with a reputation for physical aggression. As he progressed through Infant school, the problems continued. He was often non-compliant during lessons and aggressive when playing with his friends at break times. His teachers used carefully structured praise to help Jack to understand the difference between acceptable and unacceptable behaviour, and reward to support his behaviour choices. His parents were asked on many occasions to meet with his class teacher, followed by the phase leader and finally the Head Teacher. Jack was given a home–school star diary, in which positive comments were written by the teacher and responded to by his parents, who could also add comments about his achievements at home. His teacher agreed to praise him every time he finished work or followed her direction. He was also given a star chart at home in order to gain treats like watching extra TV or playing an extra game of football with his father. Sometimes it worked; sometimes it did not. Some days it appeared that he was just not interested in complying. He loved getting extra treats (especially the home treats) but he did not seem to mind if he failed to achieve a target and lost a treat – in fact, sometimes his mother felt that he enjoyed the battle of resisting homework or bedtime far more than he enjoyed a treat.

Because Jack was in a school where praise and reward were seen as the most appropriate ways to modify behaviour, the star charts were increased, as were the size of the treats on offer, as Jack moved through Junior school. Unfortunately, Jack had a very determined, often stubborn, personality and non-compliance increasingly became a battle of wills with his teachers and his parents. English in particular became a flashpoint and Jack often complained that he was bored because the work was too easy and was for 'little children'. He was a very quick thinker, able to assimilate the task, attempt it and abandon it when he lost interest, in record time.

He was implicitly begging for challenge, but although his teacher agreed that the work he was given lacked suitable challenge for his ability, she felt that it was important that he proved that he could complete easy work before he was allowed to move on to more challenging tasks. Because learning was viewed as a series of incremental steps, he was required to prove that he could put his feet firmly on the lower steps before being allowed to engage with greater challenge. He refused to comply with this tick-box approach to his learning – he knew the work was too easy and he did not see why he should have to prove what he already knew: that he could do it. So, day after day, work remained unfinished.

After discussing goals with his parents, his teacher set him a target – if he sat at his table and worked at a given task for five minutes, measured by a timer, he could earn stars which would build to extra computer time. He managed three minutes before he said he was bored and started investigating how the timer worked. He missed his star. The next day, he managed two minutes. A few days later, he gave up trying and was put on a behaviour diary. Then he started to disrupt the classroom by taking other children's pencils while they were writing. When he eventually started kicking them under the table to stop them telling the teacher, he was isolated in the classroom and only allowed to join other children in the afternoon if he had worked hard during the morning.

At this point, Jack started saying that his teacher did not like him and his frustration boiled over, leading to a week of lunchtime exclusions. His view of his teacher's opinion, who was following school protocol and actually cared a great deal, felt entirely justified to him. His patterns of behaviour were consistent with Deci's view that external motivation left Jack feeling controlled. His parents, whom he should have been able to see as his greatest allies, followed the approach that the school adopted, believing that consistency with the school's aims and values was the best way to support their much-loved son. Star charts and incentivised living were part of his home life just as much as his school life. But instead of seeing Jack make positive learning and social behaviour choices, his parents watched helplessly while he continued to seize control by making bad choices. When he was referred to an educational psychologist, his behaviour deteriorated to the point of fixed-term exclusion.

As well as perfectly illustrating Deci's theory about autonomy, competence and relatedness, none of which Jack experienced with any consistency, this case study also demonstrates Kohn's assertion that praise and reward systems do nothing to consider the root causes of the behaviour. This would have helped Jack much more than a star chart, because the backdrop to Jack's school life deteriorated along with his behaviour. His sibling, born while he was at Nursery, suffered from a serious illness and the family's life became a series of hospital visits and extended stays. As his behaviour deteriorated, the wide circle of friends who initially rallied round to help gradually disintegrated as Jack's reaction towards their children became increasingly aggressive. Unable to keep up with the pace of his career in a constant round of hospital visits and childcare, his father was made redundant.

A range of agencies was involved as the family became increasingly isolated, all offering different support at different times but with no consistency or connection. But, as David Brooks points out in his book *The Social Animal* (2011), an emergent system dictates that Jack's behaviour was not due to any single factor of his classroom attitude, his playground aggression or his family trauma – all of the issues needed to be tackled simultaneously, both for Jack, the school and his family, if he was to break out of the pattern into which he had settled. The use of praise to teach Jack the difference between acceptable and unacceptable behaviour was a reductionist approach and it was actually superfluous – he understood the difference very well; he was unwilling or unable to comply.

Jack's case demonstrates the core issue with regard to both learning and social behaviours, which is the extent to which an individual internalises the values, beliefs and expectations of the community. And the problem with contingent reward is that it both requires, and produces, compliance without internalisation. Jack, whose desire to please and develop a sense of relatedness both with his family and his school was genuine, found his life controlled by incentives in both contexts. Often, he complied for several consecutive days and he was rewarded and told that he was a good boy. But then he would get bored with his work or fall out with a friend, the cycle of conflict would start again, and because he was a 'good boy' when he was rewarded, it appeared entirely logical to Jack that he must be a naughty boy when he lost rewards. As he moved through Primary school, his self-view became increasingly determined by the praise/punishment cycle with which he lived and he became almost permanently anxious to please and be accepted. Fortunately, what he never appeared to lose was a clear sense that he was capable of engaging with levels of challenge beyond anything which he met in school.

To understand how contingent praise affects the very roots of learning, consider Jack's case in the context of Deci's research, which showed that motivation depends on feelings of autonomy, competence and relatedness. First, consider the rules that Jack and his peers were required to keep. The majority of the parents in the school identified with the school's values, as Jack's own parents did. The majority of the children complied with the rules, so they enjoyed a strong sense of relatedness and the home–school community worked well. Jack identified just as strongly with the intention of the rules – he wanted to be respected, respectful, to belong and to have friends like his peers, but he did not have a compliant nature, obedience was hard work and control mechanisms often made him resentful.

His sense of relatedness was transient and dependent on keeping the rules and getting rewards. Because his family supported the school's approach so comprehensively, his sense of relatedness within his family was also affected. What difference might it have made to Jack if, instead of being asked to follow a list of rules which were posted on the classroom wall, he had been involved in formulating them? Whether rules are provided by the teacher or whether they are arrived at through class discussion, the intention and outcome are the same. But the first approach tells children quite clearly that power and authority lie with a teacher who should be obeyed. The second approach gives pupils autonomy in the decision making process about their classroom environment. The first approach produces compliance with the rules. The second approach produces internalisation of the values which underpin the rules.

Jack's sense of social competence was also transient and depended on whether he was being well behaved or naughty. When he was behaving well, he was able to start forming friendships, only to find these fledgling friendships disintegrating every time his teacher banned him from the playground either to complete unfinished work or for inappropriate physical behaviour. His sense of social competence was slowly eroded as he became identified by his class teacher, his peers (compliantly following his teacher's example of isolating him), his former friends and eventually his parents, as a naughty child. Because he had not internalised the expectations of the adults in charge of his world, Jack was dependent on adult judgements to evaluate and reinforce his behaviour choices. His feelings of social competence followed the same roller coaster track as his praise and reward cycle, eventually leading to a significant feeling of social incompetence as his family, too, became increasingly isolated.

In his academic learning also, Jack's motivation was almost entirely dependent on adult judgement. He quickly rejected the incremental, worksheet-based learning with which he was expected to comply and in doing so, found himself with a constant diet of worksheets which were far too easy, which bored him and which he saw no need to complete just to prove a point in order to be given more challenging work. Because of the way that learning was organised, the classroom was strictly hierarchical; Jack was not anywhere near the position in the hierarchy which his ability suggested he should be and he knew it. But there was one area of his academic learning in which Jack's motivation was fully intrinsic, to the point of flow.

Early in his life, Jack had been introduced to a Library and he had discovered books. He learnt to read quickly, with little apparent effort. That nearly ended when he started school and was told that he was not allowed access to the school library as a free reader until he had finished the reading scheme which the school used. Jack was already reading independently, but his teacher said that he must follow the phonics programme and reading scheme along with all the other children. This met with outright rebellion and a refusal to comply, in spite of the offer of double stars for each book he completed. Fortunately for Jack, his mother disagreed with the school when they advised her to buy some books that Jack wanted but to use them as rewards when he complied with the reading scheme.

As a result, his in-school performance and his private reading behaviour inhabited two different places, separated by a huge gulf. Where reading was concerned, or any activity which depended on reading skills, Jack felt highly competent and it was this which enabled him to maintain a steady pace in all of his learning, in spite of, not because of, praise and reward. Because his mother supported his love of reading, he enjoyed a high degree of personal autonomy over his reading choices and there were occasions in his Infant school classroom when he felt as though he belonged, as other children quickly realised that he possessed valuable currency – the ability to read worksheet instructions which freed them from teacher dependency and reprimands for not listening. Reading was the one area of his learning in which Jack achieved mastery, demonstrating Dweck's assertion that mastery orientation is often an outcome of autonomy-supportive parents, which, in the case of his reading behaviour, Jack's mother was.

Goal setting formed a key part of his school's work to change Jack's behaviour. He was given goals for behaviour and goals for learning, but at no point was he involved in the discussion either about the goals, the reason for them being set or how he himself thought he might achieve them. In fact, he often did not have a clear idea of how to achieve the goals (which may have been as much to do with his rejection of the strategy as anyone's failure to show him the route to achievement) so he regularly failed to reach them. Where his academic learning was concerned, this was because the goals were entirely regulated by performance. He was required to complete worksheets, complete tests and complete tasks before being praised or rewarded.

As Dweck (1999) points out, performance goals, which are measuring ability, nurture dependent learners and are the route to learned helplessness. Fortunately, Jack had such a secure sense of his own ability that he was able to blame the boring work rather than his own performance for his failure to achieve his goals. But how many other children in his school, more inclined to compliance than Jack, were failing to achieve their potential when the only measure of success was a tick in a box or a score for a test?

If Jack's school had adopted learning goals, in which each pupil evidenced their learning through discussion, Jack's teachers would have quickly realised that his claims of boredom were quite justified. Does it matter how learning is evidenced as long as learning has taken place? But because of the rigid, incremental structure, with its narrow definition of learning, Jack was trapped in a classroom where the right answer (carefully scaffolded by the teacher to demonstrate knowledge) and neatly filled worksheets were valued. He was rarely able to demonstrate what he had actually learnt.

Teacher questioning is significantly affected by the stance taken on praise. In the transmission model of teaching which behaviourism fosters, right answers are valued as they prove that good teaching has taken place. Children are praised when they follow the teacher's signals to the required answer and a wrong, or unintended answer is met with feedback like, 'Good try', which leaves unsaid, '. . . but wrong'. Open-ended questions are not asked in regulated classrooms and children's questions are nearly always functional, relating to task completion. Children are immobile for large parts of the day, usually facing the front. For children like Jack (and boys in particular), this generates passive learners who must sit and wait for their minds to be filled by their teachers. Except, of course, that sometimes children like Jack fail to comply, because they need to be able to investigate, explore, ask questions and have opportunities to formulate and answer their own questions.

Although it would be ideal if all learning was intrinsically motivated, teachers know that part of every school day must involve tasks which are not immediately interesting or captivating. In a regulated environment, children will be praised and rewarded for their compliance in the successful completion of these required tasks. This is external regulation, which is the logical outcome of behaviourist practice. In classrooms where children are involved in some of the decision making, where the routine nature of the tasks is acknowledged and where their views are valued, children are more likely to identify with the need to engage in routine tasks in order to learn. This form of motivation, whether it is identification regulation or integrated regulation as defined by Deci and Ryan's research, will lead to more effective learning and therefore increased perception of competence.

For Jack, who found compliance and unquestioning obedience difficult and who enjoyed standing his ground in an argument, the routine tasks of his day were an ideal opportunity to demonstrate non-compliance. Because his learning environment had not fostered internal regulation at any point, his refusal to comply with routine tasks like spelling, handwriting and tables tests was a straightforward matter of resistance to external control, with no understanding (although plenty of external comment from his teacher) that he was harming his own long-term learning. If what Deci asserted is correct, then Jack's school failed him. Deci *et al.* stated,

> We believe a) that people are inherently motivated to internalize and integrate within themselves the regulation of uninteresting activities that are useful for effective functioning in the social world and b) that the extent to which the process of internalization and integration proceeds is a function of the social context.
>
> (Deci *et al.* 1991: 328–9)

Jack's lack of internalisation led to seven years of conflict and increasing resistance to external regulation.

Deci also makes the point (Deci *et al.* 1991) that children's learning motivation and in-school engagement is influenced as much by home experience as school. He quotes studies which show that the children of autonomy-supportive parents demonstrated more self-regulation than children with controlling parents. This was consistent across the age range of education and demonstrates how home and school contexts parallel each other.

Return to Jack's case study – his parents, who tended towards control, selected a school which matched their parenting style so that they could support their children's school values at home. Whilst this should have worked in their children's favour, it became increasingly clear that Jack needed more autonomy in his choices than either his parents or his school was willing to allow. As his behaviour deteriorated, both his parents and his school actually became more controlling rather than less. Nobody used Jack's frame of reference as their starting point for discussion so his motivation, apart from his personal reading, remained largely extrinsic and he had limited opportunities to develop the personal and social skills which he needs for his future life. As Deci observes, 'With a general attitude of valuing children's autonomy . . . we stand the greatest chance of bringing about the types of educational contexts that facilitate conceptual understanding, flexible problem solving, personal adjustment and social responsibility' (Deci *et al.* 1991: 342).

Controlling teachers

In 1982, an unpublished doctoral thesis written by B. M. Jelsa of The University of Rochester, New York (quoted Deci *et al.* 1991) found evidence that the behaviour of teachers was also, to some extent, controlled by their students. In this research project, teachers were found to be more controlling with students who fidgeted and appeared to be inattentive and more autonomy supportive with students who appeared to be engaged – this put Jack and a succession of teachers into fixed patterns of behaviour with each other.

Some years later, these research findings were pursued further by Luc Pelletier of the University of Ottawa and Robert Vallerand of the University of Quebec. They organised an experiment in which teachers were asked to teach students how to solve puzzles. Teachers were told that some students were intrinsically motivated and some were not, although the students in each group were actually randomly assigned. The teachers who had been told that their students were extrinsically motivated were very controlling of the teaching situation leading to low motivation from the students. The reverse was true of the teachers who were told that they were teaching motivated students. So although the students had been randomly grouped, their teachers acted according to the information they were given and created their own realities.

Public policy and high-stakes testing

So, classroom interaction can be shaped and reflective teachers should be aware of the need to be autonomy supportive for all pupils. However, the external regulation of teachers by policy is of more concern. As highlighted in Chapter 7, research has shown (Roth *et al.* 2007) that teachers who are controlled are much more likely to control their students and rely on contingent reward to achieve what is required. This is of particular significance in the current climate of high-stakes testing and the publication of league tables of results. In the US, this has been extended to pay determined by students' test results (Strauss 2011) and proposals to publish lists of teachers ranked using the same criteria (Goldhaber 2011).

Apart from the issues of accuracy and the effect of parents clamouring for their children to be placed with the best (according to the listings) teachers, there is no consideration of the effect of this on pedagogy. There are a limited number of ways that teachers can respond to this and they all involve teaching to test and narrowing the focus of learning. This is usually reinforced with contingent praise which, as research has shown, causes short-term gain in test results without building effective learners. And in spite of this drive to raise standards through high-stakes testing, the National Academies of America, in a pre-publication press release of *Incentives and Test-Based Accountability in Education* stated that,

> Despite being used for several decades, test-based incentives have not consistently generated positive effects on student achievement . . . The report examines evidence on incentive programs, which impose sanctions or offer rewards for students, teachers, or schools on the basis of students' test performance. Federal and state governments have increasingly relied on incentives in recent decades as a way to raise accountability in public education and in the hope of driving improvements in achievement.
>
> (Hout and Elliott 2011)

The conclusion of the report is that standards have not been raised, except in some limited contexts such as schools involved in the No Child Left Behind programme, where slight gains have been reported.

In a UK context, league tables and performance targets now dominate the educational landscape. In 2009, a group of researchers at the University of Manchester's Edge Hill campus examined the effect of SATs on levels of anxiety in 120 eleven–year-olds in three English Primary schools. They found that,

> Poorer SAT grades in English, maths and science were significantly associated with higher levels of self-reported test anxiety and lower levels of resilience, with one pupil articulating the view that, '. . . you have to get a level like a level 4 or a level 5 and if

you're no good at spellings and times tables you don't get those and so you're a nothing.'

(Connor *et al.* 2009)

It was observed that this may be due to the overt pressure on teachers to meet targets and achieve good league table positions. The findings of the study concluded that,

> Teachers conveyed a desire for autonomy in regard to their delivery of a curriculum, their teaching practices and approaches to assessment. Teachers believed that the ongoing assessment that takes place in school was of far more benefit than the externally imposed SATs and that other aspects of the curriculum were as, if not more, important as the key skills assessed by SATs.

(ibid.)

There is also a perception by many parents that SATs results impact on their child's banding or setting at the commencement of Secondary school. With Lord Bew's report into Key Stage 2 testing (Bew 2011) suggesting that teachers' accountability to parents is strengthened, this pressure is likely to remain for the foreseeable future.

In the Secondary sector, figures in 2010 showed that students taking vocational qualifications have increased at twice the speed of those taking just GCSEs (General Certificates of Secondary Education), leading to suggestions (Paton 2010) that pupils were being entered for 'easier' courses in order to boost league table positions. The problem is that whenever external regulation dominates outcomes, many schools will compete to improve their positions at the expense of a broader and richer experience for their pupils – compliance is induced at every level of the system.

If motivation research is correct, then the current move in government circles towards the use of contingent praise is of concern. Addressing the Labour Party Conference in his keynote speech in September 2011, the Labour Leader Ed Miliband mentioned the word 'values' 40 times and the word 'people' more than 50 times. But there was another subtext in the speech which went on to say that if he obtains power, he is going to reward 'producers who train, invest, invent and sell things'. He's going 'to change the values that are rewarded not just in our schools but right across society'. He's going to reward effort, praise people who work hard, reward the right values in the benefit system and punish the 'runaway rewards at the top'. He's going to link reward to hard work to create a 'something for something' culture. What he is actually promising is a return to a behaviourist paradigm in which society is externally regulated through praise and reward. But according to the research, rewards are about control, power, compliance and dependence. The person holding the rewards decides the criteria leading to control of industry, commerce, business and education through rewards. The American Federation of Teachers declared, 'No system really works unless it operates with incentives' (Shanker 1990, cited in Kohn 1999: 143). However, research suggests that controlled communities and societies are not creative and innovative ones.

Just weeks after this speech was delivered, the local council in Bolton, Lancashire, adopted a praise-based scheme in order to increase recycling rates from 30 per cent to a target of 40 per cent. The Council is spending £100,000 sending out congratulatory text messages to people who remember to put their recycling bins out on the correct day. The scheme was immediately branded 'patronising' by some, as praise was being given to people who already recycled (presumably because they agreed that recycling is a good thing to do); however, the Department for Environment, Food and Rural Affairs (DEFRA), praises it as 'innovative'. A spokesperson for the Council said that,

> This has the potential to make a real difference to the borough's recycling rates, and will encourage a lot of people who aren't currently recycling to do so . . . The evidence from previous studies shows that this sort of scheme can go a long way to changing behaviour both individually and in a community . . . Also, because the texts will make people who receive them more involved in the recycling process, I hope it will encourage them to act as champions in their area.
>
> (Gye 2011)

It remains to be seen if praising people for what they already do because they believe in it will actually raise recycling percentages – research suggests that when praised, people are less inclined to repeat a behaviour which they have previously engaged in autonomously as the praise makes them feel controlled. The agenda of praise as a means of producing adaptive behaviour is clearly defined by DEFRA, as a spokesperson stated that, 'Rewarding and recognising people for doing the right thing can encourage a range of positive behaviours, including recycling. More than half of us would recycle more if we were given a reward' (ibid.).

So, if contingent praise produces compliance, is there ever a case to knowingly create such a culture? Many teachers think so. Look back to the first school described in Chapter 1. Children in this school were almost totally regulated externally, but the Head and staff built this ethos carefully in order to provide some order and structure for children whose lives outside of school were often chaotic and for whom there were limited life choices. However, in 1981, a group of researchers (Fabes *et al.* 1981) researched the effect of external regulation on algorithmic and heuristic tasks. Seventy-six female students of similar age and ability were divided into four groups to perform a range of algorithmic tasks and a range of heuristic tasks. One group was not rewarded at all and the other three groups were given non-contingent, contingent and social competition rewards. The latter three groups demonstrated similar performance on both sets of tasks. However, the non-rewarded group performed significantly better on the heuristic tasks.

This phenomenon has also been extensively researched by Teresa Amabile of the Harvard Business School. In an article entitled *How to Kill Creativity* (Amabile 1998) she asserts that, 'creativity gets killed more often than it gets supported'. She suggests that creativity is not just restricted to the way people think or approach problems, but that it is also about expertise in a subject and motivation. If motivation is not intrinsic, expertise and creative thinking skills may well be untapped, or diverted into areas beyond the classroom. She argues that the time-consuming issue of influencing motivation often makes it easier to opt for extrinsic control. Her research also confirms that freedom, autonomy, support and encouragement are all important factors in nurturing a motivating learning environment.

Pink develops this consideration of the function of extrinsic motivation in performing certain tasks, saying, 'Amabile and others have found that extrinsic rewards can be effective for algorithmic tasks – those that depend on following an existing formula to its logical conclusion' (Pink 2011); however, he goes on to say, 'But for more right-brained undertakings – those that demand flexible problem solving, inventiveness or conceptual understanding – contingent rewards can be dangerous. Rewarded subjects often have a harder time seeing the periphery and crafting original solutions.'

So, although the teachers outlined in Chapter 1 firmly believed that they were providing the best possible education for those children in that context, the research suggests that they were actually limiting the ability of the children to perform heuristic tasks with any degree of creativity. Far from their education providing a stable platform for social mobility, it is actually shaping these children for a future of algorithmic task performance in the workplace, thus limiting their mobility. As Pink (2011) points out, as the workplace calls increasingly for creative and conceptual skills, the gap between fulfilled workers and those performing routine tasks (or working at all) will continue to widen. Arguably, it is those very children in schools such as Jane's who need to move away from a culture of compliance if they are to have access to an economically successful future.

Points for reflection

- In what ways do teachers, parents and carers limit autonomy?
- Define the tasks for which contingent praise would be appropriate.
- With three children in mind, define for each child a task where reducing praise might increase creativity.
- How can you increase pupil or child autonomy in your current context?
- Discuss this statement made by Alfie Kohn (2000) about using praise to enforce a teacher's rules: 'The point is to get the trains to run on time in the classroom, never mind whom they run over.'
- How are you as a teacher controlled by external agencies? What effect does this have on your teaching?
- How would you advise Jack's teachers and parents to support his academic and learning behaviours?

Chapter 14

Creating resolute and resilient learners

Mastery

More than 40 years ago, the Israeli Educator Dr Haim Ginott wrote, 'Praise, like penicillin, must not be administered haphazardly. There are rules and cautions that govern the handling of potent medicines . . . There are similar regulations about the administration of emotional medicine' (Ginott 1965: 39). He advised parents and fellow educators to be cautious in the use of praise, saying that dependence fosters hostility and that children should be given as much autonomy as possible, within defined limits. In the same way that rules and timing determine medicinal doses, so there should be rules about the use of praise. This stemmed from Ginott's belief that as a teacher, he was the 'decisive element' in his classroom and that he alone was responsible for creating the learning climate.

So, how is a teacher to exercise this level of responsibility in the creation of a motivating learning environment where praise is used carefully? And what are the rules for the administration of effective praise? As research has shown, praise should:

- be communicative and give immediate feedback information about achievement;
- be sincere and honest;
- be given within a relationship of mutual respect;
- be fair in acknowledging the work and achievements of each individual;
- usually be given privately;
- be descriptive, not evaluative;
- not be contingent, as this creates dependency and leaves the recipient feeling controlled;
- be used carefully for effort, as it may create in the recipient a perception of lack of ability;
- avoid creating hierarchies and competition.

Whatever model is adopted to nurture learning (some of which will be examined later in this chapter), there is no short cut to mastery. As Pink says,

> . . . the path to mastery – becoming ever better at something that you care about – is not lined with daisies and spanned with a rainbow. It if were, more of us would make the trip. Mastery hurts. Sometimes, many times, it is not much fun.
>
> (Pink 2011: 124)

He goes on to outline the work of Anders Ericsson of Florida State University, who has researched the psychology of mastery and expert performance. Ericsson states that, 'The development of genuine expertise requires struggle, sacrifice, and honest, often painful, self-assessment . . . Genuine experts not only practice deliberately, but also *think* deliberately', also adding that, 'Deliberate practice involves two kinds of learning: improving the skills you already have and extending the reach and range of your skills' (Ericsson *et al.* 2007). He estimates that it takes about ten thousand hours to achieve mastery, but his point is that mastery is not just about working the hours, but about how you think whilst you are working. He asserts that most people focus on things they already know how to do, rather than devoting effort to mastering something which they cannot do well or which they have never tried before. If, as Ericsson says, 'Living in a cave does not make you a geologist' (ibid.) then going to school does not makes you a student – an analogy with significant implications for those schools which reward or pay students simply for attending school and designated lessons.

Deliberate practise of learning skills is needed to ensure mastery. Children who develop these skills intuitively transfer them across all of their learning – one Head Teacher, commenting on his observation of the most effective learners over many years of his career, said that children who were involved in music or sport were always successful learners because they understood that the route to mastery involved many hours of focused practise, an approach which they took into every academic lesson. The maxim of one sports coach in the school was the unattributed quotation that amateurs practise until they get it right, but professionals practise until they cannot get it wrong. His role, as he viewed it, was to show his students what to practise and how, and encourage them as they practised.

Interest

So how do educators teach and foster such a learning attitude? There are a range of different answers to this question, particularly when pupils need to engage in tasks which are not, of themselves, intrinsically interesting. The role of the teacher is not just to motivate the necessary desire for mastery and effort for learning, but also to ensure that necessary knowledge structures are scaffolded as learning takes place.

This is discussed in some detail by David Palmer, of the University of Newcastle, Australia (Palmer 2005). His research is centred on motivational teaching in science, as Palmer notes that although there has been much research into motivational learning and constructivist practice in recent years, very little of that research has been subject specific. Many of Palmer's observations, though, relate across the curriculum when considering the nurturing of resilient learners.

First, Palmer discusses the concept of interest, describing two types of learning interest: personal interest, which concerns students' long-term preferences for particular subjects, and situational interest, which is short-term and immediate. Although teachers may be aware of their students' personal interests, it is the latter form of the interest construct which teachers can use to focus attention on classroom content. For this to be most effective, the event should be novel in order to arouse curiosity, meaningful to current learning and it should involve students in some form of activity. This is the thinking behind the use of hooks in unit and lesson planning.

Palmer then analyses the concept of expectancy belief (a student's belief in their own ability to complete a task), and task value (the value of the task to be performed according to the perception of the learner). He identifies three types of the value construct: attainment value, which concerns the relationship of the task with the learner's self-view and desire to achieve; utility value, which is the inherent value of the task in the learning journey; and intrinsic value, which is the enjoyment of the task for its own sake. In order for pupils' value beliefs to develop positively, they need to experience success on a regular basis. The role of the teacher in this is to promote the value of the task in hand, explaining to pupils why it is useful or necessary to engage with it, allowing as much autonomy as possible within the task and expressing enthusiasm for the inherent learning.

Palmer says little about the role of praise, but he does present a model for learning which obviates the need for contingent praise. In addition to the role of the teacher in nurturing positive value beliefs, he suggests a further role of the teacher in supporting learning. This is to demonstrate confidence in the pupils' ability to complete a given task, to select tasks which provide challenge, to tell pupils that this is the case and then provide detailed feedback when the task is complete. This will lead to increased self-efficacy in learning.

Self-efficacy

Self-efficacy (Bandura 1982) is a two-fold concept, constructed of a learners' belief that a task can be successfully performed and a belief that doing so will achieve a desired outcome. It is specific to each learning situation, so pupils may experience fluctuating levels of self-efficacy from one subject to another, or from task to task within one subject area. According to Bandura's theory (1997) there are four external factors, within the teacher's influence, which increase self-efficacy. The route to mastery needs to be scaffolded by the teacher, in incremental learning steps which allow for regular experience of success. Students themselves need to see that these learning goals are achievable, or at least trust the assurance of the teacher that this is the case.

Modelling increases the perception that a task is achievable and it is important for a teacher to demonstrate that mistakes and errors are not only inevitable when learning, but they are also opportunities. This is more likely to increase a student's resilience in coping with mistakes or failure than teacher modelling, which demonstrates perfect mastery. Verbal feedback should be detailed and specific, showing the student what has been achieved and why. Finally, Bandura observed that anxiety when learning has a significant effect on the actual learning process. Where anxiety is perceived to indicate low ability to complete a task, learning will be inhibited. Where stress is considered a by-product of challenge, learning is not affected.

Palmer concludes his article with the statement that, 'Motivation is a prerequisite and co-requisite for learning, so the essence of a constructivist-informed classroom is that it is one in which the teacher explicitly plans strategies for student motivation and integrates these at all stages of the learning process' (Palmer 2005). To achieve this, he suggests a three-fold approach to planning. Firstly, concepts to be taught should be appropriately challenging and presented in a way that allows students to experience success in every lesson (although this does not mean that a new concept should be taught in every lesson). 'Dual purpose' teaching strategies should be employed which allow teachers both to motivate and develop learning. This could include anything from discussion, collaborative group investigation, real-life context and active learning, to the use of ICT (information and communication technology).

Finally, the ethos of a classroom should foster motivational belief, by allowing pupil autonomy, using specific, communicative praise and articulating belief that each pupil can experience success. Teachers should model coping strategies to deal with challenge and error, providing detailed assessment feedback in the case of both success and failure.

Paideia

One model which seeks to incorporate all of these concepts is Paideia, from the Greek *pais*, which means 'the upbringing of a child'. This is a style of learning which was developed in the 1980s by a group working with the American Professor, Philosopher and Educational Theorist, Mortimer Adler. It led to the formulation of the Paideia Proposal, and its Declaration of Principles (Adler 1982). This states that learning begins in the activity of a child's mind and it cannot therefore be created by a teacher. Adler believed that all children are educable, that education should include a range of teaching strategies and that learning should be a lifelong process. The aim of Paideia schools is to prepare students for a full life, engaging both their hearts and their minds. The role of senior school managers is also defined, with a belief that the school principal should be a leading teacher who is fully involved with the planning of the school as a learning community. It is also suggested that school managers should themselves engage in learning.

For students, learning is evaluated both in terms of the acquisition of organised knowledge and the development of the mind to understand issues and ideas. To achieve this, the Paideia Group identified three 'pillars' of teaching: didactic lecture, coaching and discussion. Didactic teaching should take up about 10–15 per cent of each learning session, with the purpose of introducing knowledge whilst students assume a more passive role as recipients. The next 70 per cent of the session should be guided work, which supports intellectual development, with the teacher working in a coaching role. The final 10–15 per cent of the session should permit collaborative discussion (which also facilitates the development of social skills) in which students can expand their own thinking in dialogue with peers and resolve conflicting views and understanding. Questions should be open-ended in order to promote exploratory discussion.

The type and quality of questioning and dialogue is a key factor in the development of resilient learners. A range of questioning techniques and when to use them is an essential part of the teacher's toolkit. Sometimes it is entirely appropriate to ask questions which just elicit knowledge. Sometimes procedural questions have to be asked. But the frequency and intention of probing questions is an indicator of the style of teaching (and therefore learning) which is happening in the classroom. The type of questioning which pupils engage with is even more indicative.

Mercer and 'exploratory talk'

Through their research, the team at Cambridge University led by Neil Mercer, have defined the concept of 'exploratory talk' (cf. Chapter 6). They found that much of children's talk in collaborative work became cumulative (everyone agreed and added comments without any meaningful discussion), disputational (leading to individuals asserting their own views without listening to those of others) or presentational (in which one person dominates the group with their personal view). A research project (Robins 2011) using materials from the team's Thinking Together website (Mercer 2008), found that this was not only a limiting factor in collaborative group work, but it also reinforced the dependencies and hierarchies which were already in existence in the classroom. Exploratory talk strategies overcame this by teaching pupils to challenge each other's thinking through questioning, in order to deepen understanding in genuine dialogue.

Pupils struggled with the idea of challenging each other's thinking at first, regarding it as the province of the teacher and therefore quite impolite. However, once the group of pupils involved in the initial project realised the potential, it became an embedded strategy in their learning. They found that questions which they asked of each other were often more relevant to their understanding than those asked by a teacher, and there was a significant increase in motivation and learning when working collaboratively as group work no longer stalled or ended in dispute.

Another significant finding of the study concerned ability grouping. The initial project involved able pupils, but continuing research encompassed several children who were temporarily grouped together due to a range of needs which had led to delayed learning. They showed themselves equally capable of challenging each other, but they needed more time to access language and organise their thoughts than their more articulate peers. They were only willing to take this time when they did not feel under pressure to keep up. Once they returned to mixed-ability groupings, they stopped talking and became passive, unable to cope with the speed of the exchanges. One boy, in particular, remained virtually mute in spite of regular use of praise and reward to motivate him when he did engage. It was not until he went to Secondary school that he engaged with genuine enthusiasm in a dialogue-based learning process and he attributed this to his placement in the lowest band of his year group. His route to becoming a resilient learner was to be with others who, like him, found learning a real struggle.

Quest to Learn

In an age when the nature of knowledge is being redefined and the needs of the workplace are changing, some educators are making effective use of social media which are attracting users in huge numbers, even amongst young people who do not engage effectively with learning in school. This is seen as a means of motivating learners. In 2009, Quest to Learn, a digital school based on game-design principles, was opened in New York, supported by the MacArthur Foundation. It rethought the very nature of learning by moving away from a transmission model of teaching to one of active investigation and problem solving. The school is designed using gaming principles: children are involved in integrated learning which is carefully scaffolded, and engaged in enquiry-based exploration. The attractions of gaming include instant, detailed and personal feedback and the opportunity to select challenge level. When applied to learning, it supports incremental steps in which the learner selects their own challenges (autonomy) and feedback which shows progress with immediacy and clarity (competence leading to mastery). Quest to Learn is not just a different way of organising learning; it is an innovative pedagogy, which redefines key literacies in a digital age as design, collaboration and systems thinking. The curriculum, examples of which can be viewed at the Quest to Learn website http://www.q2l.org, is rigorous and extremely challenging.

Quest to Learn also considers it an important part of motivating pupils to have a facility for them to export their knowledge to other contexts which are personally meaningful to them, for example their after-school clubs or their homes. This is also proving its value in traditional schools which engage in blogging. Children at one such school, Heathfield Primary School in Bolton, Lancashire, regularly blog their work on the school's website. The change in learning engagement has been spectacular.

Social media and learning

In 2009, whilst considering the inspirational value of a creative curriculum, the attention of the Deputy Head of the school, David Mitchell, was captivated by the concept of blogging. Within weeks, the initial interest had developed from the Deputy Head writing his own blog to the Year 6 class having a blog. Whilst the pupils were curious about his passion for blogging, David comments in an article for *The Schools Network* (Mitchell 2010) that most of the Year 6 pupils, 'were still defiant and not impressed'. Then it snowed. Frustrated with the bad press which teachers were receiving because of school closures, David texted an offer to host online lessons and found, the following morning, 23 out of 30 Year 6 pupils waiting expectantly online. They watched winter videos, wrote descriptive sentences and created settings and mood. Then pupils measured the depth of the snow in their own gardens, reporting their measurements and analysing their data online. They shared pictures of their snowmen, parents joined in and it was all picked up by the local and national press. Blogging was suddenly cool.

From that point, pupils seized the initiative, engaging in their learning in a new way and enjoying the social status that blogging afforded. They requested evening lessons online and a range of social networking resources started to change the way that learning happened in school. By Easter 2010, every class in the school was blogging as pupils became 'enthused, excited and engrossed in their learning'. Writing levels in SATs (Standard Assessment Tests) soared from 9 per cent to 63 per cent at Level 5. In the first nine weeks of the Autumn term of 2011, the Year 6 class blog received over 25,000 hits, 300 posts and more than 1400 comments from 70 countries.

So what provoked this success? The blogging experience, of itself, could not have caused the astral rise in SATs writing scores, which must have been supported by several years of detailed, rigorous and committed teaching. But if blogging is the key to unlocking this learning, then it is important that the reasons for it are understood. Pupils have a global audience so they are motivated to produce the best work possible – learning carries increased significance when it can be demonstrated to others and virtual visitors create a real audience beyond the school. Pupils are able to work collaboratively at both class and home-based learning whilst parents have much more access to their children's learning and so become more directly involved.

When pupils were asked to comment on their view of blogging in order to participate in a video about the blogging project, this is what some of the Heathfield pupils blogged:

> Blogging gives me a voice that is listened to from around the world with millions of people to hear it. Blogging has helped me build my confidence because of the positive comments about my work. Comments that told me where I had gone wrong, helped me to improve. A comment makes we warm inside because it means someone has taken the time to read my work and liked it, which makes me proud. Blogging is inspirational, encouraging and makes you feel like you're somebody.
>
> (Humairaa)

> . . . blogging makes me feel like I am in a new world; a world of writing ready to publish, edit and unleash it. It's good for your education to learn more and it gives you ingredients to fulfil your writing.
>
> (Haarith)

If I get a comment on my blog I enjoy reading it and it makes me do better in class because people from all over the world like my work. The blog helped me to become more confident in school lessons and activities.

(Josh)

Blogging as it is used in this context, however, is a presentational skill which is used as the outcome of a learning process. Whilst the very public aspect of blogging may impact on a pupil's willingness to present the best work possible, it cannot, of itself, be any substitute for the quality of the teaching and learning which has taken place up to that point. In fact, it is reflective of it. The opportunity to blog motivates pupils to engage, but it is not a substitute for high quality learning experiences – it should be an outcome of them. A precipitous rush to conclude that blogging is the answer to literacy issues in the UK without empirical evidence is based on an assumptive and false perception – blogs reflect what has been taught and learnt, they do not create learning. Blogging is a key to the door. The house still has to be built on strong foundations.

A world wide example of online learning using a social medium is Mathletics. There is no doubt that it fulfils all the criteria for effective digital learning with incremental steps and instant feedback which provide each user with complete autonomy. Being able to compete against other pupils around the world is one of the most popular features of the programme. But when pupils in one school were observed using it over a period of several weeks, various patterns became apparent. Although nearly all pupils became involved with great enthusiasm and were motivated to spend many more hours engaging with maths than they ever had before, an audit of individual use revealed some interesting learning patterns.

Most children were selecting games and activities which they could do with ease, scoring points and gaining leader board positions without actually learning anything new. Many parents were impressed at their children's success and apparent prowess, without realising that they were constantly revisiting and utilising secure skills which had already been mastered. Mathletics was hailed as a runaway success which would improve standards by both staff and parents, because the children 'loved it' and spent hours engaging with it.

The implications for one gifted pupil became quite serious as he realised that his world ranking did not match his class ranking as 'the best'. The stakes became increasingly higher as the weeks passed and he eventually persuaded an older sibling to complete challenges within his account so that he could maintain a high world ranking and so retain his status amongst his peers. He cheated himself as a learner, because his priority was to protect his position. What are the implications of this mindset as he progresses through life and meets many other people who out-perform him? And, as Ericsson points out in his research on mastery, repeating known skills does not lead to mastery.

Whilst there is no doubt that Mathletics is a powerful and effective tool, this case study demonstrated that a tool has to be used effectively. There was plenty of anecdotal evidence that children were suddenly seeing themselves as successful mathematicians for the first time in their lives, which was extremely powerful. However, once they had exhausted their known skills, the novelty wore off and engagement dwindled. It did not prompt any motivation to take risks with learning new skills – that task remained in the hands of the teacher. Some pupils even seemed to think that their new-found confidence was a pause in their learning and they were successful enough not to push themselves any further – they gave themselves permission to sit on a plateau.

What it also demonstrated was that pupils engaged with social media learning in the same way as all other learning – risk-averse pupils remained risk-averse, even using their success to mask the fact that no new learning was taking place; some gifted pupils used (and diverted) it to retain their status and a handful of children who embraced learning challenge used it to explore new areas of maths and learning. The latter group of pupils was much less interested in the competitive element of the programme and they were also the pupils who linked Mathletics with classroom learning to create a virtuous learning loop. This evidence suggests that social media learning has a place, but it does not change learning mindsets – in fact, online learning may even be used by pupils to self-justify risk aversion as it creates very public, externally validated, perceptions of success.

In November 2011, Newbattle High School in Midlothian, Scotland, hit the headlines of the *Scotsman* by achieving its best results in the 42 years since it opened. The Acting Head, John Wilson, shared the reason for this in an interview (Fraser 2011). Academies, which John Wilson says, 'really motivate the young people' were set up internally in sports and expressive arts. Pupils were then encouraged to choose two of their favourite subjects from the eight subjects which they were already studying, to attend extra lessons. The extra tuition allowed for more in-depth study and yielded better exam results. But the key to this motivation is the autonomy which pupils are given over their learning choices, together with the opportunity to follow their own long term interests. These factors together lead to deeper engagement with the additional learning opportunities, as pupils enjoy increasing competence in their chosen subjects. Self-efficacy grows with mastery. As a local Councillor commented, 'By giving pupils more say in tailoring their education to their interests and desires, they are building young people's confidence.'

Perhaps the last word in resilient learning should go to various contributors to a website called Thanks for Teaching Us, which was started for students to post comments about teachers who had made a difference to their education. It demonstrates that whatever strategies are adopted, it is teachers, their expectations and their relationships with their students, which affect outcome. Some people have commented on how individual teachers have affected them up to 30 years after leaving school. Many comments are subject specific, detailing how a particular teacher engendered a love of their subject through inspirational teaching – not a single entry makes mention of praise or reward as factors in exceptional teaching. But read collectively, there is a clear indication that resilient learners need rigour, high expectations, determination and perseverance as part of their learning experience. The wording of these comments is very precise:

> Thanks for teaching me to be a non-conformist. You opened my mind to support thinking freely and not what others want me to think. You inspired me to live deliberately.
>
> (Alyssa, Massachusetts)

> Thanks for consistently setting high expectations for learning. You taught me how to persevere and overcome failures.
>
> (Debbie, Illinois)

> Thanks for being so demanding and relentless. You inspired me to try to accomplish things I didn't think my brain could do.
>
> (Amanda, Florida)

Thanks for creating a class in which knowledge was fun, in which the teacher felt like a mentor rather than a homework-nag, and where respect felt natural and essential. You inspired me to love learning, to be excited by knowledge, and to never let a question I had survive unanswered.

(Richard, Ontario)

Whatever the context and culture within which schools operate, there are certain factors which are consistent in all schools which successfully nurture resolute and resilient learners regardless of the tools which are used. Pupils are given as much autonomy as possible, supported and scaffolded as they master the necessary skills and knowledge to become competent. As a result of this, self-efficacy increases as pupils understand how and why they are learning. As maturing learners, they are no longer dependent on contingent praise to direct their social and learning behaviours. Praise becomes informative and it is the feelings of autonomy, mastery and interest which motivate further learning.

Points for reflection

- What would you define as an effective use of praise?
- What motivates the students that you teach?
- How is technology used in your teaching context?
- How would you define talk in your classroom? How can all pupils engage fully in meaningful discussion? How can this develop resilient learners?
- Discuss examples of motivational learning which interest you, either from this chapter or from your own knowledge of other contexts. What are the common factors in these settings?
- List the factors which create learning dependency. Then repeat this for supporting the growth of independent learners. Which factors predominate in your teaching?
- Carol Dweck suggests that the best way to build self-esteem is to be honest with students, telling them where they are, where they need to go next and how to get there. How does this align with your beliefs and your classroom practice?

Chapter 15

Protocol and pedagogy

Pink: The 3.0 motivation upgrade

In his 2011 book, *Drive: The surprising truth about what motivates us*, Daniel Pink highlights the dissonance between behaviourist thinking and constructivist models of teaching and learning which exists in many schools. He describes this using the computer metaphor of an operating system, arguing that society has similar operating systems which function below the surface level. Perhaps an effective way to move forward is through a willingness to question past practice, its suitability for the future and how change could be implemented in each individual context.

As Pink describes it, motivational operating system 1.0 was relevant when our ancestors were hunter-gatherers and decisions were motivated by survival – the need to find food and defend oneself. As people started to barter, trade and manufacture, an upgrade was needed to meet the needs of the newer, more complex societies and so motivational operating system 2.0, the behaviourist carrot-and-stick approach, was developed. This supported progress through the centuries of development and social evolution which led to the Industrial Revolution. But Pink argues that society needs another upgrade, to 3.0, to meet the requirements of a twenty-first century workplace. This is not a complete replacement of previous operating systems, but an upgrade which allows people to engage in creative tasks with feelings of autonomy, mastery and competence. He argues that with more than forty years of scientific research into motivation, society should be further forward with an upgrade.

He feels that many businesses have partially upgraded, but when asked in an interview (Zastrow, 2010) whether this was also true of education, he responded, 'I think schools are 2.0. I think they are in many ways – not all of them, but many of them – the purest form of 2.0'. He goes on to argue that teachers probably have a clearer understanding of intrinsic motivation than most other groups in society, yet the use of praise and reward, the 2.0 model, are still systemic.

In response, the interviewer asked Pink about his view of KIPP (Knowledge Is Power Programme) schools (cf. Chapter 8) which use reward and sanction within a firm structure. Although the attrition rate is high, students, at least up to the point of college, do well. Pink uses this as an example of the value of the 2.0 model, when schools are working with children with no structure to their lives and who lack basic learning skills. He argues that such children need scaffolding until they reach the point where they can handle autonomy. He also, however, points out that while children in rigidly controlling schools may escape poverty, they are still not well-prepared for life if this is the only educational model which they have experienced, an observation supported by KIPP's application of the Grit Scale as described in Chapter 8.

In addition to advice about the effective use of praise, Pink also describes a couple of practical examples of involving children in their own learning. In industry, the concept of 'FedEx days' (so-called because goods must be delivered overnight) is beginning to take hold. This concept was started in 2002 by an Australian company whose directors wanted to tap into the creativity of their employees. For 24 hours each quarter, all employees are allowed to work on any project which they wish, with whomever they wish. The only rule is that they must report on what they have done at the end of the 24-hour period. Pink suggests trying this in an educational context, allowing pupils to choose their own projects, working in groups of their own choosing, with the only expected outcome being a report to peers at the end of the day.

He also suggests DIY report cards, in which pupils select their learning goals for the term, then write their own evaluations at the end of the period. In fact, any form of self-assessment, whether it stands alone as this one does, or ties in with the school's form of assessment, not only gives pupils ownership of their part of the assessment process, but also sharpens focus throughout the activity as pupils have to focus on their own learning to locate evidence supporting self-evaluation. Pink suggests that teachers should audit other aspects of classroom practice: how much autonomy are pupils genuinely given? And where tasks need to be directed, how much explanation are pupils given about the reasons for those tasks and why it is important to complete them? Does homework genuinely support learning, or merely provide tasks to fulfil the need to set homework?

So if the world of education needs an upgrade, how is this best achieved? Real progress is only made when risks are taken and to be most effective, change needs to be systemic, at every level from national policy to the pedagogy of each individual teacher. This challenge is addressed in part by the Innovation Unit and Paul Hamlyn Foundation 'Learning Futures' project. Although it relates to the Secondary phase curriculum, the questions and challenges are common to all phases of education. Writing on behalf of The Innovation Unit, Lord Puttnam argues that, 'It means reworking our assumptions about how and where learning takes place, whether in school, at home, online, or in the community; it means celebrating teachers' and children's achievements wherever and whenever we find them. Crucially, it means identifying the knowledge, skills and responsibilities that must be nurtured in our children.' He continues, 'Our emphasis needs not to be on proving the residual value of outdated curricula, tests and league tables, but on inspiring and challenging children so that they in turn can inspire and challenge us' (Paul Hamlyn Foundation and The Innovation Unit 2008: Foreword).

So the debate should not be about standards and achievements, but about how people learn, what motivates learning in a school context and how to achieve these environments – rising standards should be an outcome of this. In addition to the 'Learning Futures' project, there are other organisations asking the same questions, including the Young Foundation and the RSA. Guy Claxton's 'Building Learning Power' approach is also widely used, as is Philosophy4Children, although there is a need to ensure that these do not become ends in themselves but a means of providing learning tools.

One system which encapsulates much of this thinking is the Kunskapsskolan group of schools in Sweden, which also sponsors three English academies through the Learning Schools Trust. Responsibility for learning is placed firmly in the hands of students as they select what, when and where they learn in the course of the day. The curriculum is sequenced and learning targets are carefully planned with a mentor. The building has open study areas for collaborative work, private study areas and multifunctional spaces to facilitate flexibility. It moves away from traditional fixed-length or set numbers of lessons. Much of the learning is ICT-based (information and communication technology) with blended learning also an option. Parents have access to learning programmes and outcomes for their child via a learning portal.

Another school which has taken risks in order to engage students and motivate learning is Monkseaton High School in North Tyneside. The design of the building supports a range of learning practices, the temperature is kept at a constant 18.5 °C, which is shown to be the best temperature for teenagers to learn, and the day starts at 10 am. The school is also the innovator of spaced learning. This involves three blocks of eight-minute lessons on one particular topic, with ten-minute physical activity breaks between each lesson. It is used for introducing new material, revision or teaching single topics which require a great deal of factual knowledge.

There is, of course, no single solution to the nurturing of resolute and resilient learners and attempts to import and transplant successful models across contexts will not necessarily provide the answer – what works for one community will not work in every community. But there are common factors in all of these research projects and initiatives. First, someone was willing to ask questions rather than continue to accept the status quo. Second, answering the questions has revealed common outcomes, all of which conclude that personal involvement in active, real-life learning is the most effective way to engage pupils.

There will be times when didactic teaching is part of classroom practice, just as there will be times when a particular piece of technology is the most appropriate for the task. But essentially pupils in such schools are not only engaging in learning, they are sharing accountability and taking personal responsibility for it because they own it. And in that environment, praise becomes informative not evaluative: motivated learners do not need to be directed by contingent praise. Students' opinions are valued; they are involved and in belonging are more likely to find alignment of their personal values with those of their school. Learning has meaning and self-efficacy grows. In the final analysis, curriculum content may not be very different – the difference lies in holding on to information for long enough to pass a test or possessing personally constructed knowledge when time has been taken to evaluate that knowledge through peer discussion.

There is no quick answer or magic key to learning, constructing knowledge and making meaning of the world, just as there is no substitute for rigorous teaching, high expectation, commitment and sheer hard work. There are tools which teachers can use to facilitate learning and a good teacher understands that no single tool is sufficient to meet all learning needs. Minds cannot be controlled and directed through praise and an attempt to do so merely demonstrates a lack of respect for the unique social and cultural constructs of each person as an individual.

Reflection on personal pedagogy

In conclusion, reflect on the role of praise in a twenty-first century context – use the three examples outlined in Chapter 1 to provide a range of different approaches to the use of praise. First, is the praise given sincere? Does it stem from genuine appreciation of effort made, thinking explicated or learning achieved? Or does the praise comment form part of a strategy to communicate a teacher's view, which is, in fact, a judgement?

Consider what attributions are being fostered by praise. Are performance and ability being rewarded, or the route that took the pupil there? Reflect on how comments can enhance either a fixed or growth mindset in the recipient of the praise. Think about the promotion of autonomy in a learning situation and how it promotes competency and self-efficacy in each learner. And finally, reflect on how comments can convey expectation – a thought-provoking question will produce a different learning response in a student from a question which is structured to display knowledge. It will impact not only on the individual, but also the class engagement.

Table 2 provides a summary of the types of praise used by teachers and the effect that each has. The challenge in reading this book has been to consider the difference between knowledge and assumption, together with the role and identity of a teacher. Challenge to beliefs and values are rarely easy to engage with, but the need to move to Daniel Pink's definition of the 3.0 upgrade model is compelling if today's children are to be properly prepared for personally and economically fulfilling futures.

Table 2 What happens when children are praised?

Type of praise	Associated factors	Effect on recipient	Appropriate use
Contingent	• 'if / then' promise of reward • mostly closed questions are asked to encourage the display of knowledge • regulating language is used	• feeling controlled and bribed • creation of hierarchies • encouragement of competition • compliance or resentment • diverts attention away from learning to acquisition of reward	• for algorithmic tasks where the reason for the reward is made clear • en route to independence for children who require structure
Generalised	• non-specific comments like, 'Well done' or 'Good job' • may encompass everyone	• very little effect as the recipient has no specific knowledge of why the comment is made • may appear insincere	• in a teacher/class relationship where it is understood to be intended for everyone • when creating a corporate 'feel good' moment
Ability or performance related	• comments that relate to or reward intelligence • performance is valued above the route to achieving it	• creation of hierarchies • norm referencing • competition • risk aversion in pupils who need to retain ability status • feelings of inadequacy where the praise is known to be unmerited	• only where performance is an outcome of effort or persistence

(Continued overleaf)

Table 2 Continued.

Type of praise	Associated factors	Effect on recipient	Appropriate use
Evaluative	• public awarding of certificates or merits for work which is judged to deserve it • evaluation of work or achievement which does not involve the learner	• creates dependency • reaction will depend on the extent to which the task aligns with the values of the learner	• within a trust relationship where the evaluation is followed by dialogue with the recipient
Informative or descriptive	• very specific information is provided • open questioning will prompt further thinking • power is shared	• will feel valued • will experience autonomy and will see the route to mastery • willing to take future risks • growth in self-efficacy	• in heuristic tasks • to engage learners • to encourage resilient learning

Points for reflection

• Regarding teaching and learning, outline any dissonance which exists between school protocol and personal practice in your current context. In what ways do policy and practice align?

• Are you 'doing to' or 'working with' students? In what circumstances is a 'doing to' approach valid?

• Discuss how much use you make of modelling, scaffolding, guiding and sharing as teaching and learning strategies. In what contexts or subject areas is each most applicable?

• How do you build collaborative and independent enquiry into your teaching? What are the differences between this as a bolt-on extra or as an integral part of learning?

• Working with others, define an effective toolkit of strategies for twenty-first century teaching and learning. What role, if any, does praise play in this? How might your view of this be reflective of the age of your pupils?

• What are the implications of your discussion for marking, assessment, recording, reporting and testing?

• What are some possible reactions from parents if curricula and teaching styles are developed to meet these challenges? How can this be managed?

Appendices

Appendix A – Behaviourist policy documents

Behaviour policy

RATIONALE

We believe in the promotion of good behaviour through the use of a structured system of rewards. These are consistently applied by all staff in order to embed our objective of mutual respect for each member of the school.

AIMS

- To reinforce the values of the school through the use of positive reward;
- to use reward to maintain the school's Code of Conduct and ensure that the school is a safe and secure place to learn;
- to apply praise in a ratio of 5 praise comments to every 1 reprimand or sanction;
- to engage parents in a positive relationship through the use of praise notes and phone calls;
- to minimise bad behaviour by praising good behaviour.

OBJECTIVES

We will achieve this by:

- incentivising students;
- not becoming over-reliant on sanction as a means of control;
- using senior members of staff to praise good work or positive behaviour;
- using teaching time in lessons to revisit the Code of Conduct to ensure that all students are aware of the hierarchy of rewards and sanctions.

Staff will:

- provide teaching of the highest quality through delivering well-planned lessons;
- inform parents of both positive and negative behaviour;
- apply reward credits consistently and fairly for effort, achievement or improvement, to a maximum of 3 credits per lesson;

- extend privilege time during tutor periods to reinforce good behaviour;
- display praise posters containing criteria for earning credits;
- nominate students for prizes, ensuring even distribution across an academic year;
- display examples of good work;
- select star students at weekly departmental meetings;
- facilitate the exchange of reward credits for gifts during tutor periods;
- when necessary, apply a relevant sanction, discussing with the student why this action is being taken.

Students will:

- attend school daily;
- be punctual;
- dress smartly in school uniform;
- arrive at lessons prepared and equipped to learn;
- show respect for staff and other students;
- carry a diary, presenting it when requested for the notification of reward credits and sanctions;
- comply with the Code of Conduct.

Teaching and learning policy

RATIONALE

We believe that children learn most effectively when teachers are well prepared, lessons are resourced, the learning environment is quiet and children are praised when they do well.

AIMS

- To provide a safe and secure environment in which each child is valued as an individual;
- to provide high quality teaching for every pupil which is matched to individual need;
- to monitor and assess progress;
- to build a strong home/school relationship through regular communication.

OBJECTIVES

We will achieve this by:

- ensuring that detailed planning which shows incremental steps in learning is thoroughly prepared and shared with support staff;
- displaying class timetables in a form appropriate to the age of the children;
- reinforcing expectations of learning through regular classroom conversations;
- assessing progress regularly;
- informing parents of their child's progress through agreed reporting formats;
- ensuring that all staff use efficient time management strategies;
- maintaining high expectations;
- ensuring a high level of staff subject knowledge, providing training where necessary.

Staff will:

- value learning and show enthusiasm for all that they teach;
- greet children daily, ensuring that the classroom environment supports learning;
- prepare resources before the start of each day;
- prepare differentiated lessons one week in advance, giving copies to the Head Teacher every Monday morning;
- explain work in a way which is understood;
- set targets appropriate to each pupil;
- monitor progress;
- choose good work to display, mounting it in accordance with school policy;
- encourage and praise pupils at all times;
- provide guidance to pupils when reading books are changed;
- mark work regularly in accordance with school policy;
- respond promptly to parental questions;
- set and mark homework weekly.

Appendix B – Constructivist policy documents

Behaviour policy

RATIONALE

We believe that everyone in our learning community should feel respected and valued in a safe and secure environment. We celebrate the socio-cultural diversity which exists within our school. We are building a cohesive community by creating an environment to which each individual makes a unique contribution.

AIMS

- To foster a sense of pride in achievement;
- to develop empathy for the feelings of others;
- to make positive social and learning behaviour choices;
- to develop self-control and self-confidence;
- to develop persistence, emotional sturdiness and a sense of fairness;
- to cultivate an awareness of the wider community, preparing children for a meaningful role in a global society.

OBJECTIVES

We will achieve this by:

- showing tolerance and mutual respect;
- creating a sense of ownership through consultation within effective adult/child partnerships;
- maintaining high expectations;
- challenging unacceptable behaviour;
- accepting individual accountability.

Adults will:

- create stimulating classroom environments, delivering lessons which promote effective learning;
- provide children with positive role models;
- treat all children fairly, enforcing standards consistently;
- show sensitivity to children's individual needs in a learning or social context;
- build effective home/school partnerships;
- work with outside agencies as necessary to support children who present with disruptive or aggressive behaviour.

Children will:

- accept responsibility for their own actions and choices;
- treat others as they wish to be treated themselves;
- show respect for, and tolerance of, the opinions, values and beliefs of others;
- discuss any poor behaviour choices in a calm manner;
- welcome opportunities to take responsibility for appropriate jobs;
- respect the right of everyone to play and learn in an organised and caring environment.

Teaching and learning policy

RATIONALE

We regard constructive written and verbal feedback as key motivators in a child's learning. Positive feedback should focus attention on success and improvement needs, when measured against learning intentions. In this way, we believe that children will become reflective learners as they develop an understanding of the next steps in their learning.

AIMS

- To show that we value the children's work and encourage them to value it too;
- to promote self-assessment so that children can reflect on their own learning and set targets effectively;
- to promote peer assessment so that children can support each other's learning and accept guidance;
- to ensure that work is well matched to each child's ability;
- to provide a basis for formative and summative assessment, which informs future planning;
- to define a corporate approach for all adults working with children;
- to inform parents about their child's progress.

OBJECTIVES

We will achieve positive learning partnerships by:

- ensuring opportunities exist for individual, paired and collaborative working;
- providing regular and prompt opportunities for written or spoken dialogue;
- making the learning intention clear and negotiating success criteria;
- making explicit to children how they will give or receive feedback;

- agreeing together on the next steps for progress;
- joint monitoring of progress towards agreed targets;
- maintaining clear and open communication with parents.

Teachers will:

- demonstrate understanding of the role of didactic and guided teaching, modelling, scaffolding and talk strategies to support learning;
- use assessments to adjust future teaching and learning plans;
- define the learning intention, negotiate success criteria and make clear how feedback will relate to this;
- model self-evaluation and peer-evaluation skills;
- quality mark defined pieces of work, using scaffold, example or reminder comments to indicate how work could be developed;
- recognise effort as well as achievement.

Children will:

- use a range of self- and peer-evaluation strategies to assess how effectively they have met learning intentions and indicate this to their teacher;
- self-correct secretarial errors, appropriate to their age and knowledge;
- use the time given to reflect and act on feedback comments;
- provide evidence of achieved targets and engage in dialogue with their teacher to ensure that selected targets are suitably challenging;
- reflect on feedback in order to articulate their personal learning needs.

Appendix C – Praise Posters

Wallpaper Praise
is for everyone; it aims to create a positive atmosphere in our classroom.

It sounds like this:-
Great!   Excellent!   Wow!

Well done, you're all amazing!

You must be the best class in the school.

Directed Praise

notices good choices in behaviour.

It sounds like this:-
Thank you for waiting.

You were excellent representatives of the school on our trip.

Thank you for being so helpful.

Public Praise

shares your achievement with others.

It sounds like this:-

Could I use this for our display?

Would you like to share this with the Head?

Would you like to show this to another class?

Personal Praise

uses your name and aims to draw attention to your positive attitude.

It sounds like this:-
You're thinking really carefully.

You're a star for trying this.

Well done. You're getting there.

Reflective Praise

encourages you to evaluate what you have achieved.

It sounds like this:-
What are the strengths of your work?

Have you achieved what you intended?

What are you proud of achieving today?

Bibliography

Adler M.J. (1982) *The Paideia Proposal: An Educational Manifesto*. New York: Simon & Schuster.

Alexander R. (2008) *Towards Dialogic Teaching: Rethinking Classroom Talk*. York: Dialogos.

Allard A. and Cooper M. (2001) 'Learning to Cooperate: a Study of How Primary Teachers and Children Construct Classroom Cultures', *Asia Pacific Journal of Teacher Education*, 29(2): 153–69.

Amabile T.M. (1998) 'How to Kill Creativity', *Harvard Business Review*, 76 (September–October): 76–87.

Aristotle (350 B.C.E.) *De Anima*, The Internet Classics Archive, *http://classics.mit.edu/Aristotle/soul.html* accessed 8 September 2011.

Bandura A. (1977) *Social Learning Theory*. New York: General Learning Press.

Bandura A. (1982) 'Self-efficacy Mechanism in Human Agency', *American Psychologist*, 37: 122–47.

Bandura A. (1993) 'Perceived Self-efficacy in Cognitive Development and Functioning', *Educational Psychologist*, Volume 28, pp 117–48.

Bandura A. (1997) *Self-Efficacy: The Exercise of Control*. New York: Freeman.

BBC (2000) 'Blunkett Promotes "thinking skills"', BBC News online, *http://news.bbc.co.uk/1/hi/education/592220.stm* accessed 9 September 2011.

Beaman R. and Wheldall K. (2002) 'Teachers' Use of Approval and Disapproval in the Classroom', *Educational Psychology*, 20(4): 432–45.

Bew Lord P. (2011) 'Independent Review of Key Stage 2 testing, assessment and accountability', Department for Education, *https://www.education.gov.uk/publications/standard/publicationDetail/Page1/CM%208144* accessed 24 October 2011.

Boden M.A. (1994) *Piaget*. London: Fontana Press.

Booth-Butterfield S. (2011) 'Attribution Theory', *http://healthyinfluence.com/wordpress/steves-primer-of-practical-persuasion-3-0/thinking/attribution* accessed 28 September 2011.

Briggs F. and Nichols S. (2001) 'Pleasing Yourself and Working for the Teacher: Children's Perceptions of School', *Early Child Development and Care*, 170(1): 13–30.

Brooks D. (2011) *The Social Animal*. London: Short Books.

Bruner J. (1960) *The Process of Education*. Massachusetts: Harvard University Press.

Bruner J. (1996) *The Culture of Education*. Massachusetts: Harvard University Press.

Buckley K.W. (1989) *Mechanical Man: John Broadus Watson and the Beginnings of Behaviourism*. New York and London: Guilford Press.

Burgess T. (2007) *Lifting the lid on the creative curriculum*. Nottingham: National College of School Leadership.

Burnett P.C. (2002) 'Teacher Praise and Feedback and Students – Perceptions of the Classroom Environment', *Educational Psychology*, 22(1): 5–16.

Canter L. and Canter M. (1992) *Lee Canter's Assertive Discipline: Positive Behaviour Management for Today's Classroom*. Santa Monica: Canter Associates.

Capstick J. (2005) 'Pupil and Staff Perceptions of Rewards at a Pupil Referral Unit', *Emotional and Behavioural Difficulties*, 10(2): 95–117.

Carroll L. (1997) *Alice's Adventures in Wonderland*. Kindle Edition, downloaded 3 November 2011.

Cassidy S. (2011) 'Summerhill Alumni: What we learnt at the school for scandal', *The Independent*, *http://www.independent.co.uk/news/education/schools/summerhill-alumni-what-we-learnt-at-the-school-for-scandal-2373066.html* accessed 20 October 2011.

Chalk K. and Bizo L.A. (2004) 'Specific Praise Improves On-task Behaviour and Numeracy Enjoyment: A study of Year Four Pupils Engaged in the Numeracy Hour', *Educational Psychology in Practice*, 20(4): 335–51.

Chua A. (2011) *Battle Hymn of the Tiger Mother*. London: Bloomsbury.

Chua A. (2011) 'Why Chinese Mothers are Superior', *The Wall Street Journal*, *http://online.wsj.com/article/SB10001424052748704111504576059713528698754.html* accessed 12 October 2011.

Claxton G. (2002) *Building Learning Power; Helping Young People Become Better Learners*. Bristol: TLO Ltd.

Comenius J.A. (trans. Keatinge M.W. (1967)) *The Great Didactic*. New York: Russell and Russell, *http://core.roehampton.ac.uk/digital/froarc/comgre* accessed 10 September 2011.

Cooper P. and Cefai C. (2009) 'Contemporary Values and Social Context: Implications for the Emotional Well-being of Children', *Emotional and Behavioural Difficulties*, 14(2): 91–100.

Connors L., Putwain D., Woods K. and Nicholson L. (2009) 'Causes and Consequences of Test Anxiety in Key Stage 2 Pupils: The Mediational Role of Emotional Resilience', *BERA conference paper*, *http://www.leeds.ac.uk/educol/documents/184268.pdf* accessed 24 October 2011.

Corpus J., Ogle C. and Love-Geiger K. (2006) 'The Effects of Social-Comparison Versus Mastery Praise on Children's Intrinsic Motivation', *Motivation and Emotion*, 30(4): 333–43.

Covington M.V. (2000) 'Intrinsic Versus Extrinsic Motivation in Schools: A Reconciliation', *Current Directions in Psychological Science*, 9(1): 22–5.

Cunningham H. (2006) *The Invention of Childhood*. London: BBC Books.

Davidson J. (1968) *Classic Piaget*. Davidson Films, search on *http://www.youtube.com* accessed 15 September 2011.

Deci E. (1975) *Intrinsic Motivation*. New York: Plenum.

Deci E. (1997) *Why we do what we do*. London: Penguin.

Deci E., Vallerand R., Pelletier L. and Ryan R. (1991) 'Motivation and Education: The Self-Determination Perspective', *Educational Psychologist*, 26(3): 325–46.

Dewey J. (2007) *Democracy and Education*. Charleston, SC: Bibliobazaar.

DCSF (2010) Assessing Pupil Progress, *http://www.teachernet.gov.uk* (link no longer active).

DfE (2011) 'Getting the Simple Things Right: Charlie Taylor's behaviour checklists', *http://www.education.gov.uk/schools/pupilsupport/behaviour/a00199342/getting-the-simple-things-right-charlie-taylors-behaviour-checklists* accessed 19 October 2011.

DfES (2002) Further Literacy Support: Training Materials, *http//:www.standards.dfes.gov.uk/primaryframeworks/downloads/PDF/dfes-03446-2002.pdf* accessed 20 May 2009.

DfES (2003a) *The National Curriculum*. Nottingham: DfES Publications Centre, *http://curriculum.qcda.gov.uk/index.aspx* accessed 19 September 2011.

DfES (2003b) *Excellence and Enjoyment: A Strategy for Primary Schools*. Nottingham: DfES Publications Centre.

DfES (2005) *Excellence and Enjoyment: Social and Emotional Aspects of Learning*. Nottingham: DfES Publications Centre, *http://www.niched.org/docs/SEAL.pdf* accessed 19 September 2011.

Duckworth A.L. and Quinn P.D. (2009) 'Development and validation of the Short Grit Scale (Grit-S)', *Journal of Personality Assessment*, 91: 166–74, *http://www.sas.upenn.edu/~duckwort/images/Duckworth%20and%20Quinn.pdf* accessed 23 September 2011.

Dweck C. (1999) *Self Theories – their role in motivation, personality and development*. Philadelphia: Psychology Press.

Dweck C. (2007) *Mindset: The New Psychology of Success*. New York: Ballantine Books.

Dweck C. (2009) 'Developing Growth Mindsets: How Praise Can Harm, and How to Use it Well', Keynote speech, Scottish Learning Festival 2009, *http://www.ltscotland.org.uk/video/c/video_tcm4565678.asp* accessed 26 September 2011.

Education Select Committee (2011) 'Behaviour and Discipline in Schools', *http://www.publications.parliament.uk/pa/cm201011/cmselect/cmeduc/516/51614.htm* accessed 11 November 2011.

Edwards C., Gandini L. and Forman G. (eds) (1998) *The Hundred Languages of Children. The Reggio Emilia Approach – Advanced Reflections*. Connecticut and London: Ablex.

Elton Lord R. (1989) *Discipline in Schools*. London: HMSO.

Ericsson K.A., Prietula M.J. and Cokely E.T. (2007) 'The Making of an Expert', *Harvard Business Review*, *http://harvardbusinessonline.hbsp.harvard.edu* accessed 27 September 2011.

Fabes R.A., Moran J.D. and McCullers J.C. (1981) 'The Hidden Costs of Reward and WAIS Subscale Performance', *American Journal of Psychology*, 94(3): 387–98.

Fraser G. (2011) 'Pioneering School is Top Class', *Scotsman*, *http://www.scotsman.com/news/education/pioneering_school_is_top_class_1_1948307* accessed 4 November 2011.

Fryer R.G. (2010) 'Financial Incentives and Student Achievement: Evidence From Randomized Trials', *http://www.edlabs.harvard.edu/pdf/studentincentives.pdf* accessed 29 September 2011.

Gardner B. (2011) 'Practical Experiments in School Science Lessons and Science Field Trips', *http://www.parliament.uk/business/committees/committees-a-z/commons-select/science-and-technology-committee/inquiries/school-science* accessed 19 September 2011.

Ginott H.G. (1965) *Between Parent and Child*. New York: Macmillan.

Ginott H G. (1975) *Teacher and Child: A Book for Parents and Teachers*. New York: Macmillan.

Goldhaber D. (2010) 'Getting Ahead of the Teacher-Accountability Curve', *The Seattle Times*, *http://seattletimes.nwsource.com/html/opinion/2012743626_guest30goldhaber.html* accessed 24 October 2011.

Greene D. and Lepper M.R. (1974) 'Effects of Extrinsic Rewards on Children's Subsequent Intrinsic Interest', *Child Development*, 45: 1141–5.

Gruen J. (1969) 'Samuel Beckett Talks About Beckett', *American Vogue*, 154(10).

Gye H. (2011) 'Council spends £100,000 on "patronising" scheme', *Daily Mail Online*, *http://www.dailymail.co.uk/news/article-2043656/Bolton-Council-blasted-patronising-scheme-send-congratulatory-texts-people-DO-recycle.html* accessed 24 October 2011.

Henderlong J. and Lepper M.R. (2002) 'The Effects of Praise on Children's Intrinsic Motivation: A Review and Synthesis', *Psychological Bulletin*, 128(5): 774–95.

Hitt D., Marriott R. and Esser J. (1992) 'Effects of Delayed Rewards and Task Interest in Intrinsic Motivation', *Basic and Applied Social Psychology*, 13(4): 405–14.

Holt J. (1987) *How Children Fail*. Middlesex: Penguin.

Hout M. and Elliott S.W. (2011) *Incentives and Test-Based Accountability in Education*. Washington: The National Academies Press.

Huxley A. (1991) *Brave New World*. London: Longman.

Infantino J. and Little E. (2005) 'Students' Perceptions of Classroom Behaviour Problems and the Effectiveness of Different Disciplinary Methods', *Educational Psychology*, 25(5): 491–508.

Jonsson P. (2011) 'America's biggest teacher and principal cheating scandal unfolds in Atlanta', *The Christian Science Monitor*, 5 July 2011, *http://www.csmonitor.com/USA/Education/2011/0705/America-s-biggest-teacher-and-principal-cheating-scandal-unfolds-in-Atlanta* accessed 4 October 2011.

Jordan M. (2010) 'Failure', Nike Commercial, *http://www.youtube.com/watch?feature=player_embedded&v=CgW48mBQJ14* accessed 15 November 2011.

Joussemet M. and Koestner R. (1999) 'Effect of Expected Rewards on Children's Creativity', *Creativity Research Journal*, 12(4): 231–9.

Kohn A. (1999) *Punished by Rewards*. New York: Houghton Mifflin.

Kohn A. (2000a) *The Schools Our Children Deserve*. New York: Houghton Mifflin.

Kohn A. (2000b) *What To Look For in a Classroom*. San Francisco: Jossey-Bass.

Kohn A. (2011) 'The Truth About Self-Esteem', *http://www.alfiekohn.org/teaching/tase.htm* accessed 30 September 2011.

Knutson B., Adams C.M., Fong, G.W. and Hommer D. (2001) 'Anticipation of Increasing Monetary Reward Selectively Recruits Nucleus Accumbens', *The Journal of Neuroscience*, 22(9): 3303–5.

Kolbert E. (2011) 'America's Top Parent', *The New Yorker*, *http://www.newyorker.com/arts/critics/books/2011/01/31/110131crbo_books_kolbert* accessed 14 October 2011.

Leach C. (2011) 'UKedchat Too Cool for School – Some Thoughts', *http://chrisleach78.wordpress.com/2011/08/18/ukedchat-too-cool-for-school-some-thoughts* accessed 25 October 2011.

Lionni L. (2005) *Fish is Fish*. London: Scholastic.

Locke J. (1996) *An Essay Concerning Human Understanding*. Indianapolis: Hackett Publishing Co.

Locke J. (2008) *Some Thoughts Concerning Education*. Kindle edition, accessed 26 August 2011.

Lucas H. (2011) *After Summerhill: What Happened to the Pupils of Britain's Most Radical School?* Bristol: Pomegranate Books.

Maclellan E. (2005) 'Academic Achievement: The Role of Praise in Motivating Students', *Active Learning in Higher Education*, 6: 194–204.

Malone N. (2011) 'The Kids Are Actually Sort of Alright', *New York Magazine*, *http://nymag.com/news/features/my-generation-2011-10* accessed 3 November 2011.

Mansell W. (2011) 'Hidden Tigers: why do Chinese children do so well at school?', *The Guardian*, *http://www.guardian.co.uk/education/2011/feb/07/chinese-children-school-do-well* accessed 20 October 2011.

Mercer N. (2007) 'Commentary on the Reconciliation of Cognitive and Sociocultural Accounts of Conceptual Change', *Educational Psychologist*, 42(1): 75–8.

Mercer N. (2000) *Words and Minds: How we Use Language to Think Together*. Abingdon: Routledge.

Mercer N. and Hodgkinson S. (eds) (2008) *Exploring Talk in Schools*. Thousand Oaks, CA: Sage.

Mercer N., Wegerif R. and Dawes L. (1999) 'Children's Talk and the Development of Reasoning in the Classroom', *British Educational Research Journal*, 25(1): 95–111.

Meyer W-U. (1992) 'Paradoxical effects of praise and criticism on perceived ability', *European Review of Social Psychology*, 3: 259–283.

Meyer W-U., Mittag W. and Engler U. (1986) 'Some Effects of Praise and Blame on Perceived Ability and Affect', *Social Cognition*, 4(3): 293–308.

Miliband E. (2011) 'Keynote address to the Labour Party Conference', *http://www.bbc.co.uk/news/uk-politics-15081234* accessed 25 October 2011.

Miller A., Ferguson E. and Simpson R. (1998) 'The Perceived Effectiveness of Rewards and Sanctions in Primary Schools: Adding in the Parental Perspective', *Educational Psychology*, 18(1): 55–64.

Mitchell D. (2010) 'Heathfield – we have a problem!', The Specialist Schools and Academies Trust, *https://www.ssatrust.org.uk/regions/northwest/Pages/Heathfield-wehaveaproblem.aspx* accessed 4 November 2011.

Montessori M. (2009) *The Absorbent Mind*. Miami, FL: BN Publishing.

Montessori Teacher Training (2008) *http://www.montessoritraining.blogspot.com/2008/03/montessori-philosophy-praise-vs.html* accessed 5 September 2011.

Moss P., Dillon J. and Statham J. (2000) 'The "Child in Need" and the "Rich Child": Discourses, Constructions and Practice', *Critical Social Policy*, 20: 233–54.

Moss S. (2008) 'Flow Theory', *www.psych-it.com.au/Psychlopedia/article.asp?id=62* accessed 3 November 2011.

Neill A.S. (1960) *Summerhill: A Radical Approach to Child Rearing, http://www.summerhill-school.co.uk* accessed 26 September 2011.

Niemivirta M., Rijavec M. and Yamauchi H. (2001) 'Goal Orientations and Action Controlled Beliefs: A Cross-cultural Comparison among Croatian, Finnish, and Japanese Students' in Efklides A., Kuhl J. and Sorrentino R.M. (eds) *Trends and Prospects in Motivational Research.* Dordrecht: Kluwer Academic Publishers.

Nobel Lectures (1967) *Physiology or Medicine 1901–1921.* Amsterdam: Elsevier.

Norman K. (ed.) (1992) *Thinking Voices: The Work of the National Oracy Project.* London: Hodder and Stoughton.

OFSTED (1993) *Achieving Good Behaviour in Schools.* London: HMSO.

OFSTED (1999) Summerhill School Inspection Report, *http://www.ofsted.gov.uk/inspection-reports/find-inspection-report/provider/ELS/124870* accessed 28 September 2011.

Palmer D. (2005) 'A Motivational View of Constructivist-informed Teaching', *International Journal of Science Education*, 27(15): 1853–4.

Paton G. (2010) 'GCSE league tables "skewed by vocational courses"', *The Telegraph, http://www.telegraph.co.uk/education/educationnews/7215886/GCSE-league-tables-skewed-by-vocational-courses.html* accessed 24 October 2011.

Paul Hamlyn Foundation and The Innovation Unit (2008) 'Learning Futures: Next Practice in Learning and Teaching', *http://www.innovationunit.org/resources/learning-futures-next-practice-learning-and-teaching* accessed 8 November 2011.

Pavlov I.P. (trans. Anrep G.V. (1927)) *Conditioned Reflexes: An Investigation of the Physiological Activity of the Cerebral Cortex.* London: Oxford University Press.

Pavlov I.P. (trans. Horsley Gantt W. (1941)) *Lectures on Conditioned Reflexes, II: Conditioned Reflexes and Psychiatry.* New York: International Publishers.

Pelletier L.G. and Vallerand R.J. (1996) 'Supervisors' Beliefs and Subordinates' Intrinsic Motivation: A Behavioral Confirmation Analysis', *Journal of Personality and Social Psychology*, 71(2): 331–40.

Persaud R. (2005) *The Motivated Mind.* London: Bantam Press.

Pestalozzi J.H. (1895) *Leonard and Gertrude. http://www.archive.org/details/pestalozzisleona00pestuoft* accessed 10 September 2011.

Piaget J. (1959) *The Language and Thought of the Child.* New York and London: Routledge and Kegan Paul.

Piaget J. (1972) *To Understand is To Invent.* New York: Viking Press.

Piaget J. (1962) 'Comments on Vygotsky's critical remarks concerning *The Language and Thought of the Child*, and *Judgement and Reasoning in the Child*', The Vygotsky Internet Archive, *http://www.marxists.org/archive/vygotsky/works/comment/piaget.htm* accessed 15 September 2011.

Piaget J. and Coretta C. (1977) *Piaget on Piaget: The Epistomology of Jean Piaget* (video) Yale University Media Design Studio, search on *http://www.youtube.com*, 15 September 2011.

Pink D.H. (2011) *Drive: The Surprising Truth About What Motivates Us.* Edinburgh: Canongate Books.

Pivotal Education (2009) *http://www.pivotaleducation.com* accessed 6 September 2011.

Reinke W., Lewis-Palmer T. and Martin E. (2007) 'The Effect of Visual Performance Feedback on Teacher Use of Behavior-Specific Praise', *Behaviour Modification*, 31: 247.

Richardson H. (2011) 'African-Caribbean boys would rather hustle than learn', BBC News online, *http://www.bbc.co.uk/news/education-15387444* accessed 23 October 2011.

Richardson V. (2003) 'Constructivist Pedadogy', *Teachers College Record*, 105(9): 1623–40.

Rinaldi C. (2006) *In Dialogue with Reggio Emilia.* London: Routledge.

Rinaldi C. (2009) 'The Adult Role in the Early Years Setting', Spotlight Speech at the Scottish Learning Festival 2009 *http://www.ltscotland.org.uk/video/c/video_tcm4570277.asp* accessed 26 September 2011.

Robins G. (2011) 'The Effect of Exploratory Talk on the Development of Sentence Structure in Able Writers', *Literacy*, 45(2): 78–83.

Robins R. and Pals J. (2002) 'Implicit Self-Theories in the Academic Domain: Implications for Goal Orientation, Attributions, Affect, and Self-Esteem Change', *Self and Identity*, 1: 313–36.

Rogers C. (2003) *Client-Centred Therapy: Its Current Practice, Implications and Theory*. London: Constable.

Rogers C. (2004) *On Becoming a Person: A Therapist's View of Psychotherapy*. London: Constable.

Rogoff B. (1994) 'Developing understanding of the idea of communities of learners', *Mind, Culture and Activity*, 1: 209–29.

Rosenzweig S. (1936) 'Some implicit common factors in diverse methods of psychotherapy', *American Journal of Orthopsychiatry*, 6(3): 412–15.

Roth G., Assor A., Kanat-Maymon Y. and Kaplan H. (2007) 'Autonomous Motivation for Teaching: How Self-Determined Teaching May Lead to Self-Determined Learning', *Journal of Educational Psychology*, 99(4): 761–74.

Rousseau J. (2004) *Emile*. Kindle Edition, downloaded 26 August 2011.

Ryan R.M. and Deci E.L. (2002) 'Intrinsic and Extrinsic Motivations: Classic Definitions and New Directions', *Contemporary Educational Psychology*, 25: 54–67.

Salili F. (1996) 'Learning and motivation: An Asian perspective', *Psychology and Developing Societies*, 8: 55–81.

Salili F. and Hau K.T. (1994) 'The effect of teachers' evaluative feedback on Chinese students' perceptions of ability: A cultural and situational analysis', *Educational Studies*, 20: 223–36.

Schultz W. (2002) 'Getting Formal with Dopamine and Reward', *Neuron*, 36: 241–63.

Schunk D.H. (1982) 'Effects of Effort Attributional Feedback on Children's Perceived Self-Efficacy and Achievement', *Journal of Educational Psychology*, 74: 548–56.

Schunk D.H. (1983) 'Ability versus effort attributional feedback: Differential effects on self-efficacy and achievement', *Journal of Educational Psychology*, 75: 848–856.

Shreeve A. and Boddington D. (2002) 'Student Perceptions of Reward and Sanctions', *Pedagogy, Culture and Society*, 10(2): 239–56.

Skinner B.F. (1962) *Walden Two*. New York: Macmillan.

Skinner B.F. (1968) *The Technology of Teaching*. New York: Prentice-Hall.

Skinner B.F. (1972) *Beyond Freedom and Dignity*. New York: Bantam/Vintage.

Steele M.M. (2005) 'Teaching Students with Learning Disabilities: Constructivism or Behaviorism?', *Current Issues in Education*, 8(10), *http://cie.asu.edu/volume8/number10/index.html* accessed 14 September 2011.

Steer A. (2005) 'Learning Behaviour: The Report of The Practitioners' Group on School Behaviour and Discipline', *http://www.dcsf.gov.uk/behaviourandattendance/about/learning_behaviour.cfm* accessed 10 June 2009.

Steer A. (2009) 'Learning Behaviour. Lessons Learned; A Review of Behaviour Standards and Practices in our Schools', *https://www.education.gov.uk/publications/standard/_arc_SOP/Page5/DCSF-00453-2009#downloadableparts* accessed 6 September 2011.

Strauss V. (2011) 'Why merit pay for teachers sounds good – but isn't', *The Washington Post*, *http://www.washingtonpost.com/blogs/answer-sheet/post/why-merit-pay-for-teachers-sounds-good–but-isnt/2011/10/09/gIQAVb72YL_blog.html* accessed 24 October 2011.

The National Strategies (2010) *Assessing Pupil Progress: A Teacher's Handbook*. Nottingham: The National Strategies.

Thorndike E.L. (1910) 'The contribution of Psychology to Education', *Journal of Educational Psychology*, 1: 5–12.

Thorndike E.L. (2009a) *Educational Psychology*. General Books LLC.

Thorndike E.L. (2009b) *The Principles of Teaching based on Psychology*. Charleston, SC: BiblioBazaar.

Tough, P. (2011) 'What if the Secret to Success is Failure?', *http://www.nytimes.com/2011/09/18/magazine/what-if-the-secret-to-success-is-failure.html?_r=2&pagewanted=all* accessed 14 September 2011.

Tsui, Cheng-Fang (2005) 'Achievement Beliefs and Their Cultural Contexts: Voices from American, Chinese-American and Taiwanese College Students', *3rd Hawaii International Conference on Education*, *http://nccur.lib.nccu.edu.tw/bitstream/140.119/22045/1/6.pdf* accessed 14 October 2011.

UKedchat (2011) 'How can we deal with the mindset amongst children that it is not cool to do well at school?', Twitter *http://www.scribd.com/doc/62598631/Ukedchat-Archive-18-August-2011* accessed 25 October 2011.

Vygotsky L. (1962) *Thought and Language*. Cambridge, MA: MIT Press.

Vygotsky L. (1978) *Mind in Society, The Development of Higher Psychological Processes*. Cambridge, MA, and London: Harvard University Press.

Watson J.B. (1970) *Behaviorism*. New York: W.W. Norton & Co.

Watson J.B. (1913) 'Psychology As The Behaviorist Views It', *Psychological Review*, 20: 158–77.

Weber M. (2005) 'Assertive Discipline', *http://maxweber.hunter.cuny.edu/pub/eres/EDSPC715_MCINTYRE/AssertiveDiscipline.html* accessed 6 September 2011.

Wegerif, R., Littleton, K., Dawes, L., Mercer, N. and Rowe, D. (2004) 'Widening access to educational opportunities through teaching children how to reason together', *International Journal of Research and Method in Education*, 27(2): 143–56.

Wells G. (1986) *The Meaning Makers, Children Learning Language and Using Language to Learn*. Portsmouth, NH: Heinemann Educational.

Wilde O. (2011) *Lady Windermere's Fan*. London: Penguin.

Woods R. (2008) 'When Rewards and Sanctions Fail: A Case Study of a Primary School Rule-Breaker', *International Journal of Qualitative Studies in Education*, 21(2): 181–96.

Wozniak R. (ed.) (1993) *The Roots of Behaviourism*. London: Routledge.

Young M. (2005) 'The Motivational Effects of the Classroom Environment in Facilitating Self-Regulated Learning', *Journal of Marketing Education*, 27: 25–40.

Zastrow C. von (2010) 'Carrots and Sticks are So Last Century: A Conversation with Author Dan Pink', Learning First Alliance, *http://www.learningfirst.org/carrots-and-sticks-are-so-last-century-conversation-author-dan-pink* accessed 2 November 2011.

Zentall T.R. (2002) 'A Cognitive Behaviorist Approach to the Study of Animal Behaviour', *The Journal of General Psychology*, 129(4): 328–63.

Websites

http://www.bfskinner.org accessed 9 September 2011

http://www.bookit.com accessed 10 September 2011

http://www.buddhaquotes.co.uk accessed 14 November 2011

http://www.buildinglearningpower.co.uk accessed 8 November 2011

http://www.cognitiveacceleration.co.uk accessed 10 September 2011

http://www.monkseaton.org.uk accessed 8 November 2011

http://thanksforteaching.us accessed 3 November 2011

http://www.thersa.org accessed 8 November 2011

http://thinkingtogether.educ.cam.ac.uk accessed 1 November 2011

http://www.pestalozziworld.com accessed 11 September 2011

http://www.philosophy4children.co.uk accessed 8 November 2011

http://www.primarytechnology.co.uk accessed 1 November 2011

http://www.q2l.org accessed 4 November 2011

http://y62012.heathfieldcps.net/2011/11/01/blogging-video-project/ accessed 7 November 2011

http://www.vivomiles.com accessed 20 September 2011

http://www.youngfoundation.org accessed 8 November 2011

Index

ability 13, 15, 16, 17, 19, 55, 60, 61, 70, 86, 89, 94, 105, 106, 107, 108, 109, 110, 112, 114, 117, 121, 123, 127, 135
achievement gap 64
algorithmic tasks 56, 64, 121
Amabile, Teresa 121
Anselm of Canterbury 12
Aristotle 13
assessment: formative 7, 9, 41, 42, 44, 82 summative 4, 9, 22, 28, 42 peer 43 self 7, 9, 41, 43, 46
assumption 2, 11, 23, 24, 25, 29, 32, 67, 75, 105, 108, 133, 135
attribution 59, 60, 62, 80, 84, 95, 109, 110, 135
autonomy 50, 51, 52, 54, 56, 62, 115, 121, 123, 125, 127, 129 parents 117, 118, 122 teachers 24, 51–2, 57, 118, 119, 120 students 51, 52–3, 54, 65, 68, 70, 77, 114, 115, 116, 122, 125, 129, 130
autotelic experience 56, 57, 59, 116

Bandura, Albert 25, 125 self-efficacy theory, *see* self-, the Bobo Doll Experiment 25, social learning theory 25
behaviour management 1, 4, 7, 26, 28, 32, 42, 46, 66, 86, 96
behaviour: academic 12, 31, 33, 39, 44, 60, 71, 82, 87, 91, 93, 109, 131 social 6, 7, 8, 10, 12, 28, 31, 33, 42, 60, 62, 67, 71, 75, 76, 82, 86, 96, 109, 131
behaviourism 11, 17, 19, 23, 56, 77 evaluation 24–5, 33 in classroom 28–31, 117 in national policy 26–7 in research literature 31–3 in school policy 27–8 perspective 19–25
belief 11, 17, 18, 25, 27, 28, 34, 35, 36, 38, 39, 44, 48, 62, 89, 109, 110, 123, 124, 125, 126
blogging 96, 106, 127–8, 129
Blunkett, David 41
Book It! 31
Brooks, David *The Social Animal* 32, 68, 115

Bruner, Jerome 35, 38–9 *The Process of Education* 38 *The Culture of Education* 39

Canter, Lee 75, 89 *Assertive Discipline: Positive Behaviour Management in Today's Classroom* 28
Capital Gains project 63, 69, 70
cheating 6, 69, 78
Chua, Amy 107, 108, 109 *The Battle Hymn of the Tiger Mother* 107
class contract 3, 4, 5, 8, 42
classroom organisation 3, 4, 5, 6, 7, 8, 13, 28, 44,
Claxton, Guy *Building Learning Power* 133
cognitive acceleration 44
collaboration 9, 45, 127, 128
Comenius, John Amos 13 *Didactica Magna (The Great Didactic)* 13
community 6, 10, 17, 24, 30, 33, 42, 45, 67, 95, 105, 126
competence 50, 57, 60, 62, 70, 73, 106, 115, 116, 127, 130, 132
compliance 27, 29, 33, 56, 62, 64, 65, 67, 69, 87, 95, 113–8
conditioning 19, 20, 24, 25 aversive 22, 24 classical 19, 20 operant 19, 22, 24, 92
confidence 10, 50, 88
constructivism 11, 17, 56, 124 evaluation 39, 46 in classroom 44–5 in national policy 41–2 in research literature 45–6 in school policy 42–4
control 4, 5, 9, 10, 20, 21, 23, 24, 25, 27, 28, 29, 30, 33, 37, 45, 51, 53, 54, 56, 57, 60, 62, 63, 64, 65, 67, 69, 70, 77, 104, 109, 113, 115, 118, 119, 120, 121, 122, 123
Council: Class 8, 43, 78 local 120–1, 130 Parent 10, 43, School 29, 30, 84, 87
creativity 17, 23, 30, 36, 43, 56, 58, 110, 121, 122, 123
Crespi L.P. 25
Csikszentmihalyi, Mihaly 56, 59

curiosity 1, 15, 21, 23, 47, 49, 56, 64, 68, 124
curriculum 6, 8, 12, 22, 28, 35, 38, 41, 42, 43, 46, 47, 54, 105, 107, 120, 124 creative 42, 43, 82, 95, 128 spiral design 38, 41

Deci, Edward 50, 51, 55, 62, 63, 65, 69, 70, 87, 92, 95, 113, 114, 115, 117, 118 Soma Cube experiment 50, 63
DEFRA 121
Descartes, Rene 13, 18
Dewey, John 20, 35
display 3, 5, 8, 13, 27, 77, 80, 95, 96
Dodo bird verdict 85
dopamine 68
Dweck, Carol 54–5, 61, 62, 69, 80, 95, 117, 131

education policy: national 11, 26 local 11 school 27–8
education theory: holistic 13–15, 16 progressive 10
effort feedback 46, 60
Elton Report 26, 27
Erasmus 12, 13
expectation 27, 28, 31, 32, 38, 42, 53, 57, 71, 76, 107, 108, 109, 110, 111, 112, 115, 116, 130, 135, 138, 139

failure 54, 55, 57, 58, 60, 61, 62, 65, 67, 89, 94, 95, 100, 110, 117, 125, 126
fairness 31, 46, 86, 87, 97, 103, 104, 106,
fear response: conditioned 20 Little Albert Experiment 20
flow see autotelic experience
Froebel, Friedrich 17–8, 44
Fryer, Roland 63

gaming 56, 127
Ginott Haim 123
goal setting 28, 31, 32, 51, 55, 56, 117, 125, 133
Goodman, Kenneth and Yeta 28 Whole Language 28
Grit Scale 64, 133
grouping 9 by ability 5, 127 by learning need 7, 10, 44
guided learning 4, 7, 17, 25, 44, 126, 141

Harlow, Harry 49, 50, 51
heuristic tasks 56, 121, 122
Holt, John 61
Hundred Languages of Children 45
Huxley, Aldous Brave New World 19–20

independence 3, 4, 5, 7, 17

KIPP Knowledge is Power Programme 64, 70, 132, 133

Kohn, Alfie 28, 69, 75, 77, 98, 100, 115, 122 Punished by Rewards 65, 66–8 The Truth About Self Esteem 62
knowledge: construction of 9, 11, 13, 15, 16, 17, 21, 24, 35, 39, 45, 124, 134 Dewey 35 transmission of 17, 33, 35 Piaget 36 Vygotsky 37
Kunskapsskolan 133

learned helplessness 59, 61, 117
learning: active 16, 17, 36, 44, 46, 68, 82, 125 child-centred 16 enquiry-based 38 exploratory 45, 47 incremental 22, 28, 34, 37, 114, 116, 125, 127, 129 outdoor 12, 13, 42 personalised 23, 44, 54 play-based 13, 15, 17, 36 online 23, 129, 130
learning environment 28, 29, 30, 32, 46, 47, 55, 118, 121, 123
Lionni, Leo Fish is Fish 35
Locke, John 13–15, 17, 18, 25 Essay Concerning Human Understanding 13 Some Thoughts Concerning Education 14

marking 3, 4–5 feedback 7, 9, 43, 79, 100–1, 102
Maslow, Abraham 51, 72 A Theory of Human Motivation 51
mastery 28, 58, 59, 64, 68, 107, 108, 117, 123–4, 125, 127, 129, 130, 131, 132
mentor 4, 134
Miliband, Ed 120
mindset 54–5, 57, 61, 80, 89, 93, 94, 95, 96, 129, 130, 135
Montessori, Maria 44, 45
motivation 1, 2, 17, 24, 26, 33, 38, 41, 42, 49, 52, 54, 55, 63, 82, 91, 92, 93, 96, 115, 117, 118, 124, 125, 129, 130 continuum 51, 62, 66, 69, 92, 95, 117 extrinsic 38, 46, 50, 51, 56, 59, 62, 64, 69, 113, 114, 119 cultural context 107–11 intrinsic 38, 46, 47, 50, 51, 56, 59, 62, 64, 68, 69, 92, 95, 97, 113, 116, 121 upgrade 132–3

nature/nurture 15, 25
Neill A. S. 53

overjustification 62

Paideia 126
parents 5, 7, 8, 9, 10, 11, 12, 13, 14, 15, 17, 26, 30, 31, 43, 45, 46, 47, 50, 52 56, 58, 59, 61, 62, 64, 77, 78, 79, 82, 93, 95, 99, 100, 105, 106, 107–9, 110, 113–8, 119, 120, 123, 128, 129, 134
passivity 82
Pavlov, Ivan 19, 20, 59

peer: approval 43, 50, 129 conformity 111, 115 discussion 6, 36, 43, 126, 134 praise 32, 102 pressure 30, 32, 106

performance management 5, 7, 10, 43

persistence 54, 64, 70, 73, 109

Pestalozzi, Johann Heinrich 16, 17, 18, 44 *How Gertrude Teaches her Children* 17 *Leonard and Gertrude* 17

Philosophy4Children 44, 133

Piaget, Jean 17, 35, 36–7, 44, 88

Pink, Daniel 56, 121, 122, 123, 132, 133, 135 *Drive* 56, 69, 132

planning 3, 6, 11, 28, 29, 36, 38, 75, 124, 125, 126, 128

positive psychology 49, 50–7, 59

power 23–4, 33, 67, 89, 116, 120 distributed 5, 10

praise: contingent 31, 33, 39, 43, 45, 71, 74, 86–7, 95, 96, 112, 115, 119, 120, 121, 125, 131, 134 effort related 7, 43, 46, 55, 60, 70, 76, 86, 87, 97, 108, 123 evaluative 45, 48 descriptive 45, 46, 136 informative 70, 73, 101, 131, 134, 136 performance related 55, 58, 61, 65, 135 private/public 8, 32, 67, 70, 73–4, 75, 78, 80, 96, 99–100, 105, 106, 107 social comparison 68

punishment 14, 15, 16, 17, 22, 24, 27, 49, 51, 60, 61, 62, 67, 72, 115

pupil voice 10, 30, 43

Quest to Learn 127

questioning 4, 6, 7, 8, 9, 28, 38, 44, 117, 126, 127, 136

Reggio Emilia 45

relatedness 50, 53, 62, 105, 109, 115–6

Rinaldi, Carla 45

relationships 29, 43, 46, 67, 73, 84, 89, 97, 105, 108, 130

responsibility 5, 6, 9, 38, 43, 59, 109, 128, 133–4

reward: contingent 2, 14, 46, 63, 69, 86, 87, 92, 95, 113, 115, 119, 121 financial 63 performance related 65 strategies 26–7, 30–1

risk aversion 39, 55, 64, 89,130

Rogers, Carl 35, 37–8, *On Becoming a Person: A Therapist's View of Psychotherapy* 38

Rousseau, Jean-Jacques: 15, 16, 18, 23 *Emile* 15–16

Ryan, Richard 50, 51, 62, 65, 69, 105, 117

scaffolding 38, 132,

self: -awareness 41, 47, 89 -confidence 10, 39, 43, 47, 54, 93, 95 -control 1, 10, 15, 16, 24, 25, 47, 64, 89 -determination 50–1, 74 -efficacy 60, 68, 70, 88, 125, 130, 131 -esteem 10, 33, 58, 61–2, 67, 88, 93, 107, 110 -evaluation 80, 82, 92, 101, 133, 134, 135 -theory 33, 37, 38, 39, 47, 49, 54–5, 59, 61 -view 61, 65, 68, 79, 80, 88, 94, 95, 104, 108, 111, 115, 124

Seligman, Martin 49, 59, 64

Skinner B.F. 19, 22–4, 25, 39, 89, 92 Teaching Machine 22–3, *The Technology of Teaching* 24 *Walden Two* 24

social skills 39, 41, 47, 118, 126

special needs 4, 5, 7, 32, 44, 79–80

star chart 1, 8, 67, 78, 113, 114, 115

Steer Report 26, 89

Sudbury Valley School 54

Summerhill school 53–4

table points 3, 85, 86, 87

tabula rasa 14, 17

talk strategies 4, 9, 28, 44 exploratory 34, 126

Taylor, Charlie *Getting the Simple Things Right* 27

teaching styles: dialogic 13 didactic 7, 10, 60, 126, 134 transmission model 16, 17, 33, 35, 47, 117, 127 exploratory learning 17, 24, 45–7

tests 5, 7, 9, 10, 11, 69, 82, 107, 111, 128, 133

thinking 6, 9, 16, 17, 24, 37, 38, 39, 45 skills 41, 43, 44, 47

Thorndike, Edward Lee 21–2 Law of Effect 21 *Animal Intelligence* 21

Tolman, Edward 24

underachievement 68, 111–2

Vivo Miles 30

Vygotsky, Lev 17, 35, 37, 44

Watson, John B 20–1 Little Albert Experiment 20 *Psychology as the Behaviourist Sees It* 20

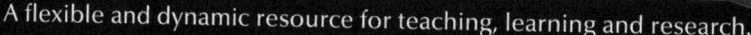